Notes from the Cracked Ceiling

CROWN PUBLISHERS • NEW YORK

Notes *from the*
Cracked Ceiling

HILLARY CLINTON, SARAH PALIN,
AND WHAT IT WILL TAKE FOR
A WOMAN TO WIN

Anne E. Kornblut

Copyright © 2009 by Anne E. Kornblut

All rights reserved.
Published in the United States by Crown Publishers, an imprint of the
Crown Publishing Group, a division of Random House, Inc., New York.
www.crownpublishing.com

CROWN and the Crown colophon are registered trademarks of
Random House, Inc.

Photograph Credits
page 136 (Janet Napolitano) and page 170 (Nancy Pelosi): *Washington Post;* page
208 (Meg Whitman): AP Photo/Steve Yeater; page 226 (Ellen Johnson Sirleaf):
AP Photo/George Osodi

Library of Congress Cataloging-in-Publication Data

Kornblut, Anne E.
   Notes from the cracked ceiling: Hillary Clinton, Sarah Palin, and what it will
take for a woman to win / Anne E. Kornblut.—1st ed.
      p. cm.
   1. Women in politics—United States.   2. Women presidential candidates—
United States.   3. United States—Politics and government—2001–2009.
4. Presidents—United States—Election—2008.   I. Title.
   HQ1236.5.U6K67 2010
   324.973'0931—dc22

                                                                              2009036286

ISBN 978-0-307-46425-5

Printed in the United States of America

Design by Elizabeth Rendfleisch

10 9 8 7 6 5 4 3 2 1

First Edition

To Jean Levy and all the others who did
not live to see a woman president

And to Miranda and Macie and all those who might

Contents

Year of the Woman?

In the last days of the 2008 presidential election, my newspaper, the *Washington Post,* ran a front-page story announcing that it had been the "Year of the Woman." The article was full of upbeat quotes from the usual suspects in the women's movement celebrating the barrier-breaking triumphs of Hillary Clinton and Sarah Palin. The trails that had been blazed! The ceilings almost shattered!

It was a heartwarming picture—at first.

But in hindsight, 2008 turned out to be just the opposite for women: a severe letdown, with damaging consequences. It revived old stereotypes, divided the women's movement, drove apart mothers and daughters, and set back the cause of equality in the political sphere by decades.

How?

It wasn't just that Clinton lost the Democratic nomination, and then Palin lost the vice presidency, in rapid succession. It was that they lost in such resounding, devastating ways. Their candidacies unleashed virulent strains of sexism across the country that many had thought were already eradicated.

Even that dated term, *sexism*, was insufficient to describe the hostility they provoked. Women, after all, were among their fiercest critics. Clinton, the former First Lady, and Palin, the popular Alaska governor, were transformed into living caricatures by men and women, liberals and conservatives, the young and the old—their flaws distorted beyond the point of recognition, their personalities mocked to the core. Each of them received the kind of national ridicule that is generally reserved for philandering politicians (like John Edwards or Mark Sanford) or corrupt ones (like Rod Blagojevich) rather than for legitimate if flawed candidates whose greatest sin was having the audacity to run—or, in Clinton's case, continuing to run after it appeared highly likely she was going to lose. Even Michelle Obama, not herself on any ballot, had to fend off accusations that she was too "strong" or too "angry" as she campaigned alongside her husband, eventually toning down dramatically her persona as a career woman.

The Clinton and Palin candidacies also dealt a blow to the remnants of the women's movement—and pitted women against one another everywhere. Traditional Democratic women's groups splintered during the primaries—some backing Clinton, others backing Senator Barack Obama, igniting internal warfare. Conservative women broke apart a few months later as they struggled with the question of whether to stand by Palin. The conservative-leaning columnist Kathleen Parker led the Republican defections, followed by Peggy Noonan of the *Wall Street Journal*, who disgustedly waved Palin off as an empty vessel who "doesn't seem to understand the implications of her own thoughts." The contrarian writer Camille Paglia, meanwhile, praised the Alaska governor's "frontier grit and audacity," and Elaine Lafferty, a former editor of *Ms. Magazine* and Clinton supporter, showed up onstage at a Palin rally.

In August, when word leaked that Obama might pick a woman other than Clinton as his running mate, her supporters erupted in outrage. Feminism, indeed. In late October, the disturbing notion that Senator John McCain, the Republican nominee, had picked Palin just because she was "hot" blossomed into a mainstream media subplot.

But perhaps the disconnect should not have been a surprise, given what had happened two years earlier, in 2006, when Nancy Pelosi made her historic ascent to become Speaker of the House of Representatives. That was supposed to be the "Year of the Woman," too. Pelosi had worked her way up the congressional leadership ranks the old-fashioned way—by earning the loyalty of her peers and spearheading a massive fund-raising blitz that fueled the Democratic takeover of Congress. It was the first time a woman had ever won the position, and it put Pelosi second in line to the presidency, making her the most successful woman ever in U.S. politics. Her victory had broken "the marble ceiling," as she put it, and produced a triumphant image: a sixty-six-year-old grandmother standing at the front of the House chamber, wielding the gavel, in charge.

Yet Pelosi's victory masked a larger truth: 2006 was a terrible year for female candidates overall. Numerous women running in close contests—most of them well-financed, qualified, and talented—had lost. By one measure, just 11 percent of the Democratic women in targeted House races won their races, compared with 95 percent of the men in similar contests. Overall, in both parties, eighteen women ran in districts with open seats, and fifty-three women ran as challengers. But of those seventy-one candidates, only ten women won—a pathetic rate of return.

The losses were stunning. Pelosi told me she had been counting on a number of new female House members to help reclaim the Democratic majority, and the chairman of the Democratic Congressional Campaign Committee at the time, Representative Rahm Emanuel of Illinois, had personally recruited strong women to run. In an article earlier that year, the *New York Times* had predicted a possible "revenge of the mommy party." Female candidates were seen as especially appealing in light of the recent Jack Abramoff scandal, in which the indicted lobbyist had curried favor with lawmakers during testosterone-heavy golfing trips and nights on the town. "In an environment where people are disgusted with politics in general, who represents clean and change?" Emanuel was quoted as saying. "Women."

And then all but a few lost. (Incumbents fared much better, with most keeping their seats, but that did not change the ratio.) The defeats were quickly swept under the rug—no one wanted to dwell on such a negative trend—but they were an important harbinger of what lay ahead.

And Speaker Pelosi, the highest-ranking woman ever to serve in Congress? Over time, her popularity sank, so that by late 2009, in one poll, more Americans viewed her unfavorably than favorably—not coincidentally, after she had been demonized in ways that the other top congressional Democrats, such Senate Majority Leader Harry Reid, had not. Called "crazy" and "mean as a snake" and "Tom DeLay in a skirt" by one especially vehement Republican, and a "hag" and a "bitch" by talk radio commentators, Pelosi was even the subject of a Republican attack video that compared her to the James Bond villain Pussy Galore. The Republican National Committee never apologized for the offensive imagery, though it appeared later to take it down from YouTube. Overall, the incident barely caused a blip.

Far and wide, double standards have persisted since the Clinton and Palin defeats in 2008. When Caroline Kennedy announced her interest in being appointed to fill Clinton's New York Senate seat later that year, a barrage of anger rained down—how presumptuous of the member of a politically connected family, who graduated at the top of her Columbia Law School class, to think she was qualified to hold the temporary caretaker job. Kennedy was mocked for her speech patterns, especially her repeated use of the phrase "you know," as if she were the first political figure to have a verbal tic, and for having a less than fully developed platform of policy ideas. When she finally withdrew from consideration, aides to New York Governor David Paterson—anonymously—spread false rumors telling reporters it was over a "tax problem" and a "nanny issue."

Paterson—under pressure to replace Clinton with a woman— wound up picking Kirsten Gillibrand, an upstate congresswoman who came under attack for being too ambitious and earned the nickname Tracy Flick after Reese Witherspoon's perky, ruthless student politician in the movie *Election*. Meanwhile, Roland Burris quickly took his seat in the Senate, replacing Barack Obama despite being selected by an Illinois governor indicted on corruption charges and being caught on a wiretap sounding as if he were bargaining for the appointment.

Similarly, Timothy Geithner sailed through his confirmation as Treasury secretary despite a failure to pay back taxes while Nancy Killefer, with a smaller back-tax blight on her record, withdrew her nomination as performance czar. Sonia Sotomayor withstood accusations of being "strident" and "sharp-tongued" and "testy" throughout her Supreme Court confirmation hearings—though under closer examination it appeared she was simply opinionated, not unlike Supreme Court Justice Antonin Scalia. At the same time, Sotomayor's detractors questioned whether she would be too "empathetic" a justice—relying too heavily on her experiences as a woman and a Latina—even though Justice Samuel Alito, in his confirmation hearings a few years earlier, had promised to draw on his own Italian background.

The original "year of the woman"—1992—had been born out of anger. Women, outraged at the dismissive reception Anita Hill received when she accused Clarence Thomas of sexual harassment during his Supreme Court confirmation hearings, ran for office in record numbers the following year. And women voted for them. The number of women in the U.S. Senate tripled; twenty-four new women were elected to the House. It was a "breakthrough" year, supposedly a harbinger of greater strides that would soon lead to the presidency.

And then it wasn't. It turned out that 1992 was just a flash in the pan, a brief surge that "ended up doing relatively little for women overall," according to Marie Wilson, who runs the White House Project, an organization devoted to putting women in the political pipeline. In fact, the electoral surge of 1992, and the "year of the woman" label, had encouraged a complacent mentality: it fed the illusion that women were on an irreversible upward trajectory.

In reality, 1992 was followed by a series of slow increases that have, by now, tapered off. From certain angles, women appear already to have peaked. Women in statewide offices—such as governor or lieutenant governor—reached a record rate, 27.6 percent, in 2001. Today, it is back down to around

23 percent, where it was more than a decade ago. Women are 50 percent of the population but 17 percent of the Congress. Women are one-third less likely than men to be recruited—or even encouraged—to run for office in the first place.

Women have gained a net seat here or there over the years, but never in meaningful numbers. "We had high expectations in 2006, but then it was kind of a very, very incremental victory. Same with 2008," said Clare C. Giesen, executive director of the National Women's Political Caucus. (In 2008, the success rate for nonincumbent female House candidates was about the same: sixty-five such women ran, of whom just eleven won.) "And I think that's the way it's going to be from now on. I don't think there's ever going to be a 'year of the woman' again. I think women are just going to have to hang in there."

The numbers are especially grim for Republicans: women are in just 15.8 percent of the GOP-held offices at the state level, which feed the pipeline into national politics—down from 19.1 percent at the peak in 1995. The party fielded a stunningly small proportion of female candidates—just 6 percent of the total—for open House seats in 2008. The proportion of women in the House Republican caucus has also shrunk, to less than 10 percent.

While there are much-celebrated gains, such as the recent election of a majority of women to the New Hampshire state senate, there are little-mentioned black holes, places where the number of women is inexplicably shrinking. In Rhode Island, the number of women in the legislature has fallen significantly, from a historic high of thirty-nine in the general assembly in the 1990s to twenty-four in 2009. In South Carolina, after the 2008 election, there were suddenly no female state senators—none.

Public opinion has stalled in some respects as well. Twenty-five percent of all Americans see men as "better suited emotionally for politics" than most women—much less than the more than 40 percent who felt that way in the 1970s but higher today than in 1993, when only 20 percent of the country saw men as better suited emotionally.

And of course, it is worth repeating, because it has been so often forgotten amid the excitement of 2008: a woman has never been elected president or vice president, or chosen as the presidential nominee of a major party.

It is a global distinction. The share of women in office in the United States is smaller than in more than seventy countries in the world, from Cuba to Rwanda to Norway. The U.S. ranking of women in politics is dropping while women's political participation elsewhere is growing. There are fewer women in the U.S. Congress today than in the assembly of Afghanistan, otherwise considered one of the most regressive countries in the world.

But if the advancement of women into the upper echelons of politics has tapered off, shrinking the pool of potential candidates for the presidency and other prominent offices, there is an even more perplexing phenomenon: few people seem to care.

The basic vibe over the last two years has been one of progress, change, and opportunity—and in that spirit there is a sunny belief that a woman will be elected to the White House soon. That assumption made sense in the summer of 2007, when Hillary Clinton was the Democratic front-runner, but it has continued even after her defeat—as if her simply having run had somehow produced concrete gains. Never mind that, after Geraldine Ferraro's losing vice presidential campaign, in 1984, more than two decades passed without a woman on a major party ticket. Now, optimists say, a female president is surely right around the corner.

The optimism is at odds with the evidence—Clinton, the most well-funded, well-connected, and famous female candidate conceivable, was roundly driven from the presidential scene, and Sarah Palin's prospects in 2012 look even worse given her abrupt resignation from Alaska's governorship in the summer of 2009—but it is prevalent. Women are everywhere, from the boardroom to the ivory tower, aren't they? Hasn't gender equality been achieved, certainly more than racial equality? No doubt, the thinking goes, an America capable of electing a black man named Barack *Hussein* Obama will have no problem electing a woman president any day now, especially given that there are even fewer nonwhites in politics than there are women. In one poll right after the 2008 election, 85 percent of adults surveyed said they thought they would see a female president in their lifetime, up from 54 percent in 1996. The allure of the "year of the woman" was strong, it turned out, even if it was elusive.

In the years leading up to her campaign, Clinton was often asked in interviews whether the country was ready to elect the first woman president.

"Well, we won't know until we try," she said cautiously.

So is the answer, after the 2008 election, simply "No"?

I began struggling with that question for the first time toward the end of the 2008 election season, after covering Hillary Clinton's campaign for two years (and then Barack Obama's, after Clinton got out of the race). Even as a woman covering mostly male politicians in Washington for the previous decade—including two prior presidential campaigns—I had never really dwelled on the gender aspect of politics before. The partisan frame seemed to trump the gender frame: it made more sense to think of Clinton in terms of the Democratic party, her health care legacy, her New York record, and the baggage of her husband's administration than to untangle what it meant that she had been a woman running for president. She was *Hillary Clinton*, after all. When Sarah Palin came along, the same thing was more or less true: she was criticized as a social conservative and a first-term governor, with gender playing a backburner role in the discussion when the Republican ticket lost.

But as I looked back across the landscape of the 2008 presidential campaign—a battlefield littered with gender-related detritus, with charges of sexism, the phrases "she-devil" and "pit bull with lipstick" and "lipstick on a pig" and "likable enough" and "Caribou Barbie" and "baby mama" scattered everywhere—it began to feel insufficient simply to chalk the Clinton and Palin defeats up to routine politics and historical accident. They may not have lost because they were women—and no one, in the dozens and dozens of interviews I conducted, ever argued they had—but their sex played an outsize role in the year's events, coloring every decision they made, every public perception, and every reaction by their campaigns.

It was no small thing that Palin was chosen exclusively by men, in an effort to win women, her strategy devised by men who had never run a woman for a high-level office before. Nor was it a minor factor that Clinton had spent so much time thinking about gender—overthinking it, arguably—and concluded that she had to run with masculine toughness, modeling herself on the British "Iron Lady" Prime Minister Margaret Thatcher.

What follow here are reflections on those decisions and many others, and on the political climate that produced such emphatic defeats for women in 2008. It is an examination of the mistakes Clinton and Palin made as women—and the mistreatment that, as women, they endured. A tour through the rest of the political landscape follows, examining questions about women now in power: How did Nancy Pelosi overcome the dilettante label to lead Congress, despite the initial dismissiveness of men who admired her simply for her looks? Who pays a "mommy penalty" for having children in public life, and why? Why are women so tough on other women? Why are there so many female elected officials who have survived breast cancer? What does former Secretary of State Condoleezza Rice, the highest ranking African-American woman in history, think of the dueling challenges of race and gender in politics?

Throughout I have interviews with some of the most prominent women in politics today—and introduce some who are running for higher office or laying the groundwork for a presidential campaign down the road.

Some, like Homeland Security Director Janet Napolitano, Senator Amy Klobuchar of Minnesota, and the businesswoman Meg Whitman of California, are still relatively unknown. But the problems they face are familiar, and serve as a warning: the political culture does not take women as seriously as we would like to think. The glass ceiling may be cracked, as Hillary Clinton declared at the end of her presidential campaign. But it is far from broken. And if no one asks why it wasn't—and isn't—it may never be.

Chapter 1

Tough Enough

Mothers vs. Daughters

Geraldine Ferraro recalls the specific moment in 2008 when she lost it. It was Super Tuesday, the day in early February when millions of Democratic primary voters across the nation headed to the polls. Ferraro, the former vice presidential nominee and at that point the only woman ever to have run on a national presidential ticket, anxiously waited for the results to come in—desperately hoping that Hillary Clinton had managed to turn around her campaign for the presidential nomination.

And then Ferraro got a call from one of her grown daughters, who had just returned from a polling station in Massachusetts.

"Did you vote?" Ferraro asked.

"Yes," her daughter replied.

"Who'd you vote for?" Ferraro asked.

There was a pause.

"Barack Obama," her daughter quietly confessed.

Ferraro flipped—becoming, in her words, "a lunatic."

"What is the matter with you?" She screamed into the receiver. "You *know* Hillary. You have *seen* my involvement with her."

Her daughter struggled to explain, saying Obama just inspired her. "What does he inspire you to do, leave your husband and three kids and your practice and go work for Doctors Without Borders?" Ferraro snapped in response.

Ferraro was livid, and distraught. What more did Hillary Clinton have to do to prove herself? How could anyone—least of all Ferraro's own daughter—fail to grasp the historic significance of electing a woman president, in probably the only chance the country would have to do so for years to come? Ferraro hung up enraged, not so much at her daughter but at the world. Clinton was being unfairly cast aside and, along with her, the dreams of a generation and a movement.

As the primaries wore on that spring, the same scene played out in living rooms from coast to coast. Mothers and grandmothers who saw themselves in Clinton and formed the core of her support faced a confounding phenomenon: their daughters did not much care whether a woman won or lost. There was nothing, in their view, all that special about electing a woman—particularly this woman—president. Not when the milestone of electing an African-American was at hand.

Clinton, the former First Lady and one of the most famous women in the world, had spent all of 2007 as the overwhelming front-runner, leading in all the national polls and raising huge amounts of cash. She looked like the inevitable nominee, and her effortless climb reinforced what young women thought they knew: pretty much every battle of the sexes had already been waged and won. Raised in a world where women made up more than half of all undergraduates on college campuses and half of the students in all law and medical schools, where discrimination was illegal, where nearly half the workforce was women and their mothers had been free to work—or not—younger women were not drawn to Clinton by any sense of history, and they recoiled at being told they should be. Feminism had long ago been declared dead, then rendered meaningless.

To the younger voters, Clinton was both a relic of that era and victim of its success. She was the wrong woman at the wrong time; she was a Clinton; she hadn't gotten there on her own; a woman could be elected another year. After all, the reasoning went, it would be easy enough next time. Look how simple it had been for her.

The generational divide would rip through families and the feminist movement, exposing a fault line that had been lurking under the surface for years. The tension between the second-wave feminists of the 1960s and '70s and their younger counterparts—the third wave, as it was known—had been growing, and now it had a focal point. Daughters heard from mothers everywhere. When Senator Amy Klobuchar decided to endorse Obama rather than Clinton, she got an earful from her eighty-three-year-old mother back home in Minnesota. "I guess some people will do what some people have to do," her mother said in an acerbic voice-mail message, adding: "But for some of us, this will be our last election."

If older women were united in their support for Clinton, that was not the case with the young. On the campus of Wellesley— the all-women college Clinton herself had attended, a place steeped in women's history and feminist thought—students were split during the primary. Ona Keller, co-president of the Wellesley College Democrats, switched her allegiance from Clinton to Obama. "I'm sure there are going to be other women in my generation, soon, who are able to run for president," Keller said. "This isn't, like, our only chance."

The same story played out at school after school. At American University, a women's studies professor held a mock caucus with her students—almost all of them female—to find that

70 percent of them were backing Obama. At Barnard College, the all-female school in New York City, there was the same divide. "For many of them, Hillary was your mother's form of feminism," Debora Spar, the president of Barnard, said—the implication being that it was time for your mother's form of feminism to go. Melody Rose, the presidential scholar at Portland State University, said that she asked for a show of hands in a women-in-politics class in 2008 and found 80 percent of her female students supported Obama. "There was just no sense that it would mean something to them as young women to see a woman elected to the highest office of the land," Rose said.

Courtney Martin, a young feminist writer, captured the zeitgeist when she confessed on a *Glamour* magazine blog that Clinton reminded her of being scolded by her mother. She was met with a torrent of fury from her older counterparts. "We old sixties feminists thought that by standing up for women as rational creatures, opening up the public world to them, and ending their dependence on men for their support, we would put to an end this image of the scolding, selfish older woman," the writer Linda Hirshmann replied. Robin Morgan, the former editor of *Ms. Magazine*, ordered young women to stop "wringing their hands because Hillary isn't as likable as they've been warned they must be.

"Grow the hell up," Morgan wrote.

But no one was more blindsided by the generational split than the Clinton campaign itself. Clinton's senior advisers had assumed that Democratic women of every age would be onboard; they had polling data to back them up and designed their campaign strategy accordingly. The real challenge, they figured, would be persuading *men* to support Hillary Clinton—and getting ready for the general election.

It would turn out to be one of many fatal mistakes.

The Iron Lady of Chappaqua

In November 2006, just after Senator Hillary Rodham Clinton was reelected to a second term, a group of her top advisers flew to New York for a meeting near her home in Chappaqua. Clinton was weeks away from launching a national campaign, a process that had been in the works for years. Yet a central mystery still loomed: how do you run a woman, even a two-term senator and former First Lady, as a viable presidential candidate?

This was not the first such gathering of the Clinton high command—they had endured several all-day sessions in New York and in Washington—but it had the greatest sense of urgency, with the start of presidential campaign season just weeks away. Mark Penn, a prominent pollster best known for guiding former President Bill Clinton through his reelection and subsequent impeachment, offered one answer using the results of some recent polling he had done.

Penn argued that people saw Clinton as tough and experienced, two positives in his view. "She has to be positioned as commander in chief. This isn't the 1990s. It is a time of international terrorism—and women have a special burden to carry," one participant in the meeting paraphrased Penn as saying. "Mark took that analysis and said, 'She's a commander in chief; we should maximize her strengths,'" recalled Patty Solis Doyle, the Clinton campaign manager, who was also in attendance. Then Penn, in a memorable flourish, said it was important to position Clinton as inevitable—to ward off competition and lock in support.

Penn had a good argument: no woman had ever come close to winning the presidency or even been taken seriously in the attempt. Women were still a small fraction of Congress—less than one-fifth—and held only a few governorships. None had ever been vice president, or secretary of defense; in the private sector, women were still scarce in corporate boardrooms and corner law offices. All available data pointed to a single challenge: convincing voters a female candidate could be tough enough to win the presidency and lead the nation in a time of war.

In December 2006, right before Clinton made her announcement, Penn invoked history in an internal memo that would set the tone of her campaign for the next year. The United States, he argued, held a firmly patriarchal view of the presidency. The campaign should not, he warned, succumb to the temptation to position Clinton as a maternal leader—should not, in other words, run her as too much of a woman.

"In analyzing the situation, regardless of the sex of the candidates, most voters in essence see the president as the 'father' of the country. They do not want someone who would be the first mama, especially in this kind of world," Penn wrote. "But there is a yearning for a kind of tough single parent—someone who can combine the toughness they are used to with the negotiating adeptness they believe a woman would bring to the office. They are open to the first father being a woman."

Furthermore, Penn said, there was already a role model for this. He flattered his client with a comparison with the towering Iron Lady of British politics. "The best role model proves the case," his memo continued. "Margaret Thatcher was the longest serving Prime Minister in British history, serving far longer than Winston Churchill. She represents the most successful elected woman leader in this century—and the adjectives that were used about her (Iron Lady) were not of good humour or warmth, they were of smart, tough leadership. As we move forward it is important to understand who we are and who we are not. We are more Thatcher than anyone else—top of the university, a high achiever throughout life, a lawyer who could absorb and analyze problems. Her mantra was opportunity, renewal, strength and choice. She was brought to power by a disastrous 'socialist' government while we are coming in after a disastrous conservative government. It is important in this process not to lose our strengths that really have positioned us to win in any attempt to shift the personal tone of the campaign."

The following month, Hillary Clinton flew to Iowa for her first visit to a nominating battleground as a candidate—the first woman in U.S. history to make such a trip as a presidential front-runner. Every piece of the Penn strategy was set in motion. Traveling in an eight-car motorcade, with a presidential-size entourage, she projected so much inevitability that she looked like an incumbent seeking reelection. Rather than greet voters in a living room, as candidates new to Iowa often do, she held a rally in a high school gymnasium with fifteen hundred guests. She did not just offer to "listen," as she had in her first Senate campaign, but flexed her rhetorical muscles at the outset. "I'm running for president, and I'm in it to win it," she told the cheering crowd.

Lest there be questions about her toughness, Clinton issued a preemptive strike, leaving Iowans with the image of her preparing for combat. "When you are attacked, you have to deck your opponent," she told Democratic party activists. "I have been through the political wars longer than some of you have been alive. We've got to be prepared to hold our ground and fight back."

It was not long after this that one Clinton adviser told me, proudly, it was as though his boss were running with a penis.

The description foreshadowed the dominant theme to emerge from the Clinton campaign over the next eighteen months.

During that time she would threaten a hard line on Iran, boast about having ducked sniper fire in Bosnia, and recall having "stood up to" the Communist Chinese government when she gave a celebrated speech on human rights in China in 1995. She would wave boxing gloves in the air at campaign events, adopting music from the movie *Rocky* as a campaign song. She would produce menacing ads, including one featuring video clips of Osama bin Laden, exploding bombs, and troops in fatigues as a male narrator declared the presidency "the toughest job in the world." A labor leader would introduce her as the candidate with "testicular fortitude." Peggy Noonan, the conservative *Wall Street Journal* columnist, would call her a "tough little tank."

Clinton would also repeat, over and over, the statement "I am not running because I'm a woman."

Indeed not: she was running, to hear her tell it, because she was tough, tested, and experienced (or at least felt that way; whether the First Lady part of her résumé actually counted as experience would remain in dispute). She was "ready on day one," "ready to hit the ground running," "ready to lead," as several of her ever-changing slogans went.

How would Hillary Clinton run as a viable woman candidate? The answer, during the course of her year and a half on the national stage, turned out to be complicated and varied. But in the beginning it looked deceptively easy: she would run like a man.

Toughness has been the core concern for women as long as they have been in public life. Campaign professionals have long found that voters hold deep doubts about women candidates, viewing them as weaker, less qualified, and more indecisive than men, putting them at a natural disadvantage in contests for jobs that are seen as requiring strength.

Some women have combated the stereotype with swagger— as was the case with Ann Richards, the Texas governor, who famously accused Vice President George H. W. Bush of having been "born with a silver foot in his mouth" at the Democratic convention in 1988. Or they have shown steely resolve, as Dianne Feinstein did during the San Francisco City Hall shooting rampage that left her to assume the role of mayor, laying the groundwork for her eventual election as a senator.

Most often, though, successful women have fallen back on a single metallurgic moniker: Iron Lady. Ever since Thatcher's hard-line stance on communism earned her the nickname in the 1980s, versions of the title have been conferred on no fewer than seven female leaders around the globe, including German Chancellor Angela Merkel (Iron Frau), former Secretary of State Madeleine Albright (Titanium Lady), and Liberian President Ellen Johnson Sirleaf (whose five female cabinet appointees are known together as the Iron Ladies). It made sense for Clinton, already viewed as battle-hardened and resilient, to take on the toughness mantle, too. She was, after all, the woman who during her husband's 1992 presidential bid had dubbed the campaign nerve center its "war room."

A student of politics, Clinton had, in truth, positioned herself as strong in 2001, when she transitioned from First Lady to New York senator. Soon after Clinton took office, the September 11 attacks hit; Islamists on a suicide mission flew two jetliners into the World Trade Center in lower Manhattan, killing thousands of her constituents in the worst terrorist attack on U.S. soil in history and triggering, under President George W. Bush, a global fight against terrorism that Clinton enthusiastically embraced. Against that backdrop, Clinton sought and won a seat on the Senate Armed Services Committee, the first New York senator to do so. Later she earned appointment to the military's Transformation Advisory Group, a panel on strategy that engaged her even more deeply with the Pentagon. She developed close relationships with military commanders—the retired Army General Jack Keane, later a vocal advocate for the so-called surge in Iraq, was seen traipsing in and out of her Senate offices—and in a few short years she earned a reputation as a hawk.

If a single moment captured Clinton's early quest for toughness, it was her vote, on October 11, 2002, authorizing the U.S. invasion of Iraq. "In balancing the risks of action versus inaction, I think New Yorkers who have gone through the fires of hell may be more attuned to the risk of not acting. I know that I am," Clinton said in a robust floor speech before the vote.

The Iraq vote would eventually haunt Clinton, providing an opening for a little-known first-term senator named Barack Obama to run in the Democratic primaries as the candidate of the antiwar left. But her advisers felt she had no choice. Clinton was a possible presidential candidate for president in 2004—even if she was leaning against running—and had her eye on the White House as a long-term goal. Even when Democratic voters began turning against the war and Obama emerged with an impassioned speech at the 2004 Democratic convention, Clinton refused to apologize for her war vote. In 2005 and 2006, she recalibrated her position on troop withdrawal and the invasion itself—calling it a mistake, and eventually attacking Bush for misleading the nation—but she never directly renounced her vote. She and her advisers were all too aware of what had happened to Senator John F. Kerry in the 2004 presidential race: he had been branded a "flip-flopper" for a variety of seemingly inconsistent views. Clinton's advisers assumed, with good reason, that as a woman she would face worse attacks than Kerry had if she made it as far as the general election.

There was ample evidence to support this point: voters viewed women more skeptically as leaders, especially when considering them for executive jobs. Men consistently ranked higher than women—both in theoretical surveys and in actual campaigns—on matters of national security, crime, and public safety. This view was so established that the Democratic group EMILY's List instructed its female candidates to "fight throughout their campaigns to establish their qualifications, power, toughness and capacity to win."

Clinton, for all her supposed exceptionalism and international acclaim, anticipated having to do the same.

Attempts over the years by various women to run for president had done little to chip away at the perception of weakness. Senator Elizabeth Dole, running in 2000, had dropped out for lack of funding, even though she ranked in second place after George W. Bush—and ahead of Senator John McCain—in some national Republican primary polls. Before that, in 1988, Representative Patricia Schroeder, a Colorado Democrat, had quit the presidential race early for the same reason, in a tearful departure that further fueled the stereotype of women as too "emotional" to be president. The rest of the women who had put their names on ballots in decades prior—Barbara Jordan in 1976; Shirley Chisholm in 1972; Margaret Chase Smith in 1964—had run quixotic campaigns to nowhere, their efforts seen as valiant but clearly doomed from the outset.

Clinton was not in this race to make a statement, or to quit after a few months. If running a serious campaign meant being tougher than all the guys, she could handle that. (She had recently held her own in a vodka-drinking episode with McCain during a congressional trip to Estonia, an incident that impressed her traveling cohorts.) Clinton hardened her image with gusto, a feat made easier by the fact that being tough was her natural tendency. As she evolved from likely Democratic front-runner to odds-on favorite over the course of 2007, she pursued a single goal: clearing the commander in chief bar.

"We were overcoming a hurdle for a woman in general to become president, and the reason why she could be the one is that she was well-positioned to overcome that," Mark Penn, the chief campaign strategist, told me in an interview the year after the campaign. Voters, he said, "already attributed that a woman would do more for health care and education and family and kids and all that stuff, and so you didn't really have to win that. Here you had someone whose core strengths were smart and strong. The question was how you connected smart and strong to her ability to get things done, to be commander in chief, to manage the economy, and to really be an effective president."

Another senior adviser—someone who frequently clashed with Penn—said this was one point on which everyone agreed from the outset. "There was concern that a woman had never really passed the commander in chief threshold, and therefore it was important to emphasize those things about her," the adviser said, adding that they "only had so much to work with" when it came to shaping Clinton's image. "It was important to actually reflect who she was, to make her actual attributes into strengths and not sort of run away from them."

And so Clinton set out to prove her toughness. One memorable display came early, on July 23, 2007. All of the Democratic contenders had flown to South Carolina for a live, televised debate. Moderators asked Obama a critical foreign policy question: would he meet "without preconditions" with leaders of rogue states such as Iran and Syria? Obama said he would. "And the reason is this—that the notion that somehow not talking to countries is punishment to them, which has been the guiding diplomatic principle of this administration, is ridiculous," Obama said.

As he spoke, Clinton's face flickered with recognition. She saw an opening. When it came her turn, she was ready. "I will *not* promise to meet with leaders of these countries," she said. "I don't want to be used for propaganda purposes."

Back in the spin room after the debate, advisers to both sides cornered reporters to try to manage the fallout, with Clinton aides gleefully declaring she had finally caught Obama being "soft." Privately, Obama advisers were apoplectic—hadn't he just handed Clinton evidence of his inexperience? Wouldn't they have to back down from what he'd said?—until Obama ordered his aides to stand by his position, which he felt confident he could defend.

Little else was remembered about the debate the next day. "Clinton: Obama is naïve on foreign policy," one headline on MSNBC read. It was, the Clinton camp felt, a victory.

Several months later, at Iowa's Jefferson-Jackson Day dinner—a sprawling event in a convention hall packed with party activists—Clinton turned in another muscular performance. With her supporters strategically positioned in the audience wearing T-shirts emblazoned with the motto "Turn up the heat," Clinton challenged Obama's readiness—and strength—in pugilistic terms. "Change is just a word if you don't have the strength and experience to make it happen. We must nominate a nominee who has been tested and elect a president who is *ready to lead on day one*," she said. "There are some who will say they don't know where I stand. I think you know better than that. I stand where I have stood for thirty-five years. I stand with you. And with your children. And with every American who needs a *fighter* in their corner for a better life!"

In an interview around the same time, Clinton told my colleague Dan Balz and me that her battle scars from the 1990s would work to her advantage, reinforcing the perception that she was tough. "It's been my observation that when you're attacked continually in American politics, you either give up, or get disoriented, or you either lose, or leave. Or, you persevere and show your resilience," Clinton told us on a bus in Cedar Rapids. "There's a sense that the country is a little bit on the ropes right now, and yes, we want . . . a uniter, but we also want a fighter."

A fighter who could stand the heat, a tough leader who would not negotiate; she sounded at times like a cross between Muhammad Ali and Winston Churchill. And it was working, at least by one measure of success. By the fall of 2007, Clinton was far and away the candidate of toughness: more than 67 percent of Democratic-leaning voters said that Clinton came to mind when they heard the word *tough,* according to a Pew survey published that September. (To understand the significance of that, consider: just 39 percent of Republicans volunteered the name of former New York City Mayor Rudolph Giuliani, a former prosecutor running on the role he'd played after the 9/11 attacks.)

And Clinton was in good company: over the course of the 1990s, women had run increasingly on toughness, gravitating more toward "men's issues," such as the death penalty and cracking down on crime. According to academic research, the trend increased further after the September 11 attacks: after 2001, female House members rushed to align themselves with national security–related legislation, sponsoring record numbers of bills sent to the Armed Services and Foreign Relations committees.

The notion that national security was the great albatross

for women candidates was enduring and widespread; female candidates knew it was a weakness they had to overcome, but they rarely did. "There is no question that national security issues make it harder for women," said Senator Jeanne Shaheen of New Hampshire, who lost her first Senate bid in a so-called national security year. "That's one of the things that defeated me in the '02 race—the focus on national security—and the belief that voters have had, historically, that women are not as good on those issues. And I wasn't the only one." Senator Jean Carnahan was another woman who lost in 2002 on national security issues, the aftermath of the September 11 attacks too much for her fledgling political career to withstand.

But 2008 was not 2002 or even 2004: it was a change election, not a national security one. And Clinton fell into a unique category: of women who were *already* seen as tough. She reminded some longtime political observers of a younger Dianne Feinstein, who, in her 1992 California race, was seen as so hardened that she finally put up an ad showing her rocking her baby granddaughter.

Woman Enough for the Job

Hillary Clinton may have been tough, but she was fumbling in another complicated arena: showing voters what kind of *woman* she was.

In truth, Clinton had been deploying more than just her "power message," as her friend James Carville later called it. She was not *all* muscle, all the time. Her manner had been more complex, more varied—to the point of being confusing, as she sent mixed signals about what it meant to her to be a woman

running for president. Clinton seemed to develop a tortured approach toward her gender on the campaign trail, sometimes embracing it, sometimes dismissing it, sometimes appearing to overcompensate for it—but rarely appearing at ease with it.

She was capable of having a light touch. Her opening announcement video, for one, was so feminine and gentle—"Let's talk. Let's chat. Let's start a dialogue about your ideas and mine," Clinton said, seated on a couch in her living room—that the comedian Jon Stewart joked about the effect it would have on men. "You might as well get on your campaign bus, the I Think We Really Need to Talk Express, to unveil your new Iraq policy, America, Let's Pull Over and Just Ask for Directions," he riffed.

And she sometimes hit on lines about gender that worked. When an Iowa voter asked how she would handle resistance to electing a woman, she delivered an answer that seemed to resonate, prompting some in the crowd to nod their heads. "I'm a woman. I'm a mom," she said in January 2007. "But I'm running because I think I'm the most qualified person to be president in January 2009."

On that same early visit, she explored gender politics at length with David Yepsen, the veteran *Des Moines Register* political reporter, as he asked her what he described as a series of "first woman" questions. For the first time, Clinton talked about the potential upside of being a woman, describing it as a "very big plus."

"I want people to vote for me on my merits, but that includes who I am as a person. I'm a woman, I'm a mom, and I've been through a lot of the same experiences that [other] women have been through. I think a lot of women have a feeling that maybe in their lives and their mothers' lives they were told they couldn't do something like this," she said.

That answer did the trick: Yepsen wrote a largely favorable column, detailing Clinton's answers at length.

Yet oddly—and to her campaign advisers' frustration—she almost never used the "I'm a woman; I'm a mom" formulation on the campaign trail again. The only part of her early rhetoric that endured was her constant use of the word *but*—telegraphing ambivalence about how to approach being a woman running for president. In our interview nine months later, Clinton sounded almost defensive about appealing to women. "Well, I think I'm appealing to men, too," she said when I asked about her women's outreach.

Over the course of 2007, she carefully adapted her stump speech to talk about gender in the most inoffensive conceivable way—saying her candidacy allowed both mothers and fathers to tell their daughters they could grow up to do anything. By late that year, it was a standard part of her stump speech. "As I go by, shaking hands and meeting people, I often hear a dad or a mom lean over to a little girl, and say, 'See, honey, you can be anything you want to be,'" she would say.

But for the most part, Clinton talked about being a woman in uncomfortable fits and starts. She rarely appealed to young women at all, the campaign blithely—and, it turned out, foolishly—assuming that they would automatically support her. And stylistically, she lurched from soft moments to harder ones, her struggle to strike the right balance playing out on the national stage. She would make explicit attempts to appeal to women voters, emphasizing the historic nature of her candidacy—briefly. Then she would downplay it, denying gender had anything to do with her candidacy or her potential appeal.

Nationally, it did not seem to matter: her support among women appeared strong in the polls for most of that first year. But bubbling beneath the surface—especially in Iowa—there were warning signs in the polls, at campaign events, in focus groups and interviews. Women, especially young ones, seemed increasingly open to Obama, and to Edwards.

Some of her advisers were on the lookout for problems. Clinton had waged an uphill battle with certain women voters in her first election, to the U.S. Senate. "Women in the educated professional class? They fucking couldn't stand her," one of her longtime advisers said of her New York contest in 2000. "We never could figure out why. We had psychologists come in." Another senior Clinton aide said that same group, consisting mainly of female urban elites, had once related to her as a Wellesley overachiever but soured on her when her marital problems were exposed—suspecting she had only stayed with her cheating husband to further her own political career. That did not matter so much in New York, where the wary women were unlikely to stray from the Democratic party, but it was problematic in a national contest, especially when there was a popular grassroots alternative in her own party.

Within months of her presidential launch, Clinton's toughness had fueled a spiraling negative campaign narrative: that she wasn't quite a woman and lacked a woman's empathetic instinct. This debate was held on both a superficial level and a substantive one, as the other Democratic candidates fought her on traditional women's issues, such as education and health care—issues that Clinton had genuinely devoted much of her life to but that were now effectively up for grabs as she emphasized the more typically male subjects of the economy and national security.

The debate over Clinton as a woman took an unseemly twist in the summer of 2007. Elizabeth Edwards, sick with breast cancer and in a fierce fight for her husband's career, made the provocative charge that Clinton would not advocate for women as strongly as John Edwards. "Look, I'm sympathetic, because when I worked as a lawyer, I was the only woman in these rooms, too, and you want to reassure them you're as good as a man," Edwards said in an interview with Salon. "And sometimes you feel you have to behave as a man and not talk about women's issues." The Drudge Report streaked a banner across its widely read web page that said: "GENDER BENDER: Wife Edwards Says Hillary 'Behaving Like a Man.'"

Days later, the question arose in a Democratic debate. Suddenly, Clinton was on the defensive about her gender—not over whether a woman could make a decent president but whether she, Hillary Clinton, was *woman* enough for the job.

"Senator Clinton, is he a better advocate for women?" CNN's Anderson Cooper asked, referring to John Edwards.

If Clinton felt incredulous about being asked such a thing, she masked it, recalling her famous speech on women's rights in Beijing in 1995. "I think it's terrific. We're up here arguing about who's going to be better for women," she said cheerfully. "Because isn't that a nice change for everybody to hear."

As if that weren't enough of an affront, Clinton was asked a related question a few minutes later. "Whenever I read an editorial about one of you, the author never fails to mention the issue of race or gender, respectively. Either one is not authentically black enough, or the other is not satisfactorily feminine," Jordan Williams, a student from the University of Kansas, said to both Obama and Clinton.

Obama replied first, with a subtle crack about not being able to hail a taxi in Manhattan, his point being that he was not worried about his blackness.

Clinton followed. "Well, I couldn't run as anything other than a woman," she said. "And I'm excited that I may, you know, may be able, finally, to break that hardest of all glass ceilings." Then she quickly changed the subject. "But, obviously, I'm not running because I'm a woman. I'm running because I think I'm the most qualified and experienced person to hit the ground running in January 2009. And I trust the American people to make a decision that is not about me or my gender, or about Barack or his race, or about Bill [Richardson] and his ethnicity. We have big challenges and big needs in our country. And I think we're going to need experienced and strong leadership in order to start handling all of the problems that we have here at home and around the world."

"Bitch Is the New Black"

The debate over toughness vs. femininity had become a maddening but real dilemma for women in elections everywhere, big and small. Female mayoral candidates in little towns encountered it; gubernatorial candidates battled it; Clinton faced it from the moment her candidacy was merely rumored. It was the problem of the "B-word"—the perception among women that she was, yes, tough, but to the point of being a bitch.

The bind was as true in business as in politics. Catalyst, an organization that researches women in business, found it as recently as 2007. "If women business leaders act consistent with gender stereotypes, they are considered too soft," the group found in a study that year. "If they go against gender stereotypes, they are considered too tough."

Academic researchers proved it time and again, even as studies showed that other dynamics for women—such as a once-relentless focus on their appearance—were changing for the better. "Women in politics are stereotyped as being less strong, being weaker leaders, and they have to compensate for that by showing strength and leadership," said Kim Fridkin, a renowned scholar on gender in politics who has studied statewide races. "But if they act in unstereotypical ways, voters tend to punish them, because they're not being a typical woman. It is this balancing act that women have to do—to eliminate people's worries about your not being a strong leader, but not so much that they think you're not being a woman. It's a very difficult line to walk."

At the same time, strategists for women candidates had long examined the merits of "running as a woman," both in style and in substance, and concluded that it worked in certain races, in certain years. Women could successfully emphasize their femininity, even motherhood, in elections that turned on social issues. That was true for Patty Murray, who ran for Senate in Washington State in 1992 as a "mom in tennis shoes," embracing, to great effect, a dismissive comment once made about her by a male colleague.

"It makes sense to run as a woman when the issue agenda is on your side," said Jennifer Lawless, who ran for Congress in 2006 and is now director of the Women & Politics Institute at American University. Hillary Clinton fundamentally misjudged what kind of year it was, she said. "If Clinton had known how attitudes toward the war would evolve, she could have made far different choices," Lawless said.

"They made the mistake of running her too much as a man, not letting some of the softness of being a woman come through," said Linda Witt, an author of *Running as a Woman: Gender and Power in American Politics*. "They didn't make any arguments that said a woman might be better."

Clinton's "ungendered" campaign style was so stark that two academic researchers started keeping track. Melody Rose of Portland State University and Regina Lawrence of Louisiana State University carefully charted Clinton's every move—from her ads to screen shots of her campaign website—to assess how much she emphasized either the historic nature of her bid or women's and children's issues. Their conclusion was that Clinton spent much of the campaign establishing a baseline "gender neutral" appeal, with some feminine flourishes, then turned deeply masculine later in the primaries. "For a general, national audience, particularly in her network news appearances and debate performances, Clinton more often than not avoided calling attention to her gender and instead focused on demonstrating her policy expertise and toughness," Lawrence said, once their research was concluded.

Clinton was caught in a classic trap—one that, even when her advisers saw it, they were at a loss to remedy. "People were telling her that she needed to cultivate the whole 'commander in chief' image to overcome a perceived liability of a woman running for president," Doug Hattaway, one of her communications strategists, said. "At a time when national security ranked high on people's priorities, and people still harbored anxiety about terrorism and an unstable world in general, there was a fear that voters would not be as comfortable trying out a woman as president. If it were a time of peace and prosperity and a little less anxiety, you might not have that concern.

"That issue aside, it's always difficult to put your finger on the gender dynamic," said Hattaway, who also worked on Jeanne Shaheen's campaign. "When you look at polling and public opinion research about candidates who are minorities or women, most people say they won't base their decisions on a person's gender or race or whatever. But plenty of psychological research shows people say one thing and do another when it comes to this. Given the context, it was considered safest for her to be decisive and tough. The challenge, then, is being decisive and tough in the commander-in-chief context, while also being approachable and personable as a candidate. Your whole persona cannot be crafted around being a tough commander in chief."

Not until *Saturday Night Live* parodied Clinton's toughness as an asset—"Bitch is the new black," the comedian Tina Fey declared. "Bitches get stuff done"—did the campaign begin to develop a consistent message about how her rough-hewn style matched her gender. ("Bitch may be the new black, but black is the new president, bitch," the comedian Tracy Morgan later countered.) By then, of course, it was too late.

"Sisterhood of the Traveling Pantsuits"

Culturally, Clinton had been navigating perilous gender waters for years, as far back as her days as the First Lady of Arkansas, with varying degrees of success.

She had gone by Hillary Rodham until her husband lost his reelection bid for governor in 1980. Then she changed her name to Hillary Clinton—and coincidentally or not, the next time her husband ran, he won. By 2007, she was famous enough to run nationwide as just Hillary, and her first name, scripted across red, white, and blue banners, became the recognizable signature of her campaign. Clinton was as succinct as her campaign banners when it came to girl talk. She had quips about her hair ("If I want to knock a story off the front page, I just change my hairstyle") and her clothes ("the sisterhood of the traveling pantsuits") and even her husband and clothes simultaneously ("In my White House, we will know who wears the pantsuits"). Questions about cooking were off the table; everyone by now knew she had never been at home baking cookies and having teas, as she controversially declared in her husband's 1992 race. She dispensed with questions about her husband's infidelity with clear, graceful lines—"You are mad, you are really upset, you are disappointed," she would say on the rare occasions she was asked, prompting women in the audience to nod sympathetically—and moved on.

Some of her advisers wanted her to open up much more; this became a central dividing point. Mark Penn argued—jokingly, he later said—that human connections were nice but "overrated," while others, including the communications director Howard Wolfson and the advertising strategist Mandy Grunwald, argued for softening the edges but were ignored. Clinton herself seemed instinctively to gravitate toward Penn's approach, serving as her own attack dog on the campaign trail and keeping the more humanizing stories—especially about her family and her childhood—at a distance.

Some aides saw it as a missed opportunity. Because for all the doubts about Clinton's womanhood, she actually had compelling personal narratives to share, as a daughter and a mother, if she had wanted to redefine herself in the public eye.

She could easily have spoken about her mother, whose story was straight out of Charles Dickens. Dorothy Rodham had led an astonishing life. Banished from a troubled household at the age of eight, Clinton's mother had moved across the country to live with unwelcoming grandparents who punished her and, at one point, locked her in her bedroom for an entire year except for school. Dorothy had gone on to marry a traveling salesman named Hugh Rodham in 1942 and to raise young Hillary and her two brothers in a household that was, even in the rosiest accounts, strict. At the same time, Dorothy was a source of intellectual stimulation and warmth, giving her daughter both the backbone and the curiosity that would propel her into national politics.

Unbeknownst to most people, Dorothy Rodham also lived with her daughter, giving the candidate another opening to connect with voters: Clinton, too, was a baby boomer juggling her career with caring for an aging parent.

But instead of incorporating her mother into her campaign in a deliberate way, Clinton mentioned her only from time to time; she did not have her mother do interviews or agree to be interviewed about her. In the end, Dorothy Rodham was an asterisk to the campaign, brought out only when things were going poorly, by which time it was too late. The same was true of Clinton's daughter, Chelsea, who was reportedly uneasy about her mother's candidacy and remained virtually off the radar screen until her mother was already irreversibly behind in Iowa.

A sometimes gruff colleague who rubbed his co-workers the wrong way, Penn bore the brunt of the criticism for Clinton's closed, commander in chief style; he was no fan of the "softer" side of politics and did not believe that having Clinton campaign with her mother and daughter would do much for her rat-ings anywhere. In truth, however, Penn was not as harsh as he was often portrayed. He advocated for some emotionally reso-nant touches, including handing out T-shirts that said "I Can Be President" to little girls at events and creating "I Can Be President" educational kits for kids (the latter idea was praised but never went much of anywhere). Penn's wife, the fund-raiser Nancy Jacobson, helped organize a successful "women's sum-mit" of female Clinton supporters. And over the course of sev-eral interviews with me throughout the campaign, Penn said that Clinton's profile as a woman should be a part, though not the central component, of her candidacy.

At the same time, an organizational flaw having nothing to do with Penn contributed to Clinton's confusing gender signals: her women's outreach division was a separate unit, cordoned off from the rest of the campaign and not involved in many of the core message decisions. The head of outreach to women, the veteran strategist Ann F. Lewis, was not on the important strategic phone call each morning. "In terms of the overall stra-tegic arc of the campaign, Lewis and her staff were not players," one senior Clinton aide said. "You could argue they should have been, but they weren't." Women voters and so-called women's issues were seen as a second-tier project—not the core mission of the Clinton team.

During her First Lady days, Clinton had surrounded herself with loyal women who came to call their universe Hillaryland and who, over time, migrated to her political operation. Patti Solis Doyle, Clinton's first campaign manager, was a founding member of Hillaryland; so was her second campaign man-ager, Maggie Williams, who replaced Solis Doyle after she was let go in the early spring of 2008. Other longtime female aides—Neera Tanden, Cheryl Mills, Capricia Marshall, Lissa

Muscatine—formed the backbone of the Clinton operation, making it difficult to argue that Penn alone was responsible for how to run Clinton as a woman.

Still, Penn was her chief strategist and pollster, and it was he who insisted that Clinton emphasize her inevitability, a strategy his colleagues complained about as the race wore on. ("Saying she was 'in it to win it' was not a message that connects with voters," one senior adviser said. Added another bitter adviser: "Oh, I loved the first slogan. The first fucking slogan, I'm in to win. No shit. I thought you were in it to lose it. You couldn't shake Penn on this.")

Penn also came under harsh internal attack for decisions that had nothing to do with gender. He was blamed for relying too heavily on polls, without conducting any focus groups to probe voters' feelings more deeply. He shared blame with other senior advisers for perhaps the biggest strategic blunders—the failure to plan past Super Tuesday, and to recognize that Obama would pick up sufficient delegate votes by winning in caucus states. And Penn took the hit for failing to grasp the underlying dynamic of the election—that it was all about change—and for wrongly positioning Clinton as a result.

"Mark was always preparing for a general election, and he doesn't have a deep feeling for Democratic primary voters, and probably not for the Democratic party," said Geoff Garin, the pollster-strategist who replaced Penn in the spring of 2008. At the same time, Garin said: "Being out of sync with the fundamental tenor of the year is not good for anyone's political health—whether it is a female candidate or a male candidate. And in a year when voters were in a frenzy over change, to be running as the candidate of experience just was more than slightly out of whack."

But Anita Dunn, the most senior woman on Obama's communications staff, said in Clinton's case it had a gender component. "They spent 2007 basically trying to credential her [Clinton] as qualified when she already was," Dunn said. "For Hillary, the opportunity for her in that race was to be a change agent who had the experience but could also bring the change. And instead they wanted to run her as Margaret Thatcher."

Objections from Clinton's inner circle about that strategy went nowhere, as Penn stood firm. Long after the campaign was over, he argued, reasonably, that if Clinton had not projected toughness, she never would have gone as far as she did. And the objections of others did not matter anyway: Penn had the ear of the two most important people in the room, Hillary Clinton and former President Bill Clinton. "It was like he had them under a spell," one aide said.

At points, as the toughness debates raged, Clinton advisers brainstormed about smarter ways to play off gender cues. One idea was to open a day-care facility inside her campaign headquarters, as a signal to working mothers about the different priorities a female president would have (not to mention a nice perk for her beleaguered staff, who by the end of the campaign were so frayed that one senior aide described it as "the most toxic experience of my life"). The day-care center never happened. Another adviser floated the idea of holding a campaign event in a sorority house, to surround Clinton with young women enthusiastic about a female president and to potentially blunt the Obama campus effect. That, too, failed to materialize. Even Penn had a clever concept—a website devoted to the first woman president, www.fwp.com—that got lost in the mix.

One especially creative idea came from outside Clinton headquarters, from Joe Trippi, the Internet-savvy former campaign manager to Howard Dean in 2004. Very early in the 2008 campaign cycle, Trippi met with the Clinton campaign manager Patti Solis Doyle, the adviser Kris Balderston, and other senior aides to pitch the idea of an online fund-raising drive to draw in one hundred dollars apiece from 5 million women—half a billion dollars, in other words, with the imprimatur of Web-smart female contributors.

"I said in that meeting, 'You're a woman, you can run as a change candidate, there's not a woman in this country who wouldn't hear that message. And I believe there are five million women in this country willing to give a hundred dollars to change Washington,'" Trippi said. "Patti looked at me and said, 'Five million? At one hundred dollars each? That's half a billion dollars. That's not possible.' And literally the other people were like, 'No way.'" Two weeks later, Trippi said, he met with David Axelrod, a senior adviser to the Obama campaign. "Axelrod said, 'You know, I read in a book somewhere that if you raised a hundred dollars apiece from five million contributors, you'd have a broad network of future support,'" Trippi recalled. "He was literally reciting my own words to me. They had a totally different attitude." A short time later, Trippi wound up in a third meeting, with the Edwards campaign, where he eventually went to work.

Thinking back on the Clinton meeting, Trippi said he was astonished that the Clinton operation did not more fully "grasp her power." "I think she could have been the nominee, and been president," Trippi said. "It was almost as if they were afraid to run as a woman."

"Hillary Is from Mars, Obama Is from Venus"

Barack Obama had no qualms about embracing his feminine side. A soul-searcher raised by a single mother and his grandparents, Obama had, as a politician, eschewed the swaggering rhetoric that usually goes with the job. As far back as his keynote speech to the Democratic convention in 2004, he took the position that America is great because of its ideals, "not because of the height of our skyscrapers, or the power of our military, or the size of our economy."

Running for president, as one presidential scholar put it, usually involves "manly men doing manly things, in manly ways." Many a male candidate has looked foolish in the process—think John Kerry shooting geese in Ohio weeks before the 2004 election, or Michael Dukakis in the tank in 1988.

For Obama, it was the opposite. As the 2008 campaign

progressed, his feminine side seemed to grow. Far from proving himself on the shooting range or in military gear, he appeared on daytime talk shows and used words like *inclusive* and *sensitivity* and *empathy*. He encouraged his campaign to foster "consensus," a tone reflected by his grassroots Internet operation. He deferred to his wife, whom he described as the "tougher" one. Obama was at ease discussing breast cancer and relating to his two young girls, whom he brought up on stage with surprising regularity. He liked to *listen,* and to rest a hand on the shoulder of an autograph seeker on the rope line—warmly, not in the backslapping style of previous male candidates.

And Obama saw his ability to twist the gender rules. In his first biographical television ad in Iowa, Obama fired what was essentially a warning shot to Clinton—he was going after her people. The ad, entitled "Mother," opened with a photograph of Ann Dunham, holding her young son Barack. "My mother died of cancer at fifty-three," Obama said, voicing over his own ad. "In those last painful months, she was more worried about paying her medical bills than getting well. I hear stories like hers every day."

Helping cast Obama in the role of the sensitive (if sometimes domestically hapless) nurturer was his wife, Michelle, a tall, confident lawyer who rarely missed an opportunity to cut him down to a smaller size—playfully, of course. She developed an entire speaking schtick around her husband's flaws. At one fund-raiser in early 2007, she pointed out that Obama had trouble "putting his socks actually in the dirty clothes." At another event that April in Beverly Hills, she went on a long, funny riff about her husband's private and public personas:

> I am always a little amazed at the response that people get when they hear from Barack. . . . A great man, a wonderful man. But still a man.

I have some difficulty reconciling the two images I have of Barack Obama. There's Barack Obama the phenomenon. He's an amazing orator, *Harvard Law Review,* or whatever it was, law professor, bestselling author, Grammy winner. Pretty amazing, right?

And then there's the Barack Obama that lives with me in my house, and that guy's a little less impressive. For some reason this guy still can't manage to put the butter up when he makes toast, secure the bread so that it doesn't get stale, and his five-year-old is still better at making the bed than he is.

Comments like those fueled a related but separate problem for the Obamas: the perception of Michelle as the critical, emasculating wife. But they nonetheless helped Obama chip into Clinton's natural base.

Stories began to emerge about the Clinton-Obama gender yin-yang. "Hillary is from Mars, Obama is from Venus," *Salon* blared, observing that Obama played the Indigo Girls at a campaign stop, typical for this "self-consciously inspirational candidate, who is always talking about things like coming 'together for a common purpose.'" A similar *Newsweek* headline read: "Obama's Campaign Bends Gender Conventions." An op-ed in the *New York Post* in early 2008 even described his appearance in feminine terms: "It's not only Obama's policies and strategies that appeal to women. He is like a woman: slim, good-looking, with long elegant fingers, appealingly dressed— all terms more typically ascribed to female candidates."

By the time the general election arrived, the narrative of Obama's feminine traits had taken hold to such a degree that Democrats were fretting. Would Republicans, and certainly the war hero John McCain, once more demolish a girlie Democratic nominee? Susan Faludi, author of the Pulitzer Prize–winning book *Backlash*, declared that the Obama vs. McCain race had "the makings of an epic gender showdown," given Obama's refusal to hew to traditional male stereotypes. And while she praised Obama for surrounding himself with "pacifist—not security—moms," Faludi warned that effeminacy canards were already lurking; television hosts were calling Obama "prissy" and a "wuss."

The gender showdown never came to fruition in the way Faludi envisioned; instead, Obama imposed a different frame on the general election, of himself as the stable, wise overseer of the failing economy vs. an erratic, slightly crazy McCain—with, of course, an even less trustworthy Sarah Palin by his side, in a separate gender Rubik's Cube.

But Clinton's supporters never stopped marveling at the role reversal that had taken place in the primaries. Here was the first viable female candidate for president, so tied in knots over trying to overcome her liabilities as a woman that it gave her main rival an opening—to run as the woman in the race. "I joked during the campaign that if Bill Clinton was the first black president, Obama could be the first female president," said the former Clinton press secretary Dee Dee Myers, referring to the poet Maya Angelou's assertion that Clinton had been "the first black president." Obama, Myers said, "had so much more latitude to act like a girl than Hillary. Because he didn't have to prove himself. He didn't have all that baggage."

"Don't Hit Me, I'm a Girl"

As the campaign rolled forward into the fall of 2007, Clinton, still the front-runner, hit a rough patch during a rocky debate performance in Philadelphia, a rare instance when she lost control of her message and seemed uncertain. In the debate on October 31, the moderator, Tim Russert, asked Clinton whether she would support giving drivers' licenses to illegal immigrants. Initially she seemed to say she would, then retracted it a few minutes later. Her six male rivals pounced, turning an already contentious debate into an all-out scrum.

Seven years earlier, Clinton had deftly turned such a moment to her advantage, when her rival for the New York Senate seat, Rick Lazio, aggressively pursued her during a debate. Lazio crossed the stage waving a piece of paper, gesturing toward Clinton and insisting she make a campaign pledge not to accept large donations known as soft money; Clinton refused, then made his hostile approach her focus, wryly telling supporters the next day: "I knew I was going to share a stage. I didn't think I was going to have to share a podium." The incident became legend.

After the Philadelphia debate in late 2007, the Clinton campaign tried a similar—but heavier-handed—approach. Advisers rushed out a video compilation of the night's attacks, calling it "the politics of pile-on." "What happens when the 'politics of pile-on' replaces the 'politics of hope'?" the campaign asked in a statement. It listed her grievances, assailing Obama for going negative and Edwards for doubling down "in his effort to become the guy best known for attacking other Democrats." "The American people are looking for a president who can stand strong and come out ahead under any circumstances," the statement posted on the campaign website said. "Last night, once again, that person was Hillary Clinton.

"One strong woman," it concluded.

Two days later, Clinton suddenly embraced the historic nature of her campaign in a high-profile manner destined to grab headlines. In a speech on the campus of Wellesley College, her alma mater in Massachusetts, Clinton made the rare declaration that voters *should*, in fact, support her as a woman. "In so many ways, this all-women's college prepared me to compete in the all boys' club of presidential politics," Clinton said. "We need to shatter that highest glass ceiling. We can make history."

It was a sentiment that some advisers had wanted her to convey much more forcefully, for months. Her candidacy *was* historic, a fact that had gotten lost in the euphoria over Obama, they felt. Advisers had been debating whether Clinton should give a sweeping address on women, to help focus public attention on how much the country had evolved and what she, as the first female president, would achieve.

But the timing was all wrong. On the heels of the Philadelphia debate—in the context of the "politics of pile-on"—the Wellesley speech came across as cheap, an effort to play the gender card. Now her rivals and commentators accused her of trying to have it both ways. "Please," Ruth Marcus wrote with exasperation in her *Washington Post* column. "The Philadelphia debate was not exactly a mob moment to trigger the Violence Against Women Act; if anything, this has been an overly (pardon the phrase) gentlemanly campaign to date. Those other guys were beating up on Clinton, if you can call that beating up, because she is the strong front-runner, not because she is a weak woman. And a candidate as strong as Clinton doesn't need to play the woman-as-victim card, not even in 'the all-boys club of presidential politics.'" The *New York Times* columnist Maureen Dowd dubbed it Clinton's "don't hit me, I'm a girl" strategy.

Campaign advisers watched in horror as the "politics of pile-on" mushroomed into its own controversy. Days after the original debate, by now all but forgotten, Obama was asked on the *Today* show whether Clinton was playing the gender card. "Well, look, I am assuming, and I hope, that Senator Clinton wants to be treated like everybody else, and I think that's why she's running for president," Obama said. "You know, when we had a debate back in Iowa a while back, we spent I think the first fifteen minutes of the debate hitting me on various foreign policy issues. I didn't come out and say, 'Look, I'm being hit on because I look different from the rest of the folks on the stage.' I assumed it was because there were real policy differences there." Obama took an even more direct swipe, noting that Clinton had been running on toughness for months. "So it doesn't make sense for her, after having run that way for eight months, the first time that people start challenging her point of view, that suddenly, she backs off and says: 'Don't pick on me.'"

The aftershocks of the "politics of pile-on" reverberated for weeks. Clinton got a question about it in another debate. Former President Bill Clinton further extended its shelf life, comparing the attacks on his wife to "when that scandalous Swift Boat ad was run against Senator Kerry" in 2004. A new narrative took off: here were the Clintons again, self-absorbed and self-pitying, blaming their political enemies for everything.

Yet it also reflected how contorted the campaign had grown over handling her as a woman, an internal confusion that had seeped into their behavior in subtle but meaningful ways for months. Was she tougher than all the men? Or was she being wrongly attacked? Should she open up more to the public, or would doing so diminish her as she tried to rise above the male fray? Could she give a sweeping speech on gender, or would she be accused of playing the gender card even more? Why didn't anyone seem to see *her* campaign as historic? If she attacked Obama, would her critics portray her as even more of a bitch?

Being tied in knots over gender affected Clinton's decision making in other ways. Her advisers knew early on that there was damaging material involving Obama's pastor, the Reverend Jeremiah Wright, going on a racial tirade—material that would later come as close as anything to destroying him and that, if it had been focused on months before, could have made it much worse. But Clinton was warned not to go after Obama too hard in Iowa, for fear of looking "shrill or bitchy," one aide said. The B-word again. Bill Clinton and Mark Penn had pressed to attack Obama from the outset, to "strangle the baby in the cradle," as one aide put it. Other advisers worried that to do so would undo whatever softening of Hillary Clinton they had been able to achieve.

A stunning turning point for the Clinton campaign came in late November 2007. Six weeks before the first nominating votes were cast, a *Washington Post*/ABC News poll of Iowa caucus goers found that Obama was not only ahead in the state but also running even among women. A similar *Des Moines Register* poll showed Obama leading Clinton among women, 31 to 26 percent. Penn's assurances to the campaign that women would turn out in droves for Clinton—or at least hold her steady in second place in the first caucus state—were suddenly in doubt.

Donors were pulling Clinton and her husband aside at events to tell them there was a real problem. She was still not connecting with voters, especially young ones, and Obama was. Her husband was increasingly irate about the way voters perceived her. "How in the world has she been defined as removed and unemotional and detached?" Bill Clinton asked one donor who spoke to him of the problems. "That's just wrong."

And the detachment gap was only about to get worse, as Obama rolled out the biggest weapon in his arsenal: Oprah Winfrey, the most popular celebrity in daytime television, who for the first time had endorsed a presidential candidate.

The Oprah Effect

By the end of 2007, prominent women had been defecting from Clinton for months, and they would continue to do so throughout the primaries, producing a steady dribble of stories about Clinton's problems hanging on to her base. Some female elected officials complained in interviews afterward that Clinton had taken them for granted—failing to call to ask for support early on while Obama was flying in to meet them for breakfast. One prominent female member of Congress said she had sought a meeting with Patti Solis Doyle to talk about doing surrogate work; the campaign manager showed up more than ninety minutes late. Another prominent elected Democratic woman said she could not get her calls returned. The results were devastating. In January 2008, Arizona Governor Janet Napolitano announced she was supporting Obama. Two days later, Senator Claire McCaskill of Missouri did the same. Two weeks after that, in a public relations coup, Caroline Kennedy wrote an op-ed comparing Obama to her late father, President John F. Kennedy; she, too, was supporting him, even though, because she was a New Yorker, Clinton was her senator. Maria Shriver did the same a few days later. In Minnesota, Senator Amy Klobuchar followed suit in late March. One by one, they signaled to other women: there is no shame in supporting a male over a female candidate.

None of them mattered to women the way that Oprah did.

Shortly after dawn on a cold Saturday in mid-December,

people from across the region started lining up outside Hy-Vee Hall in downtown Des Moines. Sleet drizzled, coating the streets in ice; it was twelve degrees. But all that was little deterrent. Anticipation had been building for weeks, with the Obama campaign giving out thousands of tickets to that event and two other similar ones, in Cedar Rapids and Columbia, South Carolina, later that weekend. The South Carolina stop drew so much interest that the campaign moved it to a football stadium. With Oprah set to make the first political appearances of her life—three cities in two days, in front of more than fifty thousand people total, across two time zones—the Obama campaign ground to a halt. Senior advisers flew to Chicago to help her prepare for what was by now dubbed "Oprah-palooza."

In Iowa, Oprah strode onstage in a lilac velvet suit, clutching a sheath of papers. Michelle Obama joined her. Some eighteen thousand people—many of them women, crushed up against the perimeter for a better look—fell silent as Oprah spoke, describing Obama as a man with an "ear for eloquence and a tongue dipped in the unvarnished truth.

"For the very first time in my life, I feel compelled to stand up and speak out for the man who I believe has a new vision for America," Oprah said, her voice booming. "I am not here to tell you what to think. I am here to ask you to think—seriously."

Clinton officials downplayed Oprah as "just a celebrity." "I'm not sure who watches her," the former Iowa Governor Tom Vilsack, an ardent Clinton backer, said, musing that her audience was "maybe young moms, maybe people who are retired." No one seemed to grasp the otherworldly quality of the Oprah phenomenon. In the two Iowa events, an estimated twenty-eight thousand people showed up to see her; that was nearly one-quarter of the total number of voters who had participated in the caucuses four years earlier. In an organizing coup, Obama volunteers were gathering names and cell phone numbers from thousands of event goers, steadily building a database of supporters to mobilize.

Yet Oprah was far more than a nifty organizing tool or a celebrity endorser: she was the embodiment of a whole way of marketing to women. The "Oprah effect" has been studied, obsessively, by Oprah's competitors for decades. One former magazine editor finally wrote Clinton a memo trying to explain what was happening.

"You ignore the Oprah phenomena at your peril," Elaine Lafferty, former editor of *Ms. Magazine,* warned, citing observations and research from other editors at women's magazines who wanted to help Clinton succeed.

The memo advised:

> We believe Oprah and her organization [have] in effect been closely advising Obama in terms of message, vocabulary and delivery.
>
> Oprah's brand is essentially negative wrapped in something that seems positive. There is always something wrong with you . . . but Oprah will fix it. In other words . . . you are fat—but Oprah will make you thin. You are poor. Oprah will make you rich. That message is now Obama's message. The way we countered this was by refusing to buy into the negative. We decided to do something different. In other words . . . "YOU ARE NOT FAT. YOU ARE PERFECT THE WAY YOU ARE AND YOU KNOW IT! CELEBRATE!" We maintained the constant celebration reinforcement, the continuous refusal to buy into the negative. It works. In my opinion, it is the only way to counter the Oprah effect.

Bottom Line: you are running against a WOMAN candidate.

Obama's language and presentation is not just poetry. He employs the vocabulary of femaleness, the vocabulary of emotion that fills women's magazines and daytime television. He speaks endlessly of that which "is deep inside of me." (How many men speak that way?) His language resonates consciously with women and unconsciously with men.

But if outsiders saw a looming Oprah tidal wave, the campaign did not. Clinton advisers tried to counter the Oprah news by announcing Barbra Streisand's endorsement. Obama advisers laughed out loud when they heard that. A talk show television diva with a daily audience of at least 7 million and her own women's magazine up against a singer whose last big hit was "You Don't Bring Me Flowers," in 1978? Bring it on.

Winning the Battle, Losing the War

Clinton desperately needed a counterpunch. With the clock on the Iowa caucuses rapidly running out, she finally introduced her last remaining surprise on the campaign trail: her daughter, Chelsea, and her mother, Dorothy Rodham.

Yet even that was botched. Chelsea and her grandmother arrived in Iowa with so little warning that some reporters missed their first appearance, at a diner in Des Moines. They made it into the eleventh paragraph of an Associated Press story, which noted that "the reluctant Chelsea Clinton's public emergence normally would have been big news, but it was a last-minute announcement that was overshadowed by hype surrounding Winfrey."

Finally convinced she needed to get more personal in an aggressive way, Clinton's advisers launched a "Hillary I Know" effort, with videos and a website featuring testimonials from her friends. Chelsea did not want to speak in public yet, so Clinton's childhood friend from Illinois, Betsy Ebeling, flew to Iowa to campaign with Clinton in smaller settings. "When she's with us, she's our girlfriend," Ebeling said.

Clinton tried a frenzy of new themes. "Working for Change, Working for You" made way for "Every County Counts," which competed with "I've Switched to Hillary" and "Ready for Change! Ready to Lead!" So many slogans spewed from campaign headquarters her senior advisers could not remember them all. The last one was practically a masterpiece, a stunning amalgam of clichés run amok. It barely fit on the side of her campaign bus: "Big Challenges, Real Solutions . . . Time to Pick a President."

Clinton headed into the Christmas holidays trailing in the Iowa polls, her support among women eroded, her best symbolic weapons as a woman fired to little effect. She was still the Iron Lady of the campaign trail, but it was not working. She produced a Christmas television ad entitled "Presents" showing her alone, in business attire, wrapping gifts labeled "energy independence" and "health care." Most other candidates, including Obama, used Christmas as an opening to send off warm, fuzzy images of crackling fires and their loving families. Not her.

Two days before Christmas, with a massive snowstorm moving across Iowa and airports throughout the region shutting down, Clinton flew in from New Hampshire to squeeze in several last hours of campaigning.

At her final stop, a "Holidays with Hillary" event at the Iowa Veterans Home, she mentioned Christmas just once. Instead she told the wheelchair-bound residents in holiday sweaters that she would never forget their military service and would fight to keep their medical benefits intact. "The commander in chief doesn't quit when the battle is over and the war is fought," she declared in her final Christmas send-off.

It was hard to quit being tough.

Chapter 2

Under Siege

"Likable Enough"

By 8:00 P.M. on the night of January 3, 2008, the results were clear: Clinton had lost the Iowa caucuses, badly. She came in third place—losing women to Obama by a crucial five-point margin. Among younger women, Clinton did especially poorly, ranking barely above New Mexico Governor Bill Richardson, a shortcoming that would come back to haunt her.

With just five days to turn the trajectory of the Democratic primary process around, Clinton flew to New Hampshire. Her supporters were apoplectic. How had the front-runner, the first serious female candidate in history, fallen so far so fast? They demanded she take some sort of action, either opening herself up more or going on the attack against Obama.

Instead, Clinton fell into a new role: that of a woman under siege.

During a debate that weekend with the four remaining Democratic contenders, one of the moderators focused on Clinton's personal weaknesses, which had been so sharply exposed by her Iowa defeat. "My question to you is simply this: What can you say to the voters of New Hampshire on this stage tonight who see a résumé and like it, but are hesitating on the likability issue, where they seem to like Barack Obama more?" Scott Spradling of WMUR-TV asked.

Clinton nodded, and paused. "Well, that hurts my feelings," she said, smiling broadly. The audience laughed. "But I'll try to go on."

With the audience warming, she stepped up her enthusiasm. "He's very likable! I agree with that," she said with a coquettish shrug. "I don't think I'm that bad."

Obama, who was looking down at the podium, barely glanced at her as he leaned into his microphone to comment. "You're likable enough, Hillary," he said.

Women in the audience exchanged irritated looks.

For the next two days, with the polls in New Hampshire suddenly reflecting a bounce for Obama after his Iowa triumph, Clinton raced from one event to the next. Her crowds seemed small, as they often do for losing candidates, and the bags under her eyes seemed to sag more. Members of her inner circle were exhausted and tense. They assumed the end was around the corner. Many were preparing to offer their resignations after she lost New Hampshire on Tuesday.

The day before the primary, at a crowded coffee shop in the coastal city of Portsmouth, about a dozen undecided women gathered. They had been hastily summoned by the Clinton campaign to meet the candidate—for an aptly named "Conversation with Undecided Voters" squeezed in between several "Time to Pick a President" events. Clinton spent more than an hour answering questions, most of them on policy, before Marianne Pernold Young, a freelance photographer, summoned the courage to ask one of the last. It would change the course of the race.

"As a woman, I know it's hard to get out of the house and get ready. My question is very personal. How do you do it? How do you keep up?" Pernold Young, sixty-four, asked.

Clinton paused, seemingly at a loss for words. Pernold Young jumped in to fill the void. "And—who does your hair?" the freelance photographer followed up.

"You know, I think, well—luckily on special days I do have help," Clinton said, initially responding in an upbeat tone. "If you see me every day and if you look on some of the websites and listen to some of the commentators, they always find me on the day I didn't have help. It's not easy."

Then she started to slow down. "It's not easy . . ." Clinton said. "And I couldn't do it if I just didn't passionately believe it was the right thing to do."

She paused again, as if the magnitude of the question had just swept over her. Her voice broke, her eyes welling up with tears. Reporters who had been drifting off snapped to attention. "You know, I have so many opportunities from this country, and I just don't want to see us fall backwards. You know, this is very personal for me. It's not just political. It's not just public. I see what's happening, and we have to reverse it."

Photographers' camera shutters whirred. "Some people think elections are a game. They think it's like, 'who's up,' or 'who's down,'" she said. "It's about our country, it's about our kids' futures, it's really about all of us together. You know, some of us put ourselves out there and do this against some pretty difficult odds."

Some of the women at the roundtable nodded, a few of them with tears in their own eyes. Clinton went on. "And we do it, each one of us, because we care about our country. Some of us are right, and some of us are not. Some of us are ready, and some of us are not," she said, settling back into her familiar message. "Some of us know what we will do on day one, and some of us haven't really thought that through enough. . . . This is one of the most important elections America has ever faced. So as tired as I am, and I am, and as difficult as it is to keep up, what I try to do on the road, like occasionally exercise, try to eat right—it's tough when the easiest food is pizza," she said. "I just believe," she said, pausing, "so strongly in who we are as a nation. I'm going to do everything I can to make my case. And then the voters get to decide."

Immediately after she choked up, BlackBerries and cell phones began to buzz at the campaign headquarters. "We heard that she was bawling and that it was a total breakdown, and we were like, 'All right, that's that,'" one senior adviser said.

Back at the hotel that night and on her campaign bus the following day, Clinton expressed dismay about the moment, her advisers said. She had worked so hard to prove herself as a viable commander in chief; was that, she now wondered, going to be overshadowed? Clinton mulled the consequences of having "shown weakness," one senior adviser said. "What she did not get was that she did not need to prove competence or steeliness anymore," the adviser, who huddled with her that day, recalled. "People needed to feel comfortable with her."

. . .

She won the New Hampshire primary the following day—with overwhelming support from women, a dramatic reversal of Iowa. Her emotional moment and the response to it had triggered a popular backlash. This time, the politics of pile-on were for real: John Edwards, upon hearing about the incident, had taunted her on camera, saying, "Being president of the United States is also tough business." Comparisons were made between Clinton and Ed Muskie, the 1972 presidential candidate who lost after an emotional outburst in New Hampshire, and Pat Schroeder, the Colorado congresswoman who teared up when she dropped out of the 1988 presidential race.

In the retelling of the 2008 campaign, that moment—the moment Clinton "cried"—quickly became a turning point of epic proportions. It marked the instant when the controlled, rigid candidate was "humanized" (or when the public realized the "ice queen is melting," as Juan Williams put it on Fox News the next night), transforming both her image and her electoral fortunes. Finally, the advocates for making Clinton more of a woman were vindicated: she had had her Oprah moment.

In reality, it was just as likely that other factors helped Clinton win New Hampshire, a state where she and her husband had deep ties and where Obama had never set foot before he started thinking about running for president. Clinton had a strong team of female advocates in place, including Kathy Sullivan, the former Democratic state party chair; Terie Norelli, the Speaker of the New Hampshire House of Representatives; and Sylvia Larsen, the president of the New Hampshire Senate, in addition to numerous other legislators. She had women lawmakers, at the state level, pretty much sewn up. In the final hours they gave Clinton an extra push with an aggressive campaign among women in New Hampshire—including sending out e-mails and distributing glossy, hard-edged flyers questioning whether Obama would firmly back abortion rights. The abortion drive came so late that Obama had virtually no time to respond.

Furthermore, Clinton did not after New Hampshire transform into some sort of touchy-feely candidate for "women" who had a new "voice." She actually adopted an even more rough-and-tumble style in the months ahead, playing the theme song from *Rocky* at her events and questioning whether Obama would be ready to answer the phone at 3:00 A.M. if a national crisis arose.

But the Iowa defeat, coupled with the two questions—about her likability and her hair—awakened voters, especially older women, to the realization that the first viable female candidate for president was about to lose. Her trials became symbolic. For the first time, people started talking about her as a woman, rather than as a Clinton, upending the frame that had been in place for years.

Anita Dunn, who would go to work for Obama as a senior adviser several months later, said even she was drawn to Clinton that weekend. "I watched, I was still neutral during New Hampshire," Dunn recalled. "I saw [Obama] walking into these adoring crowds like he was the Messiah. And I saw her out there sweating with her political career on the line and then choking up because she realized that it was almost over," Dunn said. "I would have voted for her."

She was not alone in feeling that way. And it turned out that Clinton did extremely well in the role of resilient victim: in the day after the New Hampshire primary, supporters rushed to open their wallets, donating more than $1 million in the first twelve hours after she won.

. . .

The role of aggrieved party had always suited Clinton well: her approval ratings had soared during the Monica Lewinsky scandal in the 1990s, as voters saw her showing strength and resolve. In her Senate race, Rick Lazio's aggressive finger-pointing during their debate had solidified her standing. Her New Hampshire victory could be seen as the latest in a series of trials Clinton had endured, as she overcame her male rivals and the mockery of male pundits.

Obnoxious, gender-based remarks about Clinton had been flying throughout 2007. The commentator Tucker Carlson had described Clinton as a castration threat, saying: "When she comes on television, I involuntarily cross my legs."

"Will Americans want to watch a woman get older before their eyes on a daily basis?" the conservative radio talk show host Rush Limbaugh challenged. "And that woman, by the way, is not going to want to look like she's getting older, because it will impact poll numbers. It will impact perceptions." He may have had a point. Looking old was a serious danger for female candidates, as their strategists could attest. But the observation seemed crass coming from Limbaugh, and no one mistook it for a compliment. It, in turn, had been prompted by a photograph posted on the Drudge Report of Clinton looking haggard.

After the New Hampshire primary, the commentator Mike Barnicle faulted Clinton "for looking like everyone's first wife standing outside probate court." And the talk show host Chris Matthews, provoking what became a crusade against him personally, argued that "the reason she's a U.S. senator, the reason she's a candidate for president, the reason she may be a front-runner is her husband messed around." Though he was making a point others had made, Matthews later apologized.

Her supporters had been incredulous when two young men, reportedly as a prank, stood up at a Clinton event in New

Hampshire in January 2008 with signs ordering her to "iron my shirt." That seemed so retrograde as to be ridiculous; surely it did not represent a trend. As time wore on, they were not so certain. Lists of media offenses began to bounce around the blogosphere, making their way into voters' e-mail in-boxes. For the first time in the campaign, women started keeping track.

The gratuitous remarks worsened as Obama edged permanently ahead among delegates and Clinton stayed in the race, ignoring calls for her to drop out. On CNN, NPR's Ken Rudin compared Clinton to the Glenn Close character in *Fatal Attraction*, apparently unaware that the butcher knife–wielding Alex Forrest had come to epitomize an awful stereotype of successful career women. "She's going to keep coming back, and they're not going to stop her," Rudin said, a comment for which he, too, later apologized.

Geoff Garin, the Clinton pollster and strategist at the end of the campaign, said it was Clinton's hardships—as much as anything else—that won her such a following from the lower middle class. "Women who most saw their lives in Hillary's story were the women who had not graduated from college," Garin said. "They saw that she knows what it is to struggle against all the prejudices and obstacles that women have to face in their lives. Partly it came out of her experiences as First Lady, fighting for health care. It was much more important that she'd fought for health care than that she lost health care. And much of it came out of the Monica Lewinsky situation, where lots of women felt that Hillary Clinton had experienced the kind of pain, the very personal pain, that they experienced in their own lives and handled it well, handled it with strength."

Could Clinton have done even more to capitalize on the growing sense of injustice women felt? Mark Penn thought so.

"I think that after New Hampshire, women realized they'd been had," Penn said. "Earlier, when Obama said, 'You're playing the gender card,' women backed off. They wanted [Clinton] to be tough and strong but many women voters got nervous when he said she was playing the gender card. But all that changed after New Hampshire—it opened their eyes up to what had really been going on under the surface and on cable TV."

Penn continued: "We didn't tie it all together and say, 'You're in the majority in law school, you're in the majority in education, you're struggling as professionals, you're managing kids, and you know what? You're being discriminated against in every conceivable way.' We never closed that loop."

Was all of it because Clinton was a woman? Or because she was Hillary Clinton—such a target-rich opportunity after decades in the limelight and a style that grated even on some politically sympathetic women? Were the Clinton complaints, some on the Obama side wondered, a case of politically opportune political correctness?

After all, plenty of criticism came from women, a fact often overlooked as the antimedia cry escalated. Just as Clinton had faced serious resistance from upper-income, highly educated women in New York during her first Senate campaign, she had sharp critics at the national level. Sometimes it was gender-specific, too. Anna Wintour, the editor of *Vogue*, deplored "the notion that a contemporary woman must look mannish in order to be taken seriously as a seeker of power." Clinton had, Wintour said, dropped out of a cover photo shoot for her magazine for "fear of looking too feminine." When it came to Bill Clinton, Maureen Dowd—and many others—said essentially the same thing Chris Matthews had, writing that Clinton "won her Senate seat after being embarrassed by a man."

. . .

As the primaries and caucuses progressed, with Obama gaining traction in the delegate count and Clinton right on his heels with her own repeat victories, women began to connect the dots themselves. Increasingly, the race became about Clinton as a woman, the gender component of her campaign suddenly in full view.

Media bias became an immediate target—and reasonably so. The senior Clinton adviser Ann Lewis blamed journalism in sweeping terms. In an interview shortly after the election, she declared it was the one profession where having more women in its ranks had not made a difference for women. "It was awful. I am shocked to this day," Lewis said. "Not at the sexism, or the hostility . . . but that nobody stood up and said this was wrong. I cannot forgive that."

But other Clinton aides said they were not so shocked. Veterans of her operation chalked it up to Clinton-specific combativeness, having witnessed the battles of the 1990s—when the First Lady was a target of much worse Republican venom, accused of murder, corruptness, and malice on a regular basis.

Clinton officials would eventually launch an antimedia crusade, but they were not exactly wallflowers cowering in fear of a mean male press corps. For one thing, the Clinton press team was almost entirely male. Howard Wolfson, who was in charge of all of the candidate's communications, had earned a reputation as a tough negotiator handling the New York tabloids and television networks. His deputy, Phil Singer, espoused even more of a take-no-prisoners approach, regularly declaring war on the beat reporters, many of whom were women.

Or perhaps that was part of the problem: had the Clinton team, so ready for war and in anticipation of the "right-wing attack machine," helped create a hostile climate that in the end they were powerless to defuse? Why, many of us in the press corps wondered afterward, had no effort been made to cultivate reporters, or to try to allow Clinton a connection to the press? Asked if the campaign's angry attitude toward reporters was partly to blame for unsympathetic media treatment of Clinton, Lewis conceded: "I believe that is a question."

Hostility came from the public, not just the media. T-shirts encouraging voters to pick "Bros before Hoes—Obama '08" started showing up online. An absurd rumor circulated again on the Internet that Clinton was having a lesbian encounter with her young assistant Huma Abedin; officially, the campaign dismissed it as preposterous, which it was. But it bothered people, adding to the sense that they were on an unfair cultural playing field. "I didn't hear a whole lot about Barack and Reggie," one adviser said, referring to the aide who did the same job for Obama, Reggie Love.

The Clinton communications strategist Doug Hattaway said he was constantly shocked by the words people used to describe her. "Voters would call her a bitch," Hattaway recalled. "The number of times I heard that word over the course of those months—I could not believe it. And I was in the bubble," he said, referring to the self-contained mobile campaign unit, rarely penetrated by outside noise.

Clinton herself was shaken by just one incident, advisers said: a remark by the MSNBC host David Shuster that she was using her daughter in an unseemly way. Though Chelsea still shied away from interviews, she had grown into an enthusiastic campaigner on her mother's behalf, traveling extensively and developing her own following, mostly on college campuses and in retirement homes. When it became clear in early February that party stalwarts known as superdelegates were going to play an outsize role in picking the nominee, Chelsea began placing calls asking them to back her mother. But Chelsea still refused to be interviewed. On air one night, Shuster asked about the inconsistency: "Doesn't it seem like Chelsea's sort of being pimped out, in some weird sort of way?"

Clinton did not see the comment, but Howard Wolfson described it to her on a conference call the next day, aides said. Her reaction astonished people. One described Clinton as angry; others said she wept. "She wasn't hysterical, but she teared up," one person said. "Most people on the call thought she was crying," another participant said. It was a Clinton they had never seen before—distressed, inconsolable. Chelsea, walking through an airport terminal with an aide who was on the call, got on the phone to reassure her mother and the campaign she was fine. ("Chelsea ended up being like, 'It's okay, it's okay,'" one participant back at headquarters said, in keeping with the Clinton pattern of family members being more upset by barbs aimed at others than by those aimed at themselves.)

The campaign responded more forcefully than ever before. In an acerbic e-mail exchange, Philippe Reines, a longtime spokesman, told Shuster he had been "absurdly offensive." Shuster apologized on air and in private; he told me he even offered to apologize in a personal phone call with Clinton and her daughter, a request the campaign rebuffed. Clinton aides felt the apology was insufficient, and it put them on the warpath. Eventually, they threatened to pull out of an MSNBC debate, and Shuster was temporarily suspended.

"Pimped out" may have been an unfortunate choice of words. But was it sexism? Aides said Clinton was offended not because it was sexist per se but because it involved her daughter, whom she had sought to protect for so long. Shuster had "suggested that she was a bad mother, and that she would not tolerate," one aide said. It was a glimpse of Clinton in a role that would come to embody the latter phase of her campaign: that of a protective, fighting momma bear.

In the end, how much the antimedia revolt helped carry Clinton through the last months of the primary was hard to assess. While she fell irretrievably behind in the delegate count in February, she continued to win important states, rolling up Massachusetts, California, New York, Pennsylvania, Ohio. Women over thirty continued to gravitate toward her: she won just over half of white women voters in the early contests, rising to more than 60 percent on and after February 5, and peaking in the later primaries. Clinton averaged 64 percent among white women thirty years old and up from March 4 through the end.

Was it because they were mad at the media commentators and Obama supporters who demanded that Clinton get out of the running? Was it because they had new doubts about Obama, who faltered before some important contests? Was it, in certain areas, racism?

Scholars with a grounding in gender politics mostly agreed that Clinton had received harsher media treatment than Obama, sometimes in familiar ways—stories about her laugh, dubbed her "cackle" by *The New York Times,* or about her husband. Though Bill Clinton was an exceptional case, the husband focus was something women in virtually every kind of campaign had experienced, along with an obsession with looks; strategists have long called it the "hair, hemlines, and husbands" phenomenon.

Still, when it was over, few people outside the campaign or within blamed sexism for Clinton's demise. Not one senior adviser out of many interviewed ever argued Clinton lost because she is a woman. Ann Lewis, infuriated though she was by the press treatment, said "it was not the factor" that undid Clinton. "The biggest factors were within the campaign," Lewis said.

"Not everything bad that happened to her happened because she was a woman," James Carville said. "And some of the good things that happened to her were *because* she was a woman."

Nonetheless, a new level of soul-searching began. Howard Dean, outgoing chairman of the Democratic National Committee, said in hindsight that the media had taken a "very sexist approach" in its coverage of Clinton. Most outspoken of all was Katie Couric, the CBS anchor, who delivered a forceful on-camera critique after Clinton dropped out of the race in June. "Like her or not, one of the great lessons of that campaign is the continued and accepted role of sexism in American life, particularly in the media," Couric said. Citing the Hillary Clinton "Nutcrackers" sold in airports and Tucker Carlson's comment about protecting his private parts when he heard her voice, Couric said: "It isn't just Hillary Clinton who needs to learn a lesson from this primary season. It's all the people who crossed the line—and all the women and men who let them get away with it."

Clinton herself felt the same way, her senior aides said. As one senior adviser who remained close to her after the campaign ended put it: "At the end of the day, Hillary Clinton concluded that the thing was rigged against women in a serious way."

Doug Hattaway put it slightly differently. "I don't know if the system is rigged. But the political culture is a minefield for women, and she was the first to try to make it across," he said. If political scientists had concluded that the president was seen as the "father" of the nation, then it remained a code that women had not cracked. "There's a lot of emotional baggage wrapped up in the presidency," he said. "There isn't all that much wrapped up in who is your senator or your state legislator. It's just not the same thing. The president symbolizes so much about the state of the nation, and society, and how we feel about ourselves."

Representative Jim McGovern, a Democrat from Massachusetts and one of the Clinton supporters who spent the most time with her on the campaign trail, said he came away from the 2008 experience less certain he could tell his young daughter that she could be anything—including president—when she grows up. He recounted going into a restaurant in Worcester, Massachusetts, and running into one of his constituents, who lambasted him for endorsing Clinton, telling him, "The last thing we need is a woman as president of the United States."

"Look, I think sexism is a huge problem in this country. I mean, the people who say it isn't, they're just full of shit," McGovern said.

Bill's Spotlight and Shadow

Hillary Clinton may have been under siege, but no one felt more aggrieved than Bill Clinton, who repeatedly found himself in the midst of controversy, his comments increasingly construed as dismissive of Obama. When Clinton told one audience that Obama's antiwar stance was a "fairy tale," he was widely chastised in the black community for discounting what Obama had accomplished. The criticism mounted when Clinton implied that Obama would win South Carolina for the same reason Jesse Jackson had, because of a large black electorate. A narrative

emerged: of Bill Clinton angry and off the reservation, lashing
out at reporters and critics to the chagrin of his wife's advisers.

Clinton, along with a number of prominent women, felt that
Obama had been given both a free pass and undue historical
blessing—in short, that race trumped gender. Gloria Steinem
wrote a widely circulated op-ed in the *New York Times* asking
whether a woman who had been a community organizer with
two young daughters before serving a single Senate term would
be a viable presidential candidate. (Her answer: No.)

Geraldine Ferraro took it a step further. "If Obama was a white man, he would not be in this position," Ferraro told her local paper, the *Daily Breeze,* in Torrance, California. "And if he was a woman of any color, he would not be in this position. He happens to be very lucky to be who he is."

Such passion may have resonated with older white women, but it produced a fierce backlash elsewhere. Their complaints added ammunition to critics who were making another case against the Clintons: that they were injecting race—and racism—into the campaign. Yet however inelegantly Bill Clinton and Ferraro put it, there was an underlying point to be made.

Built into the framework of Barack Obama's biography-heavy candidacy was the implicit idea that electing an African-American as president would represent enormous change and a historic landmark all at once—an idea so powerful that, when it came to fruition on November 4, 2008, it prompted supporters across the country to weep. Obama had already written a best-selling autobiography about coming to terms with his bi-racial identity. When he began running, he placed himself in the context of the American dream, citing the "fierce urgency of now" (a phrase borrowed from the Reverend Martin Luther King, Jr.) and encouraging people to "bend the arc of history." The Obama campaign gently guided people to the conclusion that to vote for him would be to fulfill King's dream.

Both Obama and Clinton had traveled to Selma, Alabama, on a civil rights pilgrimage in March 2007, their first joint appearance of the campaign. No similar nod to women—no joint trip to Seneca Falls—ever occurred.

When Obama won the Iowa caucuses, news accounts declared that he had made a historic breakthrough—although he was not, in fact, the first African-American to win a primary battle. Jesse Jackson had won five primaries and caucuses in 1984 and another eleven in 1988. Nonetheless, *Time* magazine called it "Obama's Historic Victory," while other accounts made note of the fact that he had won in the predominantly white state, sentiments repeated over and over on television in the days that followed. "They said this day would never come," Obama said in his victory speech the night of the Iowa caucuses, further cultivating the sense of awe that a special day had, in fact, arrived.

Yet just a week later, when Clinton won the New Hampshire primary—becoming the first woman to win any primary contest, *ever*—it was barely discussed as a landmark. It was as if it did not count; she was, after all, supposed to be winning. Much was made of her choking up, but the idea that her winning represented a leap forward for women in politics was hardly touched upon, in her speech or in the coverage. "Clinton Escapes to Fight Another Day," the headline of a *New York Times* analysis read.

The coverage described Clinton on her own terms: as inevitable, a semi-incumbent, who then failed to live up to the soaring expectations she had set.

When it came to Bill Clinton, his statements did not happen in a vacuum, nor get him in trouble in isolation. They were part of a larger thicket of complicating factors—not least of which was his uncharted role as the husband of a female presidential candidate, itself made more extraordinary by the fact that he had been president himself eight years earlier. The Clintons' relationship had been a source of fascination and revulsion during his presidency; when his wife ran, it became an incalculable part of the political equation.

Lost in the discussion was the fact that the Clintons were operating much as the rest of the world does: with women sharing power with their male relatives and leveraging their familial relationships into office. Globally, over the course of history, women from the Queen of England to Indira Gandhi of India have inherited status from male relatives—husbands, fathers, brothers.

Even in the United States, women have long derived political power from their husbands: many of the earliest women in Congress got there by filling their husbands' seats after they died. The first woman elected to the Senate, Hattie Wyatt Caraway of Arkansas, started out as a replacement for her husband, who had been a congressman and a senator before his death in the middle of a term. Since then, countless female politicians' careers have arisen out of tragedies. Senator Olympia Snowe started out in the Maine state senate as a replacement for her husband, Peter Snowe, who died in a car crash. Former Senator Jean Carnahan of Missouri filled her husband's seat in the Senate after he died in a plane crash a few days before the election. At least five members of the House—Representative Lindy Boggs of Louisiana, Representative Jo Ann Emerson of Missouri, and Representative Lois Capps, Representative Mary Bono Mack, and Representative Doris Matsui of California—were elected after replacing their husbands.

But in Hillary Clinton's case, this phenomenon was criticized as odd, as parasitic. One young female student at American University told me that even though she supported Clinton she was worried that she would win—and send the wrong message, that the route to success was through marriage to a powerful man. When Clinton lost, she said, it was a "huge relief."

"Give 'Em Hill"

By late February 2008, Clinton was losing and would never recover from the delegate lead Obama had built up. Her advisers had failed to preserve enough money or to plot strategy across the states that held caucuses, where Obama would gain his permanent advantage. Clinton herself "never understood caucuses," one senior adviser said.

But as a matter of style, Clinton started, for the first time, to win.

Or at least to make sense. No longer running as a distant, steely Margaret Thatcher, no longer at pains to be "humanized," Clinton had turned into a fist-throwing populist fighting on behalf of needy people everywhere. Her toughness routine merged with the central issue in the late-contest states—the economy—to form a coherent message that would carry her through the last race in June. She was not there just to prove her own resilience but also to serve as a protector. Coming across as a "momma bear," as Dee Dee Myers put it, Clinton found a model of female leadership that worked.

Fighting images overwhelmed the Clinton campaign. A supporter in Ohio gave her a pair of blue boxing gloves for Valentine's Day, and she waved them enthusiastically onstage. Kelly "the Ghost" Pavlik, the middleweight boxing champion and a native of hardscrabble Youngstown, endorsed her in early March, and she brought him out on the road. She put up an ad, entitled "Fighter," narrated by Ohio Governor Ted Strickland: "We need a president who first of all is going to be a fighter. That's the way I see Hillary Clinton. . . . She's fighting for us. And that's the kind of president we need."

"I do think we need a fighter back in the White House," Clinton said in a one-on-one debate against Obama in Cleveland.

Five days before the Ohio and Texas primaries on March 5, Clinton released the most memorable advertisement of the season: her "3 A.M." ad asking voters which candidate they would rather have in office when an emergency strikes in the middle of the night. It showed images of children asleep in the middle of the night, with a male narrator's voice asking: "It's 3 A.M. and your children are safe and asleep. But there's a phone in the White House and it's ringing. . . . Who do you want answering the phone?"

She autographed yet more boxing gloves in Indiana, where a local steelworkers' union president introduced her as having "testicular fortitude." Signs at events encouraging Clinton to "Give 'em Hill" multiplied. For the first time, Clinton had a persona that was consistent and that worked. The contests kept coming, and Clinton kept fighting, to the end.

Mark Penn was a strong proponent of the fighter strategy. "I wanted her to fight back against the attacks on her, and just about everybody else thought that was off-putting and she shouldn't do it. And then she was out there, she just started to do it," Penn said. "I'd write to her and say, 'This is great, you let it out, about time. Keep it going.' And I think her fighting back was critical to her transformation in the latter part of the campaign."

Penn acknowledged that he was against just bringing out her family to show who she was; to this day, he stands by the fighter motif as her best. He remains unconvinced that her emotional moment in New Hampshire turned the race around. "In looking back, people sometimes confuse a genuine moment and the power of it with soft family moments," he said. "Showing she was a good mom and traipsing around with her daughter and mother made for good copy but didn't really do much—having a moment that showed how much she cared and how much of a fighter for people she was—time and time again those moments made a real difference."

Other advisers—in fact, almost every other Clinton adviser—believes a completely different version of events, namely that Clinton began doing better once she shed Penn's advice and started connecting to voters rather than worrying so much about being commander in chief.

"I thought 2007 was wasted," Doug Hattaway said. "It wasn't until 2008, after throwing caution aside, that she found her voice and her stride, and people saw it and responded well. She did pretty well after February. She got more votes and more delegates. It was just too late."

Representative Debbie Wasserman Schultz, a Florida Democrat who campaigned relentlessly for Clinton in the primaries, said it was almost painful to watch the candidate fritter one of her greatest assets away. "It was a missed opportunity simply because the first half of the campaign didn't capitalize on her gender like the advantage it was," she said. "In a change election, which this was, people are looking for something that is not the same old same old," she said. "I mean, they were sick of Bush. They were sick of white men. *Obviously.*"

Wasserman Schultz, herself a young mother, was part of a new generation of women who embraced womanhood as they campaigned. And even though running for national office was different, she said she wished Clinton could have capitalized on it more, just a little. "I mean, she was the only woman in the race. She was absolutely one of the most qualified candidates running, she had a tremendous base of support, and I just don't think she was able to use her gender as the asset it was. She *decided* not to use her gender as the asset that it was," she said.

Failure to Launch

On Saturday, June 7, 2008, a sweltering summer day, thousands of Clinton supporters and volunteers—and news crews—gathered outside the National Building Museum in Washington waiting to get in. An air of sad anticipation hung over the crowd as they awaited the announcement of what they already knew: the contest was over, and Hillary Clinton, having campaigned across hundreds of thousands of miles and every time zone, was finally dropping out.

No one quite expected what came next.

Clinton stepped to the wooden podium, smiling, almost radiant. "Well, this isn't exactly the party I'd planned, but I sure like the company," she started, drawing laughter.

But as she continued—delivering, for the first time, a stirring address on what her achievements as a woman meant—women,

and men, in the crowd began to cry. "Now, on a personal note, when I was asked what it means to be a woman running for president, I always gave the same answer, that I was proud to be running as a woman, but I was running because I thought I'd be the best president," she said. "But—*but*. I am a woman and, like millions of women, I know there are still barriers and biases out there, often unconscious. And I want to build an America that respects and embraces the potential of every last one of us. I ran as a daughter who benefited from opportunities my mother never dreamed of. I ran as a mother who worries about my daughter's future, and a mother who wants to leave all children brighter tomorrows," she said.

"As we gather here today in this historic, magnificent building, the fiftieth woman to leave this Earth is orbiting overhead. If we can blast fifty women into space, we will someday launch a woman into the White House," Clinton continued, as people in the audience turned to look up toward space.

"Although we weren't able to shatter that highest, hardest glass ceiling this time, thanks to you, it's got about 18 million cracks in it," she said. "And the light is shining through like never before, filling us all with the hope and the sure knowledge that the path will be a little easier next time. That has always been the history of progress in America."

It was unlike any speech she had ever given—open, resonant. Reporters shook their heads in disbelief. Where had this Hillary Clinton been all that time?

The question is still the great what-if about her candidacy. What if Clinton had given a version of that speech at the beginning of her campaign, instead of at the end? It is impossible to know whether the narrative of the race would have unfolded differently, whether she could have stirred the passions of a generation by painting a vivid picture of how far women had come and still had to go. Clinton's advisers had struggled with the notion of a "gender speech" for more than a year—planning such an address, then scrapping it, then reviving it again when she began to falter.

Yet right up until the very end, she was ambivalent about the idea—she truly meant it when she said she was not running because she was a woman—and that discomfort, picked up and shared by some of her senior aides, had political implications. "We never embraced the idea of the first woman president as a strategy," Patti Solis Doyle said in an interview months afterward, with a touch of remorse. "There was always a reason not to—whether it be turning off male voters, a polling reason, a get-out-the-vote reason," she said.

Clinton campaign advisers had made a set of calculations— about money, about putting resources into early primary states, about skipping most of the caucuses, about targeting men and older women, about deploying her husband, about attacking Obama, about planning only up until Super Tuesday—that all contributed to her demise. In hindsight, it is tempting to pick one and declare it "the reason" she lost, though in fact it is impossible to know how a different set of decisions would have played out.

But one thing is for certain: the campaign counted on a collective uprising from women and achieved it, but only after the candidate was too far behind to recover. The campaign "would sometimes talk about the 'X factor,' the moment when the women of America would realize that she was a woman and coalesce around her," Howard Wolfson said in a later interview. "There was a recognition that this could happen, and it was important for it to happen—but it didn't really coalesce until it was too late."

· · ·

Running as a confident, unstoppable heir apparent had severely damaged Clinton—and not just because it blinded her to Obama's ascent, or alienated voters with its arrogance, or because its unraveling the following year would be so spectacular. It also telegraphed that there was nothing all that challenging about electing a woman president.

At times in 2007, it felt as if Clinton had been inevitable for so long that the country had already had a woman president. And, in fact, when her credentials were questioned, she responded that she had already been a co-president of sorts, traveling to eighty-two countries and having a front-row seat on her husband's administration.

That attitude failed to tap into whatever potential enthusiasm there might have been among young women—who were already a tough crowd to reach. They considered themselves postfeminists, to the extent they thought about it, and preferred not to view the world in terms of gender. Supporting Barack Obama was proof of their liberation: they were free to choose whomever they favored for president, unburdened by any old-fashioned notions of loyalty or sisterhood, a sign that women were now diverse and evolved enough to disagree.

And if young women felt fully liberated—or were even totally oblivious to the barriers that had once existed, in many cases before they were born—it was hard to blame them. Nothing in 2008 *felt* unequal. Women had worked alongside men as peers in every profession for decades, with discrimination and sexual harassment laws on the books. Women were heads of corporations and universities, as senators and governors and chiefs of police. Sandra Day O'Connor, once denied a job as a lawyer because she was a woman, had already served more than two decades as a Supreme Court justice and retired. A woman had been U.S. attorney general; two had served as secretaries of state. Women had been White House press secretaries in both Democratic and Republican administrations. Every year seemed to bring a new achievement, making the next one less remarkable: Nancy Pelosi was chosen as the first female Speaker of the House of Representatives in 2006, the same year Katie Couric became the first woman to sit solo in the anchor chair of a major television network's evening news program.

All the inequity that persisted—the limited number of female CEOs, the slim percentage of women in Congress, the lingering pay gap between men and women—had been hidden behind a few bright, shining exceptions and "year of the woman!" pronouncements. Young women had been taught they could be anything and have it all; electing a president must not, therefore, be that big a deal.

By Iowa, it was official: Clinton was not the candidate of young women. Half of all women between the ages of eighteen and forty-four voted for Obama in that first contest; 15 percent of those young women voted for former North Carolina Senator John Edwards; Clinton came in third overall, including among young women.

The younger the women were, the worse Clinton did: she won just 14 percent of women under thirty in Iowa. Part of the problem may have been unique to Iowa—a state that has never elected a woman as a governor or member of Congress—but as the primaries continued, Obama kept winning young women, even as older women rallied enthusiastically around Clinton and her performance overall improved. In the primaries with exit polling data, Obama won more than half of all women under thirty, becoming, in other words, the preferred choice of most of Chelsea Clinton's peers.

Clinton's failure to win young women was more than just an interesting footnote. It marked a major strategic error on the part of the campaign, and helped lead to her defeat. If she had done 10 points better among women under forty-five in Iowa, she could have won the caucuses and stopped Obama in his tracks.

Mark Penn had been convinced that young voters not only would support a woman for president but would relish the opportunity to do so. "This [sexism] is now an objection we can turn on its head. Ninety-four percent of young women will come out to vote for the first woman president. This is a powerful movement for us, not against us," he wrote in one 2006 memo. His recommendation: "Understand the life issues of young women." That never happened. His 94 percent prediction was wildly off base.

Ann Lewis said the campaign faced a generational zeitgeist that was impossible to overcome. Young women, Lewis said, given their own ease in life so far, did not accept the premise that electing a woman president might actually be difficult. "Young women did not understand how few women there are, or why it mattered," Lewis said.

There were, though, many additional factors working against Clinton. Young women, like young men, could not remember a time when there was not a Clinton or a Bush in the Oval Office. And young female voters could remember the Monica Lewinsky scandal—and were, in fact, in the same peer group as the young intern who had an affair with Bill Clinton.

But above all, said Celinda Lake, the Democratic pollster, Clinton was campaigning uphill in trying to convince younger voters that gender mattered. "Race is much more powerful to them than gender," Lake said. "Gender doesn't seem that new to them, that interesting to them."

Could Clinton have made it seem new? Was the cultural view of gender so firmly cemented, the women's movement so irreversibly uncool, that she could have never overcome it? Or could she have given a gender speech early on and set the tone for the entire campaign in a different way?

Clinton had, after all, given a famous speech on women in Beijing in 1995, declaring that "women's rights are human rights." But she was reluctant to make a similar speech as a candidate. Her advisers worried it would turn off older, more conservative women, or men, if she started talking about women's issues out of nowhere. The last thing they wanted was to revive the image of Clinton as a bra-burning radical, though that had never been who she really was. If she was going to talk about gender, it needed context—or an excuse.

One opportunity had arisen in the spring of 2007, very early in the campaign, when the radio host Don Imus referred to the Rutgers women's college basketball team as "some nappy-headed ho's." Clinton quickly responded, accepting a long-standing invitation to speak at Rutgers's prominent Center for American Women and Politics, where she would call on society to say "enough is enough." Aides worried that it would be seen as opportunistic, but bigger problems arose: on the day Clinton was scheduled to speak, the worst rain in more than a century flooded northern New Jersey, forcing her to postpone. That same day, April 16, a deranged gunman opened fire on the campus of Virginia Tech and killed thirty-two people—an event that dominated the headlines for weeks. When Clinton finally gave the rescheduled address, four days later, the moment was lost. It was as if the stars had aligned against her, aides mused in hindsight.

Seven months later, when Clinton was mocked for mentioning gender in her speech at Wellesley—during the "politics of pile-on" episode—many of the women in her campaign decided to drop the idea of a major gender address altogether. "If she gave a gender speech, it would have been, 'Oh, there she goes again whining,'" Lewis said. "I felt terrible about arguing against it."

Ironically, Penn, the author of the masculine Iron Lady strategy, said he pressed for Clinton to talk about gender, finding himself arguing against women in the campaign. "Look, if you're Hillary Clinton, who are you going to listen to about what to do for women, me or Ann Lewis?" Penn told me afterward. "You're going to listen to Ann Lewis."

Other advisers said Clinton herself was uncomfortable with the concept of a gender speech, especially one drawing attention to the "firstness" of her candidacy, something that, by definition, required her to make it all about herself. She had "mixed feelings," one aide said—perhaps because she wanted so much to be the first woman president and was afraid of drawing attention to her personal ambition.

And what, exactly, would a gender speech say, anyway? Would it talk about women's achievement over time, or focus on inequality? Would it be aimed at the fathers of young girls, making the case that any child could grow up to be president in the United States? Would she talk about sexism, and risk sounding like a "harridan," as Lewis feared and as one columnist had already called her? Or was there a hunger for a gloomy diagnosis, something that acknowledged how far the country still had to go when it came to talking to, and about, women?

Aides and speechwriters passed around memos and drafts, but it never went far. After Obama gave a major speech on race in April 2008, there was near consensus that having Clinton give a gender speech would look "contrived." The time for that had come and gone.

. . .

In the end, it took defeat for Hillary Clinton to talk about being a woman in an expansive way.

She and her husband had flown home to New York from South Dakota after campaigning for the final primary there, on June 2. On that last flight of the campaign, they sat silently at the front of her plane, barely speaking. Clinton was despondent. People who visited with her at home in the immediate aftermath said she was full of gallows humor, deflated, and angry at the process.

She still had to bow out officially—to give a final farewell, thanking supporters who by now numbered in the millions. A speech she gave at Baruch College on June 3 was interpreted in the wrong way; she did not acknowledge that Obama had clinched the necessary delegates for the nomination, leading to stories that she intended to put up a fight (a plotline aided by the fact that Terry McAuliffe, her national chairman, introduced her as "the next president of the United States"). For the final, final farewell, Clinton had to make everything clear.

Her speechwriting cast, already large, expanded for the effort. For three days, two of her top speechwriters, Lissa Muscatine and Sarah Hurwitz, circulated drafts among advisers. Jim Kennedy, a former Clinton spokesman turned Sony executive, offered a line about having put "18 million cracks" in the glass ceiling—hadn't she, after all?—a line that would come to define the speech. Clinton herself did some work on the remarks; in interviews, aides disagreed on how engaged in the process she was, with some saying she focused on it only as the moment closed in.

After reading it, Clinton expressed discomfort with the gender parts of the speech, several aides said. She had not made breaking the glass ceiling the focus of her campaign, she argued, so why start now? She pushed back against some of the personal language. Several advisers, especially Howard Wolfson and Doug Hattaway, told Clinton that she needed to give her supporters a vehicle for their feelings, assuring her she was not in danger of seeming too self-absorbed.

"There was a huge fight about it," one adviser said. Clinton's resistance "went back to her original ambivalence about running as a woman." In the end her advisers won out, and the speech proceeded—and turned out to be, in the estimation of virtually everyone, her best.

Hillary Clinton had always been seen as a flawed test case for a woman presidential candidate: she was unique, having led an extraordinary life that was unlikely to be repeated. It was impossible to untangle the unique threads of her life—as a former First Lady, the wife of a complicated former president, with her own tortured history with the public and the press—and it did not seem wise to extrapolate any larger meaning from her experience. She was not just any woman, the reasoning went; she was Hillary Clinton, and that was a different ball of wax.

Or was it?

Any woman who could mount a serious campaign for president was bound to be extraordinary in some way, and to have an unusual marriage, and baggage. Could it be that Clinton seemed like the exception because getting to that point required being exceptional? Might there be similarly extreme responses the next time?

Sarah Palin, still an unknown figure sitting at a desk in Alaska, was about to find out.

Chapter 3

Hunting Season

The Men's Choice

As rumors of a surprise Republican vice presidential pick began to seep out on the morning of August 29, 2008, a wave of confusion swept across the political establishment. Television crews had been hovering outside the houses of candidates on the short list, waiting for one of them—presumably either former Massachusetts Governor Mitt Romney or Minnesota Governor Tim Pawlenty—to emerge with a smile and a thumbs-up. No one guessed that the nominee, secretly flown in thousands of miles from Alaska, was a young woman whom Senator John McCain had met only twice before.

By the time Sarah Palin took the stage alongside McCain in Dayton, Ohio, for her first appearance that Friday afternoon, party stalwarts were in a state of shock. They knew the seventy-two-year-old veteran had an impulsive, mischievous streak, but had he really chosen an unknown forty-four-year-old governor from the Arctic as his running mate? Democrats, fresh from a convention intended to heal women's wounds, were galled; were the *Republicans* now going to break that barrier?

And who the hell was this woman?

As Palin stepped up to the podium, it quickly became clear that she was unlike anything voters had ever seen. Her political profile as a maverick who had taken on the "old boys' network" in Alaska was just the beginning. What made her truly alien to the nation was her profile as a woman. Beautiful and poised, her brunette hair swept up on top of her head, Palin beamed and waved, speaking in a western, nasal twang. She immediately introduced her young family, including her four-month-old infant

with Down syndrome and her husband, whom she described as her high school sweetheart and "still the man that I admire most in this world."

She was, she told the massive television audience hungry for information about her, just an average "hockey mom" who joined the PTA, eventually running for city council of her hometown, then mayor, then governor. Along the way she had developed a passion for rooting out corruption and waste, she said. Her selection as vice presidential nominee was a great honor, she said, but also a natural progression of events. Palin heralded her new place in history without hesitation. "It's fitting that this trust has been given to me eighty-eight years almost to the day after the women of America first gained the right to vote," Palin proclaimed. Citing both Geraldine Ferraro and Hillary Clinton by name as the "two other women who came before me in national elections," Palin proposed picking up where they had left off.

"It was rightly noted in Denver this week that Hillary left 18 million cracks in the highest, hardest glass ceiling. But it turns out the women of America aren't finished yet, and we can shatter that glass ceiling once and for all," Palin said, to some boos but mostly cheers from the Republican crowd.

Palin's confidence matched her stage skills—she was, one of McCain's senior advisers later told me, focused on rehearsing her speeches "as seriously as a Shakespearean trained actor"—but it was not an act. In those first few days, she expressed no self-doubt about her ability to serve as vice president, no hesitancy toward the white-hot media environment she was stepping into, according to several people who worked with her during that phase. McCain and his top advisers admired her fearlessness; it was among the reasons they picked her.

Even so, his campaign manager, Steve Schmidt, tried to

impress upon Palin the extraordinary scrutiny she would face in the nine weeks between her selection and the election on November 4, and beyond, if they should win. At a secret meeting in Flagstaff, Arizona, two nights before her selection was announced, Schmidt and Mark Salter, McCain's top speechwriter, sat down with Palin at a ranch belonging to Bob Delgado, a business partner of Cindy McCain. It was, an aide said, a "brutally frank conversation about the total loss of privacy for her family, the intrusions of the media and others into her family's private life, a warning that she would be attacked in vicious and personal terms," because the McCain campaign "believed she would provide an existential threat to the Obama candidacy."

Palin's response to Schmidt and Salter was quick, and sure. "No problem," she told them.

That, advisers said, was the total extent of the McCain campaign's preparation for putting a woman on the Republican ticket for the first time in history.

The casual approach was stunning: unlike the Clinton campaign's epic internal deliberations over how the public would perceive a woman in high command, the McCain camp made a calculation based on gut feelings and vague electoral math.

The campaign had found that none of the men under consideration moved the needle in their polling. Nor, they concluded, would someone predictable, like Pawlenty or Romney, generate the kind of media buzz the moment required. McCain was waging an uphill battle for the presidency, with only a few months left to detach himself from the Bush legacy and repair the badly damaged Republican brand, and he needed an instant game changer. He was trailing badly with women, despite the earlier fractures in the Democratic party; and he needed to shore up his support among conservatives. Palin, a popular governor with a reformer style—and those looks!—seemed tailor-made both to lure some of those 18 million Clinton voters away and to excite the conservative base.

It made a certain amount of sense, but the decision was missing a critical perspective: that of a woman. Not one female strategist was involved in the selection process—not out of hostility but because the already bare-bones McCain campaign had very few women on staff. Nor were there senior advisers with expertise in running women's campaigns. Most of the staff members were alumni of the most recent Bush White House operation; the rest had been with McCain all along. Schmidt and Rick Davis, another senior McCain aide, put Palin on the original short list, floating her name in a meeting with a group of other male advisers. McCain himself made the final call, telephoning Palin at the Alaska State Fair to invite her to consider joining him. By the time Palin arrived in Arizona the week before the convention, her selection was more or less a done deal; McCain offered her the position the next day.

Had a council of Republican women met to discuss the Palin choice ahead of time, they might have cautioned McCain that women are usually held to a higher standard, especially on questions of toughness and competence—and that women won't switch party affiliation just to vote for a woman. Female candidates also have to remember that women can be deeply suspicious and critical of one another. Palin's appearance was another obvious red flag; a group of female advisers could have gently reminded the McCain men that women are not always thrilled to see a young, attractive woman step into the limelight, and they might need to prepare for the long knives.

The "mommy wars"—over whether women should work or care for their children—might have been taken into consideration, to prepare to counter effectively the inevitable questions about how a mother of five children planned to balance her life with the vice presidency. News that Palin's teenage daughter was pregnant, which she disclosed to the vetters the night before she was picked, might have triggered alarm bells among women in a way it did not for the McCain team.

But the only severe risk the McCain inner circle foresaw was Palin's lack of experience, especially on foreign policy. All the gender stuff seemed irrelevant. After all, Hillary Clinton had proven the country was basically ready to elect a woman. No problem. Right?

"They had no idea what they were unleashing," one female adviser who worked with Palin during the campaign, and remained sympathetic to her, said. "This wasn't just a risky pick because of her experience. It was a risky pick because of what she represented and what she looked like. If she'd been a Rhodes scholar it would have been risky."

After the announcement was made, Jane Swift, the former Republican governor of Massachusetts—who had given birth to twins in office—sent the campaign a seven-point memo of lessons she had learned during her tumultuous tenure. Advisers read it, but it did not seem to penetrate. "I don't think they needed a woman in every meeting, but they needed great strategists who've worked with women candidates," Swift told me, looking back. The lack of gender awareness in the McCain campaign was so glaring that Swift later began telling college audiences about it, saying in a speech at Williams College that McCain advisers "either chose to ignore previous experience or were just completely unaware of it."

At the White House, President George W. Bush watched the selection with the wary eye of a veteran. Bush was as shocked as anyone: he learned who the vice presidential pick was from television and had, like most, assumed Pawlenty—

someone he knew far better—was the leading choice. Once he realized what McCain had done, it did not take long for Bush to process what was happening, even from a distance. He had been there when his father picked Dan Quayle, an unknown senator, as the vice presidential nominee; he knew how well surprises go over, which is to say not very well. Later that first day, Bush asked his press secretary, Dana Perino: "How's it playing?" She told him things looked really good.

Bush seemed skeptical. "He said, 'She might have been a good pick, but I don't know if she has any idea what's about to hit her,'" Perino later recalled. "The president had seen what had happened to his dad. And then he had been a candidate two times. He could anticipate what it was going to be like. And he said, 'She has no idea.'"

Perino herself—the second female White House press secretary in history, the only one to serve in a Republican administration—had an even more dubious reaction. Perino had worked hard to neutralize stories about her own good looks and clothing, and to be treated as a peer by the administration and the press corps. As a Republican woman, she knew that the scrutiny could sometimes be extra sharp—and that there were far fewer Republican women to stand up for one another. Watching the Palin announcement on television from her office in the West Wing, Perino told a reporter on the phone, "I don't know her, but I can tell you one thing. The gender politics is about to get really ugly."

At first, it appeared Palin was simply a polarizing force, which had its benefits. Though she horrified many Democratic women, pushing them away with conservative views on abortion and the teaching of abstinence, her arrival thrilled a Republican base that had never fully trusted McCain after his primary campaign against George W. Bush in 2000. Conservative female voters, a long-neglected demographic, responded ecstatically. It seemed that all Republicans needed to do was drive up their party's turnout, as Bush had done two elections in a row, and steal some moderates, and victory was within reach.

After Palin ad-libbed a quip about being a hockey mom in her convention speech ("I love those hockey moms. You know, they say the difference between a hockey mom and a pit bull . . . lipstick," she said), Republican women started showing up at her events carrying giant red plastic lips along with signs that read "Hockey Moms 4 Palin" and "We love you, Sarah!" Her crowds were instantly huge. Copies of her square, rimless eye-glasses sold out at designer stores. Palin-mania, as it was called, consumed even the McCain operation. From the moment she was introduced, through the convention, and until her first major television network interview, Palin was the darling of the campaign, her success wildly outpacing their imagination of how she would perform, and upstaging the presidential nominee. "We didn't have any idea if we were going to win, but we definitely had a too-close-to-call race. And she was a big part of that," Mark Salter told me of that period.

The euphoria lasted about two weeks. But even before the Palin phenomenon began to unravel, after a series of faltering interviews, there were signs that the torrent of passions she had provoked was excessive and uncontrollable—far beyond anything the men on McCain's vice presidential short list would have generated.

The first sign was the rumor about her youngest baby.

As the Republican convention was getting under way and Democratic operatives were melting down over what effect Palin might have, an anonymous contributor to the liberal blog Daily Kos posted a comment accusing Palin of fabricating her fifth pregnancy earlier that year—to cover up for the fact that the baby belonged to her teenage daughter Bristol. Palin's latest pregnancy had some components that seemed odd—she had reportedly flown home to Alaska from Texas as her water broke and she started going into labor; she did not look pregnant in public photographs as far as seven months into her term—but this anonymous allegation did more than raise doubts.

"Sarah, I'm calling you a liar. And not even a good one," the poster, under the pseudonym Arc XIX, wrote. "Trig Paxson Van Palin is not your son. He is your grandson." The posting flashed across cyberspace, reaching thousands (including me and every mainstream political reporter I knew). Andrew Sullivan, a political blogger at the prestigious *Atlantic* magazine, picked it up, encouraging reporters to ask McCain officials questions about the circumstances of Palin's last pregnancy, which they promptly did.

McCain aides, perhaps naïvely, were blown away by the questions. "I will never forget the first phone call I got from a real reporter, from a real newsroom, about the maternity of the infant," Nicolle Wallace, one of the few senior women consultants on the campaign, said. "He started asking me about amniotic fluid, and whether or not it had leaked. . . . I said, 'Are you asking me to respond, on the record, to a charge that amniotic fluid came out of her vagina?' He was so mortified, he hung up." Back at McCain headquarters, where aides had been out of the loop on Palin's selection in the first place, advisers did not know whether to believe the baby was hers.

The conspiracy theory had a familiar ring in one sense: it was reminiscent of the frenetic response a decade and a half earlier to another ambitious woman who had appeared suddenly on the scene. In First Lady Hillary Rodham Clinton's case, the allegations were not that she had covered up a pregnancy but that she had participated in corruption and murder, or secretly been a lesbian. Of course, the Clinton questions, often tinged with gender, came from outraged conservatives rather than the mostly liberal crowd who drove the Palin inquisition (the main exception being Sullivan, a quirky libertarian at the forefront of the pregnancy charge).

And the "fifth baby" frenzy stood in obvious contrast to another baby rumor that had been circulating for some time—to much less effect. Some reporters and political operatives heard rumblings that former Senator John Edwards had carried on an illicit affair and fathered a love child around the time he began running for president, in 2007. Except in Edwards's case, much of the rumor turned out to be true. Several close Edwards operatives even refused to work for him out of disgust. Only the *National Enquirer* pursued the story, breaking news of his affair in October 2007; Edwards denied allegations of infidelity point-blank, making it difficult for mainstream news organizations to responsibly pursue them—until he admitted it in 2008, after he had dropped out of the race. Still, two Edwards aides later said they were surprised no other gossip pages—or serious news outlets—raised the question more often, given how many people suspected the affair was happening.

They had a valid point in political terms: had there been intense interest in proving the Edwards allegations earlier, it could have affected the outcome of the Democratic primary. A damaged Edwards could have shifted votes to Clinton in the early contests. By the time Palin emerged, that was neither here nor there, but the contrast—between the ungrounded hysteria over a fake pregnancy and the arm's-length treatment of a real one—was striking.

Fair or not, the Palin pregnancy ordeal quickly led to another upheaval, this time rooted in fact: unbeknownst to all but a few senior McCain aides, Palin's oldest daughter, seventeen-year-old Bristol, was actually five months pregnant.

That development, once revealed, would refute questions about a faked pregnancy—Bristol could not have given birth four months earlier—but aides, conscious of the earthquake it would produce, had hoped to postpone releasing it as long as possible. When people at the convention began scrutinizing photographs of Bristol over Labor Day weekend, Steve Schmidt approached Palin to tell her the pregnancy secret could not hold much longer. The campaign issued a release from Palin and her husband, Todd, attempting to put the whole controversy to rest. "Our beautiful daughter Bristol came to us with news that as parents we knew would make her grow up faster than we had ever planned," the statement said. "As Bristol faces the responsibilities of adulthood, she knows that she has our unconditional love and support.

"We ask the media to respect our daughter and Levi's privacy, as has always been the tradition of children of candidates," it read.

Maybe a male candidate could have avoided triggering an uproar with such an announcement in the middle of a political convention—though it is hard to imagine. Palin certainly did not. The news rocked the Republican gathering in Minneapolis and consumed the political oxygen nationwide.

McCain aides tried to beat back questions about Palin's complex family life by claiming a double standard. "She's been a very effective governor," Steve Schmidt said at the convention in response to a question about whether Palin could serve as vice president while coping with so much personal activity. Frustrated, he argued: "I can't imagine that question being asked of a man." Protestations about Obama's having two young daughters fell on deaf ears. This was different, reporters persisted, because she had a newborn child with special needs. Wasn't motherhood itself supposed to be one of her credentials? Schmidt, like the other men on the McCain team, appeared especially ill at ease having to discuss such questions, the likes of which they had never faced in their professional lives.

What most disoriented Palin's defenders was that the barrage of personal questions was coming not just from the conservative defenders of family values but from the media, and from liberals, blurring the traditional battle lines over motherhood and the workplace. Democrats, the usual advocates of women's careers, demanded to know how Palin could care for her family and also manage the vice presidency—a job that would put her just a heartbeat away from an office held by a seventy-two-year-old president, if McCain were elected, they noted. Reporters were just as curious. It was not sexist, they argued, to want to know how that would work logistically. And voters wanted to know, too. One woman pulled me aside at a Palin rally to ask: Was it true that Todd Palin stayed home full-time with the children? It was not; Palin herself said many times that he worked part of the year on an oil rig on Alaska's North Slope.

Suddenly, the "Mommy Wars: Special Campaign Edition," as a *New York Times* story put it, were on in full force.

"If you were facing the same family issues as Sarah Palin would you have accepted John McCain's offer to run for vice president?" *People* magazine asked on its website.

"The role of vice president, it seems to me, would take up an awful lot of her time, and it raises the issue of how much time will she have to dedicate to her newborn child," CNN anchor John Roberts said to the correspondent Dana Bash. Bash replied that, from the McCain camp's perspective, it was probably not a question that would have been posed to a man.

"A mother's role is different from a father's," the columnist Sally Quinn retorted in the *Washington Post*.

"They were questioning whether a mother can be president, vice president," said Representative Kay Granger, a Republican of Texas and one of the longest-serving female members of the House. "Here you've got this exceptional woman who is governor of a state, who has a young baby, has children, and all during this time they are just questioning, 'Well, shouldn't she be at home?' And that was astonishing."

Actually, given public opinion shifts against working mothers, it was not *that* astonishing: by a two-to-one margin, the public opposes the trend of more women working outside the home, according to a study by the Pew Research Center in 2007. Some 41 percent said it was a bad thing for society for mothers of young children to work, compared with 22 percent who said it was a good thing. (Among working mothers themselves, just 21 percent said that it was ideal for them to work full-time, down from 32 percent who said the same a decade earlier.) And the split broke heavily along partisan lines, with Republicans opposing working motherhood the most.

Still, in the upside-down world that Sarah Palin's arrival created, it was Republicans who found themselves defending the idea of a gender-neutral society, where fathers were just as suitable to care for children and women professionals should not be treated differently from their male counterparts. Biological differences were out the window. The McCain campaign issued a statement deploring a "faux media scandal designed to destroy the first female Republican nominee," and a group of Republican women, led by former Hewlett-Packard chief executive Carly Fiorina, banded together to denounce what they described as "sexist attacks" on Palin. (They were a vigilant group: when Obama described McCain's policies as trying to put "lipstick on a pig," the Republican council of women rose again to defend Palin's honor, accusing him of a veiled attempt to compare her to a sow.)

Former New York City Mayor Rudolph Giuliani took especially dramatic umbrage, sounding almost politically correct. "How dare they question whether Sarah Palin has enough time to spend with her children and be vice president?" Giuliani asked a raucous crowd on the floor of the Republican National Convention. "When do they ever ask a man that question?"

Democrats were giddy about the turnaround. "Have conservatives discovered sexism?" a writer gleefully asked on the website of the National Organization for Women.

Not all conservatives were so adamant—Dr. Laura Schlessinger, consistent in her advocacy of stay-at-home motherhood, declared herself "extremely disappointed" that McCain would pick such a dangerous role model—but the Republican party figured out several ways to embrace Palin. They told two narratives about her: as a superhuman mother goddess, able to raise four children, give birth to a fifth, and return to work in under a week, all, presumably, while keeping up with her jogging and moose hunting (her ability to "field dress a moose," a tough-sounding activity few could envision, was a constant theme of the Republican ticket). This was the rugged, western story of Palin, one that mythologized her stamina and set her apart from ordinary women, who might feel overwhelmed at the prospect of simultaneously being a mother of several young children and helping run the free world.

The other narrative about Palin was that she was human—
all too human, with everyday flaws, regular-folk values, and a
working-class sensibility. Here, her daughter's pregnancy and
her own strange delivery story were part of what made her real,
just an average hockey mom, warts and all. ("The Palins are
a busy clan," the narrator in her convention video said, allud-
ing to the chaotic nature of her brood.) The McCain campaign
argued this quality would help her connect to ordinary voters in
a way Obama could not. In addition, her decision to keep her
disabled baby and her daughter's decision to go through with
her own pregnancy were proof that she walked the conservative values walk. "Some of the chattering class still don't quite
get it. We appreciate a mother who gives the unconditional love
and support that a daughter needs, deserves, and would want to
have, and she has only affirmed our own appreciation for Sarah
Palin," said former Arkansas Governor Mike Huckabee, an
evangelical Christian.

The two extreme Palins—the superhuman one and the everyday hockey mom—were sometimes difficult to reconcile, but
together they formed a recurring theme. Palin had been brought
in to save the McCain campaign, the only extra-powerful vice
presidential nominee who could do so. But when she failed in
that task, she was not just average, she was trailer trash: "a
diva," a "whack job," matriarch of a bunch of "Wasilla hillbil-
lies," in the words of McCain aides who soured on her and her
family and began leaking negative stories to reporters.

Then a third Palin emerged: the idiotic beauty queen who
paraded well onstage but could not answer basic questions about
why she should be vice president or what she would do if she
got the job. This Palin—the Tina Fey version on *Saturday Night
Live*—was the one that stuck, the one that became the enduring

frame for the whole Republican ticket and, some women felt by the end, the reason why Palin's candidacy represented a setback for women in politics everywhere.

If one group remained relatively calm about Palin throughout, it was the Obama campaign. Opposition researchers at the Obama headquarters in Chicago, on the instructions of the senior Obama adviser Anita Dunn, had put Palin on their short list of possible McCain choices early in 2008. But they had removed her from their A-list when news broke over the summer that she was being investigated for "Troopergate," a messy personal scandal involving her efforts to fire an Alaska public safety commissioner when he did not remove her former brother-in-law from the state police force.

Dunn, a widely respected, no-nonsense Democratic operative, had the unique perspective of having run a campaign against Palin two years earlier, as an adviser to the Alaskan gubernatorial candidate Tony Knowles. She considered Palin a formidable and charismatic politician; she also had a grasp of Palin's thin record and her history on the so-called bridge to nowhere, a federally funded roads project symbolizing government pork that Palin had supported before distancing herself from it. Dunn had also sat through numerous Palin-Knowles debates.

That Palin expertise, shared by few in the country, would steady the Obama campaign at a moment when national Democrats embarked on what Dunn described as "two weeks of total hysteria" over the Alaska governor. Dunn had ordered her own research staff to stop putting so much energy into Palin, convinced that she could not pass the vetting process. "How was I to know that *they* weren't going to vet her?" Dunn asked with a laugh afterward.

The initial Obama response, at Dunn's direction, came from Press Secretary Bill Burton, who dismissed Palin as too inexperienced—getting the idea into the ether immediately, so it would stick. Then the Obama team dialed back even that criticism, not wanting to be seen as piling on or to give Palin a legitimate shot at playing the victim. Obama called Palin from his campaign bus to congratulate her on her nomination. The rest of the Democratic staff was under orders to stay focused on pursuing McCain—and not to touch personal stories about Palin.

Obama himself drew a firm line, declaring Palin's family off-limits. "Our people were not involved in any way in this and they will not be," he said, sounding angry when asked about the pregnancy rumor at a press conference. "And if I ever thought there was somebody in my campaign that was involved in something like that, they'd be fired, okay?" He pointed out that his mother had had him at age eighteen. "How a family deals with issues and teenage children, that shouldn't be the topic of our politics," Obama said. "I would strongly urge people to back off these kinds of stories."

But that cool response from the Obama campaign only made Democrats more apoplectic. A Democratic female member of Congress went into a frenzy, calling Dunn and demanding action. Why, the congresswoman wanted to know, wasn't Obama hitting Palin over the strange circumstances of her fifth baby? "She felt so strongly that we needed to make a direct issue out of the fact that Palin had gotten on the plane after her water had broken to fly home to Alaska. And how no ob-gyn in the country would have recommended that. And that either meant that she hadn't really delivered the baby or—worse—that this was just showing what a totally unfit person she was and that we should make an issue of it," Dunn recalled.

Dunn said she thanked the congresswoman for her advice— "I thanked everybody during those days for their advice," she said. Going after Palin in such a way made little political sense. "To me it was a very good example of how differently elite women were reacting to Palin from normal women," Dunn said. "Not that normal women wouldn't raise an eyebrow at that story, but they would not ever want to have that discussed in a campaign. They would not see that as a character point they wanted to have debated. Because in their lives they have to make trade-offs all the time."

Early in the race, so-called normal women did seem to relate to Palin—and to move toward her in the polls. Obama aides denied it at the time but later acknowledged that their internal polling showed younger white women shifting toward McCain after he put Palin on the ticket. (They had gone through a similar period of public denial around the New Hampshire primary, when Clinton started winning women, a source of rare internal dissent in Obamaland.)

The female shift to McCain was brief—lasting only about two weeks in September—but it was real. Most of the drift came from independent women, not hard-core Democrats; the few prominent Clinton supporters who defected, such as Lady Lynn Forester de Rothschild, were not representative of a larger trend.

Clinton herself stayed noticeably quiet. Her advisers held a meeting immediately after Palin was chosen to debate her response—with Ann Lewis and Cheryl Mills advocating that Clinton welcome the new vice presidential candidate and acknowledge the historical implication of her run. "Their argument was, we spent the last year and a half talking about a woman for president. There might be some women who don't want to see us beating up on another woman," one senior adviser said. "It was like, we've got to recognize girl power here."

And so Clinton did, calling Palin, in her first public statements, "an important new voice to the debate" and urging people to "be proud of Governor Sarah Palin's historic nomination, and I congratulate her." She rebuffed a preliminary request by the Obama campaign to speak out against Palin, telling the team, through intermediaries, that anything she said along those lines would produce ugly stories about a catfight. She clung, with iron discipline, to her criticisms of McCain rather than his running mate.

Former President Bill Clinton was even less critical. "I come from Arkansas, I get why she's hot out there . . . why she's doing well," he said a few weeks after Palin was picked. "People look at her, and they say, 'All those kids. Something that happens in everybody's family. I'm glad she loves her daughter and she's not ashamed of her. Glad that girl's going around with her boyfriend. Glad they're going to get married.'" Voters, Clinton said, would likely think to themselves: "I like that little Down syndrome kid. One of them lives down the street. They're wonderful children. They're wonderful people. And I like the idea that this guy does those long-distance races. Stayed in the race for five hundred miles with a broken arm. My kind of guy.

"I get this," Bill Clinton said, his competitive tone softened dramatically since the primaries. "My view is . . . why say, ever, anything bad about a person? Why don't we like them and celebrate them and be happy for her elevation to the ticket? And just say that she was a good choice for him and we disagree with them?"

Joel Benenson, the lead pollster for Obama, said the campaign never really worried about retrieving women drawn to Palin, but they did redouble their efforts to lure them back. The chief targets were affluent, suburban parents and rural, independent, middle-class women. "We obviously thought there'd be some excitement because she was a woman, she had a compelling story, her rise to the governorship in Alaska and so on, but the bottom line was that we actually made a conscious decision that we were running against John McCain and didn't need to really spend a lot of time focusing on Sarah Palin," Benenson said. "We believed that whatever attraction that she held in the early days would fade pretty quickly."

Other Democratic officials who had run against Palin before marveled at the mistakes the McCain team made in fundamentally understanding her. Celinda Lake, the Democratic pollster, said there were three obvious missteps from the outset: not recognizing the Cold War mentality that native Alaskans are raised with; not understanding how her western dialect would sound on the East Coast; and not starting her off with interviews in small media markets, where her aw-shucks approach might work. But it was her Alaskanness that tripped them up most. "One-third of Alaskans came up around the military. They came up for the Cold War," Lake said. "They came up in support of people who were up there. So when Sarah Palin used to say all the time in Alaska, 'We see the Soviet Union from our front porch,' Alaskans would say, 'Yeah, damn straight. I remember when we came up here to defend America in the Cold War.' People in the Lower 48, and particularly east of the Mississippi, were going, 'Is she a nutcase? What is she talking about?'"

In the end, the attraction of the Republican ticket faded for most people because of the economy. The financial firm Lehman Brothers collapsed on September 15; McCain responded by declaring that the fundamentals of the economy were strong. The Obama campaign mounted a deliberate campaign to describe

McCain as "erratic," depicting him as aging, and out of touch. Soon afterward, the trajectory of the race was set.

Still, though it was not all Palin's fault, the polling numbers showed she had become an unmistakable drag.

If a single event encapsulated Palin's drag on the Republican ticket, it was her interview with Katie Couric. In fact, it was not a single interview but a devastating series—each more painful than the last, conducted over consecutive days in late September, just as the economy was imploding.

The details of how the CBS interview came about were, like so much else in the McCain operation in late 2008, a source of internal dispute.

When confronted with accusations that the campaign "set up" Palin to fail, McCain advisers point out that Palin granted her first network interview to ABC's Charles Gibson weeks earlier as part of a broad media strategy designed to get several big networks out of the way so she could concentrate on preparing for the one vice presidential debate, in early October. In keeping with that plan, Palin flew home to Alaska after the Republican convention, and an ABC crew took over a hotel down the block from her house for several days. Gibson interviewed her there, doing his live shots at the edge of Lake Lucille, where Palin's home in Wasilla sits, her husband's seaplane parked on the water in the background. It was among the more exotic moments of any recent presidential campaign.

The interview was not perfect, but it was passable. Palin's confidence was on full display. When Gibson asked if she had any moments of doubt before accepting the nomination, she replied: "I didn't hesitate, no.

"I answered him 'yes' because I have the confidence in that readiness and knowing that you can't blink," Palin said, repeating

Gibson's first name throughout the interview. "You have to be wired in a way of being so committed to the mission, the mission that we're on, reform of this country and victory in the war, you can't blink. So I didn't blink then, even when asked to run as his running mate."

Senior campaign aides had flown to Wasilla to monitor the Gibson interview and prepare Palin for her next sit-downs, and they gathered in a bar decorated with giant stuffed bears and moose heads to watch it with reporters over beers. Palin may not have blinked at the vice presidency, but Steve Schmidt winced several times as he watched her on the big screen with Gibson—it was one of the first times that her odd locution, replete with "even" and "also, too, though," was plainly evident. Still, there was no suggestion that she would not proceed with the next interviews on her list.

According to numerous people in the McCain orbit—both sympathetic to Palin and not—something happened to her between the convention and the time she saw Katie Couric. Her allies said she grew increasingly nervous, "spooked" about the position she was now in and conscious of gaps in knowledge she had not known she had. One ally of Palin said that, cooped up in hotel rooms all day without any familiar faces to talk to, she started to lose her bearings.

Internal critics said Palin simply stopped listening to advice. Instead she grew distracted by off-topic questions—such as her popularity in Alaska, at one point demanding that Schmidt conduct a poll of Alaskans to make sure she was not suffering for being away campaigning in the Lower 48. A newspaper in

Alaska had written up ten sample questions that Couric might ask Palin, and she fixated on those as well.

Whatever the reason, Palin was not ready when it came time for her to talk with Couric, despite repeated conversations about how important it was for her to do her homework. McCain advisers were aware that, while Gibson might risk appearing condescending if he stumped Palin, any similar blowback from the Couric interview would rest at Palin's feet. Katie Couric could not, by definition, be scapegoated for going after Palin because she was a woman. Palin, aides said, did not seem to grasp the added significance of the CBS interview, her first with a prominent female reporter. "She was aware of the plan, she heard the plan, and she refused to prepare for the Katie Couric interview. She would not engage in Q-and-A beforehand," one senior McCain adviser said. "She was unprepared. She was unfocused. And the results were a disaster.

"Katie Couric was prepared, and Sarah Palin was not," the aide said.

Her defenders pointed out—repeatedly—that the McCain team picked Palin, not the other way around. "They say she wasn't ready for prime time? It was their job to *make* her ready for prime time," John Coale, a D.C. lawyer and prominent Clinton supporter who crossed over to support Palin, said. "They had no idea what women were about. Who the hell thought it was a good idea to have her first three interviews with the big network anchors?" Coale's wife, the Fox News anchor Greta Van Susteren, would go on to become a Palin defender on the airwaves.

Another senior McCain adviser countered: "We had explicit and frank conversations about what was involved in this, and I just don't buy the 'poor little me' act, this 'I was in over my head.'

We paid painstaking attention to detail, deliberately going through all of these things with her for hours."

McCain aides had arranged for Palin to tape several interviews with Couric to run over the course of a few nights, to mask the fact that she would be out of view doing debate preparation. Palin emerged from the first day shaken, reporting back that it had gone badly.

Sensing a fiasco, she tried to put a stop to it. "I knew it didn't go well the first day, and then we gave [Couric] a couple of other segments after that. And my question to the campaign was, after it didn't go well the first day, why were we going to go back for more?" Palin told the documentary filmmaker John Ziegler after the campaign ended. "Because of however it works in that upper echelon of power brokering in the media and with spokespersons, it was told to me that, yeah, we are going to go back for more. And going back for more was not a wise decision either." McCain aides confirmed to me that Palin had asked to stop the interviews but was told, in the words of one, that pulling the plug on Katie Couric was "not an option."

It is difficult to do justice to the interviews in print. Some of Palin's most-ridiculed answers—such as her seeming inability to name a newspaper or magazine that she reads—could be explained as defensiveness. At one point, Couric pressed her three times for the name of a news source; Palin demurred, replying that she had read "all of them, any of them that have been in front of me all these years.

"I have a vast variety of sources where we get our news, too," Palin said. "Alaska isn't a foreign country, where it's kind of suggested, 'Wow, how could you keep in touch with what the rest of Washington, D.C., may be thinking when you live up there in Alaska?' Believe me, Alaska is like a microcosm of America." Her allies said she was simply irritated that Couric would imply she did not keep up with the news. Jane Swift, the former Republican Massachusetts governor and a fierce defender of Palin's during the campaign, said: "When I saw the Katie Couric interview, my reaction was, 'She is furious with the national press. She sees them as the enemy. She thinks all they want to do is embarrass her, embarrass her family.' And when you asked her what she reads all she's thinking is, 'You're just trying to make me look stupid.'"

But there were some moments that are much harder to explain. One—so cringe inducing that Tina Fey reenacted much of it verbatim—involved Palin's inability to make a convincing case that John McCain would overhaul Wall Street practices:

> **Couric:** You've said, quote, "John McCain will reform the way Wall Street does business." Other than supporting stricter regulations of Fannie Mae and Freddie Mac two years ago, can you give us any more examples of his leading the charge for more oversight?
>
> **Palin:** I think that the example that you just cited, with his warnings two years ago about Fannie and Freddie—that, that's paramount. That's more than a heck of a lot of other senators and representatives did for us.
>
> **Couric:** But he's been in Congress for twenty-six years. He's been chairman of the powerful Commerce Committee. And he has almost always sided with less regulation, not more.
>
> **Palin:** He's also known as the maverick though, taking shots from his own party, and certainly taking shots from the other party. Trying to get people to understand what he's been talking about—the need to reform government.
>
> **Couric:** But can you give me any other concrete examples? Because I know you've said Barack Obama is a lot of talk and

no action. Can you give me any other examples in his twenty-six years of John McCain truly taking a stand on this?

Palin: I can give you examples of things that John McCain has done, that has shown his foresight, his pragmatism, and his leadership abilities. And that is what America needs today.

Couric: I'm just going to ask you one more time—not to belabor the point. Specific examples in his twenty-six years of pushing for more regulation.

Palin: I'll try to find you some and I'll bring them to you.

Senior McCain allies, once they saw the interview, were appalled. All of the questions about Palin's competence, which had been growing since the first week in September, were now clearly justified. But they had no time to dwell on it, with the economy melting down alongside their poll ratings. Palin was whisked into debate preparation in Arizona, the campaign hoping to stop her from going into total free fall.

Beauty Is Beastly

If the Palin candidacy thrust the question of sexism back into the spotlight, it was with a twist: her good looks were problematic in their own right, drawing attention that could be superficially seen as positive but was really a liability in political terms. The sexualization of Palin—as commentators fawned over her appearance and cable news channels aired a videotape of her strutting in a bathing suit as a beauty pageant contestant two decades earlier—posed a dilemma without much precedent. Hillary Clinton had been mocked for her "manliness," her raw laugh and her square-cut pantsuits, but she had rarely been dis-

missed as an object of desire. What did it mean, politically, that men wanted to sleep with Palin? Did that kind of thing draw *any* votes, or was it sheer insult? Could Caribou Barbie, as she was called, be taken seriously as a vice presidential candidate?

The McCain campaign, having blithely concluded that her looks were an unalloyed asset, began to see a potential downside after just a few days—as buttons declaring Palin the "Hottest VP" at the Republican convention gave way to more sinister pop culture references, mainly sex fantasies. The phrases "Sarah Palin naked" and "Sarah Palin bikini" rocketed to the top of a list of political Web searches. Larry Flynt, the porn mogul, produced a video entitled *Nailin' Paylin,* featuring a seductive look-alike. An artist in Chicago painted a large portrait of Palin naked, holding a machine gun; his wife hung it in her North Side bar, and the *Chicago Tribune* wrote it up uncritically as a local feature.

But even if McCain advisers wanted to complain, they could not do so effectively. Their early use of the sexism card—starting with expressions of over-the-top outrage at the GOP convention—left Republicans with an exhausted arsenal once the focus on Palin's sexuality kicked into high gear. And it opened them up to further ridicule, most crushingly on *Saturday Night Live*, where Tina Fey (as Palin) stood alongside Amy Poehler (as Hillary Clinton) for a joint "address" on sexism that made Palin look absurd.

"Sexism can never be allowed to permeate an American election," Fey said. "So please—stop Photoshopping my head on sexy bikini pictures."

"Stop saying I have cankles," Poehler added, with a bitter smile.

"Don't refer to me as a MILF," Fey said. "Reporters and commentators, stop using words that diminish us—like pretty, attractive, beautiful."

"Harpy, shrew, boner-shrinker," Poehler interjected.

The comedians had a point—could Palin really complain about being seen as too beautiful after Clinton had weathered such brutal insults?—but there was ample evidence that Palin's looks contributed to the narrative of her as an idiotic pawn. Peter Hart, the Democratic pollster, conducted a focus group several weeks before the election with undecided voters in Ohio, asking which of the four candidates each of them would most like to sit next to on an airplane. "Geez, I'm a twenty-nine-year-old male," one said, picking Palin. Then, sounding embarrassed, he changed his mind to say he'd rather sit next to Obama.

After the election, researchers at the University of South Florida submitted a paper concluding that Palin's appearance had diminished people's perceptions of her competence. "Focusing on Palin's appearance reduced intentions to vote for the McCain-Palin ticket," the researchers found. The notion that sexually objectifying a woman diminishes her is hardly new—it is at the core of feminist theory—but it is not exactly one that had made the rounds of a presidential campaign. It was strange, uncharted territory, and the McCain campaign had no idea how to respond. Should they ban all discussion of Palin's looks, reverting to a more traditional feminist model decreeing that focusing on her appearance insulted her intellect? Or should they embrace her appearance, portraying her as part of the newer generation of women who own their attractiveness and use it as a powerful tool?

Long before Palin came into the national eye, social psychologists had conducted experiments to assess the impact of attractiveness on job performance—and concluded that women could be perceived as *too* attractive to be considered competent or intelligent. Dubbed the "beauty is beastly" phenomenon, it seemed to affect only women, not men. "There's a tipping point—when a woman gets too attractive, she gets downgraded on leadership and intelligence," said Lee Sigelman, a political science professor at George Washington University, adding that it is basically "the dumb blond idea." In the early 1980s, Sigelman applied the beauty-is-beastly theory to politics with a test: he showed people two photographs of Rose Bird, the chief justice of the California State Supreme Court—one before she had a makeover and another afterward. People liked the prettier Justice Bird but respected her less. "In terms of personal attractiveness, the more attractive Rose Bird was seen as the more attractive person," Sigelman said. "But the other perceived characteristics—leadership capability, intelligence— did not go up as she got more attractive. They downgraded her on those dimensions."

In actual electoral situations, voters responded the same way. When Jennifer Granholm, an attractive blonde with cropped hair, first ran for governor of Michigan in 2003, her strategists found that people in focus groups—mostly women—saw her as too pretty to be a governor. Those kinds of looks were associated with models, Barbie dolls. Granholm could not change her appearance, so her campaign made a creative decision: to shoot her advertisements in black and white, and show mostly still photographs of her rather than video. "Women could not envision a female governor with her beauty," one adviser said. "When we took it down a notch, people said, okay, she can be governor."

These were surely not problems that John McCain had grappled with in advance, if he had even heard of them. In fact, many McCain confidants did not seem to grapple with Palin's beauty at all: they were just blinded by it. Fred Barnes of *The Weekly Standard* found her "exceptionally pretty"; William Kristol called her his "heartthrob"; Jay Nordlinger of the *National Review* had written about her as a "former beauty pageant contestant, and a real honey, too," though he had not, to his credit, said those qualifications would carry her into national politics. This was not just neoconservative chatter: even in the McCain headquarters after Palin was picked, one senior adviser told me, people routinely referred to her as "hot."

Democrats I spoke to, all too pleased to see Palin on the decline, argued that there was nothing wrong with pointing out the obvious in her appearance. Anyway, hadn't Obama been objectified, too? A young woman had starred in a video, "I've Got a Crush on Obama," that had seemed only to boost his popularity. Photographers had shot him on the beach bare-chested in his swimsuit (a photo that was brought back out at the end of his first hundred days in office, on the cover of *Washingtonian* magazine). And before that, John Edwards had been a "pretty boy," his head of gleaming brown hair no less commented on than Palin's high cheekbones.

But political operatives rarely worry about male candidates being too attractive; the concern is that they might seem too effeminate. Looks may have helped bring Democratic control of the House in 2006: Officials that year recruited a number of good-looking candidates—almost all of them male—to run for competitive seats. A *Washington Post* piece by Shailagh Murray tallied them: Heath Shuler (a former football quarterback), Brad Ellsworth (a swaggering Indiana sheriff), and Mike Arcuri (described as having "piercing Italian eyes and a runner's physique"). One woman, Gabrielle Giffords, was on the list of good-looking recruits.

To the extent that Sarah Palin was discussed less than respectfully inside the campaign, such discussion did not seem to be sanctioned at the upper levels. Palin was certainly approachable: she showed aides pictures of her family on her BlackBerry, talking casually with them on the campaign plane, usually with either Bristol or Willow in tow. Sometimes she did not seem to recognize herself as the principal. One campaign aide recalled a conference call in which Palin referred repeatedly to Steve Schmidt as "sir," replying to his directions "Yes sir, yes sir." Afterward, Schmidt called her with protocol instructions, telling her that she was the "ma'am" in that situation and that he was to be referred to as "Steve," the enlisted officer.

Still, several women in the McCain office expressed quiet discomfort to one another and to outside allies with the strategy devised for Palin. She seemed lonely and out of place on the road. She complained about not being given enough time to jog, the one activity that cleared her head. Her role as an attack dog—though traditional for the vice presidential nominee and one she appeared to relish—did not seem to be working for her as a woman. At one point, one said, several women separately lobbied the McCain campaign scheduler to send out a friendly face to accompany Palin on the campaign trail. When it became clear that McCain operatives were fanning the flames of negative stories about her, and in some cases leaking them themselves, several prominent women—including Carly Fiorina and the spokeswoman Nancy Pfotenhauer—tried to defend her. (In the aftermath of the campaign, the internal sniping continued: a senior aide derisively suggested "postpartum depression" as an explanation for what they thought was Palin's erratic behavior.)

Eventually, Fiorina herself was benched, after remarking on television that neither McCain nor Palin would have been qualified to run her former company. Fiorina's treatment only made the women of the campaign feel more isolated. Newer allies, including Elaine Lafferty, a former editor of *Ms. Magazine* and a Clinton supporter, tried to intervene.

Lafferty was an unusual fit inside McCain's world: a feminist and a Democrat, moved by Clinton's defeat, she offered her expertise as a writer and a communicator after Palin was selected (she had also, five years earlier, coauthored a book with Van Susteren). During the Democratic primaries, Lafferty had written a strategy memo to Clinton suggesting she combat Obama's Oprah effect more aggressively. Now, in late 2008, Lafferty found herself volunteering at McCain headquarters as the Republicans tried to win over disaffected Clinton voters. "I had been obviously brought on to have something to do with women voters, but couldn't get anywhere with any of that, despite memo after memo after memo," she said. "People would say, 'What do you do on the campaign?' I would say, 'I write memos.'"

Lafferty was insistent that Palin could be more effective if she tried to talk more directly to women, rather than repeating her stock lines about being a "maverick." "My point was that you've got to use certain language. Women wanted to support her. The ones who are lukewarm can be passionate, the ones who are passionate can convince others, the ones who are uncomfortable can be brought around. I was trying to push language, and push a speech," Lafferty said.

Remarkably enough, Palin did give a speech on women, on October 22, in Henderson, Nevada. It went almost completely unnoticed at the time, buried under a cascade of daily events and viewed cynically by the traveling press corps—another cheap effort to win women over, just as the Palin pick itself had been. Palin was still drawing big crowds, but by then she was such a problematic running mate that few in the political establishment took her seriously.

Palin gave the address nonetheless, and it included several shots at Obama that, though they paled in comparison to some of her other allegations (such as his tendency to "pal around" with terrorists), were in some ways more provocative. She portrayed herself as a modern feminist, joined with a more fearless pro-woman candidate, McCain, than any seen on the Democratic ticket. "Our opponents think they have the women's vote all locked up, which is a little presumptuous since only our side has a woman on the ticket," Palin said. "When it came time for choosing a vice president, somehow he couldn't bring himself to choose a woman who got 18 million votes in the primaries.

"You've got to ask yourself: Why was Senator Hillary Clinton not even vetted by the Obama campaign?" Palin said. "Why did it take twenty-four years, an entire generation, from the time Geraldine Ferraro made her pioneering bid until the next time that a woman was asked to join a national ticket?" She raised one sore subject, then another. Palin brought up a pay disparity question involving Obama's Senate staff, which had been found to pay women a lower salary than did McCain's office (Obama's aides countered, somewhat weakly, that he employed women in lower-ranking positions). "Does he think that the women aren't working as hard?" Palin asked. "Does he think that they are 17 percent less productive? And Barack Obama can't say that this is just the way that it's always been done around the Capitol, because I know one senator who actually does pay equal wages for equal work, Senator John McCain."

The speech was brazen, a radical departure from the Palin script about energy independence and rejecting the old boys' network. It also raised a question that cut to the core of the women's movement in the 2008: What did it stand for now, anyway?

Was feminism, and the feminist movement, geared toward helping women everywhere advance—regardless of their politics, especially their views on abortion? Or was the movement, to the extent it still existed, now deeply, irretrievably anchored in the Democratic party, willing to support men over women if the politics lined up that way? Hadn't the movement, in failing to secure the nomination for Clinton, proven the inefficacy of staying within partisan lines? Would the movement work to elect a woman president or vice president, or was that a secondary goal?

If Clinton had epitomized the feminist movement's dream, Palin was in many ways its worst nightmare, and almost all of the traditional groups—NOW, the National Organization for Women, being the most prominent—rejected her reflexively. That left some big-tent feminists, such as Lafferty, feeling alienated—even, at some points, bombarded with insults. When Lafferty wrote a piece for The Daily Beast defending Palin's intellect, she was pilloried in over-the-top terms across the blogosphere (one posting on the popular women's site Jezebel .com bore the headline, in huge type, "As Far As I'm Concerned, Former Ms. Editor Elaine Lafferty Can Go F*** Herself"). It has gotten more than 18,300 views.

Debora Spar, the president of Barnard College, said she had raised the idea of inviting Palin to speak on the all-girls' campus and was immediately shot down by horrified colleagues. That only got Spar thinking further about what Palin represented, and the dilemma she posed for feminists. "Despite all the Tina Fey stuff, and all the comedy that came of the whole event, she threw a real wrench into feminism," Spar said after the election was over. "I think her success was very painful for traditional feminists to watch. . . . I heard from older Barnard alums, who were part of traditional feminism and really embraced Hillary Clinton, and when Sarah Palin came along it was like cold water being thrown on everybody. But in many ways Palin represented exactly what feminism had always fought for. She was young, she was in what appeared to be a healthy, loving marriage, she didn't get her success by marrying into power or being born into power. She got it on her own merits. She was everything feminism was supposed to represent."

Spar went so far as to suggest that Palin had helped put a nail in the coffin of the old feminist alignment, whose borders had been shifting for decades. "Within feminism there was an assumption of ideology—that people who were in favor of women's achievement were also in favor of access to abortion and liberal politics and a more interventionist government.

And it lined up that way for thirty years, but I don't think it lines up that way anymore," she said.

Yet if there was a seismic shift among women over time, it was *away* from Palin, not toward her, with some conservative female intellectuals leading the way when her public performances and her ideas proved weak. Most prominently, the columnist Kathleen Parker—who initially defended Palin and pilloried "the Left's hypocrisy in questioning Palin's qualifications to be vice president against the backdrop of her family's choices"—abandoned her in the midst of a financial crisis that she said demanded a vice president more up to the task. "It was fun while it lasted," Parker wrote at the end of September. "Like so many women, I've been pulling for Palin, wishing her the best, hoping she will perform brilliantly. I've also noticed that I watch her interviews with the held breath of an anxious parent, my finger poised over the mute button in case it gets too painful. Unfortunately, it often does. My cringe reflex is exhausted.

"If Palin were a man, we'd all be guffawing, just as we do every time Joe Biden tickles the back of his throat with his toes. But because she's a woman—and the first ever on a Republican presidential ticket—we are reluctant to say what is painfully true," Parker wrote. Weeks later, Peggy Noonan made an equally forceful case against Palin in the pages of the *Wall Street Journal.* "We have seen Mrs. Palin on the national stage for seven weeks now, and there is little sign that she has the tools, the equipment, the knowledge or the philosophical grounding one hopes for, and expects, in a holder of high office," Noonan wrote. "No news conferences? Interviews now only with friendly journalists? You can't be president or vice president and govern in that style, as a sequestered figure. This has been Mr. Bush's style the past few years, and see where it got us. You must address America in its entirety, not as a sliver or a series of slivers but as a full and whole entity, a great nation trying to hold together. When you don't, when you play only to your little piece, you contribute to its fracturing. In the end the Palin candidacy is a symptom and expression of a new vulgarization in American politics. It's no good, not for conservatism and not for the country. And yes, it is a mark against John McCain, against his judgment and idealism."

The questions about the movement's obligations to women candidates, and the obligations of women to support other women, raised another one: Did Palin consider herself a feminist?

"I do," she replied when asked that directly by Katie Couric. "I'm a feminist who believes in equal rights, and I believe that women certainly today have every opportunity that a man has to succeed and to try to have it all anyway. And I'm very, very thankful that I've been brought up in a family where gender hasn't been an issue. You know, I've been expected to do everything growing up that the boys were doing. We were out chopping wood and you're out hunting and fishing and filling our freezer with good wild Alaska game to feed our family. So it kind of started with that. With just that expectation that the boys and the girls in my community were expected to do the same and accomplish the same. That's just been instilled in me."

Couric followed up: "What is your definition of feminism?"

"Someone who believes in equal rights. Someone who would not stand for oppression against women," Palin replied.

But a month later, asked the exact same question again, Palin gave a different answer. The NBC anchor Brian Williams asked: "Governor, are you a feminist?"

"I'm not going to label myself anything, Brian," she answered.

Her most honest answer—one that perhaps made Palin seem naïve but echoed the confusion of many women nationwide— came a few days after the election. Unprompted, in response to a question about why she and McCain had not won more women, Palin replied: "I truly believe that we have more in common than we have differences, when we want to make sure that our communities are healthy and safe and that we have health care for our children and that our daughters have equal opportunities in the workforce. All those things that we have in common, again, certainly outweigh the differences that perhaps we have."

She continued: "So I would like to see, perhaps, some of these feminist women—sometimes, you know, I consider myself, too, as a feminist, whatever that means." In another context, it was the kind of comment that many women might have related to; from someone else's lips, her riff on solidarity could have been a rallying cry. But by then Palin was a caricature of her former self, her Tina Fey persona more real than reality, her profile cluttered with stories about her as a shopaholic in the waning days of a bitter, losing campaign.

First Dude

Todd Palin, never a major figure in the campaign, brought a new archetype to national politics nonetheless: that of a rugged "first dude," as his wife called him, a supportive husband happy to care for the children and let his more publicly successful spouse take the limelight.

Hillary Clinton had been at the opposite end of the spousal spectrum—both saddled and blessed with a larger-than-life husband whose earlier successes constantly lurked at the edges of her candidacy. While many women come to politics through their husbands, it is probably safe to assume that few future female candidates will run for president with a former two-term-president husband in tow.

But the question of husbands—be they successful career men or oil rig workers—is a looming one for women in politics as they try to navigate what voters consider "normal." Experience has shown that the husbands of female candidates draw close scrutiny, especially in their business dealings. Dianne Feinstein was not picked as Walter Mondale's running mate in 1984 in part because of questions about her husband, Richard Blum, and his business. The woman Mondale did pick, Geraldine Ferraro, then faced questions about *her* husband's tangled finances, which became one of the targets of the Reagan campaign. In 2006, Claire McCaskill, in her Senate race, weathered an almost identical inquisition over the business operations of her husband, who ran a line of Missouri nursing homes. A smattering of stories about Cindy McCain, the Republican nominee's heiress wife, in the general election never came close to matching the level of scrutiny that Bill Clinton faced in just the primary. "Women candidates are far more accountable for their husbands' behavior than male candidates are for their wives' behavior, and that's really not fair," the Clinton strategist Geoff Garin said.

"If they're married, their husbands are part of the package, and it becomes 'We're going to check into him and expose his dealings' and not in a way that usually happens with candidates' wives," said Dianne Bystrom, an expert on women and communication in political campaigns. "If you're a married woman, you can expect your husband to be thoroughly investigated. If you're a married woman with young children, it becomes, 'Who's going to take care of your children?' The best thing to be is a widow with older children if you're running for office."

To the extent that Todd Palin drew scrutiny, it was for his constant presence in Sarah Palin's political life. Critics in Alaska complained that he spent too much time in her office, meddling in her official duties. In particular, he was cited in an ethics investigation for trying to pressure Alaska's public safety commissioner into firing his brother-in-law, who was divorcing Governor Palin's sister. (Todd Palin said he had simply met with the safety commissioner, not taken part in any effort to pressure him.)

For the most part, though, Todd Palin was a silent, stoic figure at his wife's side, sometimes looking like a stray Secret Service agent as he stood next to her and McCain at campaign events. His profile—as a commercial fisherman and a champion snow machine racer—guaranteed that no one would see him as an emasculated counterpart to his wife, and it helped bolster her middle-class claims. But he could not help her where she needed it most: on the questions of her competence and experience as an executive leader.

Extreme Makeover

One of the most frustrating aspects of Palin's candidacy, for her and for the McCain advisers, was that no one seemed to take her experience as governor seriously. Democrats argued that she had only briefly been governor of a sparsely populated state, with experience as mayor of a tiny suburban town before that; Republicans countered that she was, nonetheless, a governor, the youngest and only woman ever elected governor in Alaska, and that that should count.

To the extent that any lessons were learned from the Palin candidacy, one clearly was the importance of proving a woman's credentials, regardless of how obvious they seem at first blush. If Clinton had gone overboard with that maxim, Palin did not seem to consider it much at all. (The Obama campaign, meanwhile, demonstrated the same lesson in reverse: when running against a woman, challenging her résumé, whether as First Lady or as mayor of Wasilla, can be highly effective no matter how inexperienced your own candidate is.)

In addition to the women's speech she gave in October, Palin did try to give her campaign heft at moments—she gave addresses on special education and energy—but the efforts were dwarfed by the overall negative story line about her. "If [earlier on] Governor Palin had done the speech on special education that she did in Pittsburgh the last week of the campaign, or the speech on energy, then you would have established a baseline of credentials for her around issues people expected a governor to be fluent on," Jane Swift said. "And it would have thwarted this emerging narrative of 'She's stupid'—partly because she's good looking—'and she talks different than us.'"

If Palin's credentials were not respected, it should not have been a surprise. Mountains of research have been accumulated on the subject over the years. Several prominent organizations—including the nonpartisan Barbara Lee Family Foundation in Boston—devote themselves to studying how women are uniquely perceived when they run for higher office. It is a topic that has spawned entire programs of study at universities across the country and been the subject of countless doctoral dissertations. Not all of the literature is ivory-tower theoretical; some of it, in fact, hinted at the exact problems Palin would face. In a brochure for gubernatorial candidates entitled "Positioning Women to Win," the Barbara Lee Family Foundation warned that women sometimes "[need] to let down their hair," with voters reacting badly to a woman who's "so well-dressed and so well put together that, to some people, that didn't appeal to them." In other words, women candidates need to be aware of the problem of perfection, with women who appear too organized and coiffed failing to connect with people, just as women who are less than perfect have been judged.

The same brochure warned that party identification will almost always outweigh gender—meaning it was foolish for Republicans to assume they could pick up women voters just by having a woman on the ticket. "At some point, partisanship trumps gender," the brochure stated. The same supposition had been challenged repeatedly elsewhere. "The idea that by putting a woman on the Republican ticket, that that was somehow going to fundamentally alter even independent voters' perceptions of the party or John McCain, was just off," said Danny Hayes, an assistant political science professor at Syracuse University, who studied the 2006 midterm elections to see which was stronger, party or gender, and found that partisan ties consistently won out. Asked whether that was something the McCain campaign should have recognized, he said: "I would say they should have read some more political science and thought a little more carefully about it."

But by the fall of 2008, the campaign was flying at top speed. There was little time to think carefully about anything. And that fact would lead to the final, devastating blow.

"I started getting e-mails from friends of mine in Alaska about her clothing," Anita Dunn said. "They said, you know, she doesn't dress this way. She doesn't own anything this nice. Somebody has done a total makeover on her. You guys need to go investigate."

Reporters did the investigating. Late in October, Federal Elections Commission reports showed that more than $150,000 had been spent at department stores and designer shops over the course of the campaign, and Republican National Committee officials—furious at the campaign—quickly confirmed that they had been directed by the McCain headquarters to pay the bills.

Nothing about the story added up: while everyone agreed that Palin had been instructed to buy three new suits and employ a stylist to carry her through the campaign, at a cost of $20,000 to $30,000, no one could quite account for how the tab had gotten so much higher. Anonymous allegations flew. One report, later discredited, suggested Nicolle Wallace, a former adviser to President Bush had taken Palin shopping (a McCain aide said the story had been an attempt by Palin to divert blame). McCain advisers said Palin directed low-level campaign staff members to go shopping for her and her husband, putting charges on credit cards, all the way through the end of October, with the eye-popping totals only discovered when they submitted expense reports. Palin said repeatedly that was untrue. "It's so ridiculous," she said, addressing it at a rally after trying to ignore the story for several days. She declared that she usually bought her hockey-mom clothes from a consignment shop in Anchorage and had borrowed the clothes for her public performance as the vice presidential running mate, "just like the lighting and the staging and everything else that the RNC purchased."

What was not in dispute was that Palin was wearing much nicer outfits than she'd had in her Alaska days. And it quickly became apparent that this was the worst kind of story she could face: What more pernicious narrative for a woman is there than that she had been out on a credit card bender, picking up shoes and designer suits rather than prepping for the biggest race of her life?

Republican donors were appalled, as were McCain aides, Steve Schmidt, and McCain himself. The news undercut the argument that McCain and Palin were reformers, committed to frugality and smart spending decisions. Calling Palin on the carpet for the shopping spree was not about her as a woman but about her as an irresponsible running mate. "I don't think it's a gender issue; it's a Sarah Palin issue," one aide said.

But for women—both inside the political orbit and not—the story struck a resonant cord. Some high-profile professional women I know reacted sympathetically, arguing that it is costly to look good on the national stage every day—something men don't understand. Others expressed a mixture of horror and fascination; how did she manage to spend so much? *Vanity Fair* had its fashion department try to spend a theoretical $150,000 on designer clothes for Palin and came up with only $50,000 worth. Why hadn't she or the campaign hidden the bills until after the election? Didn't she—or anyone—anticipate the furor this sort of thing would cause? To argue that the issue was not politically relevant was fruitless; the money had been spent by a political committee, and it was a matter of public record. Even McCain staff members did not try to label coverage of "the shopping spree from hell" an unfair double standard.

The additional twist of the alleged involvement of Nicolle Wallace only worsened matters, reviving the stereotype of frivolous women. In fact, the clothes had been put on men's credit cards; a portion of the wardrobe appeared to have been bought for Todd Palin. But that did not matter much. When stories spilled out alleging that Wallace and Palin were not on speaking terms, yet another caricature emerged. "The fact that it descended into a catfight between her and me, as if we were throwing Jimmy Choos at each other, and the fact that people, mostly on the right, presumed I had gone shopping for her was so silly and such a sign of how far we have not come, either as candidates or as people," Wallace said.

"It certainly made me question what I've been doing for the last twelve years," she went on. "When the story broke, everyone assumed I had gone shopping for her, what, because I'm female, or I like clothes? After six and a half years of being taken seriously, and never treated like a girl in the Bush White House, it was a real gut blow to be treated like a girl who must have gone shopping at Neiman Marcus."

The campaign seemed to awaken Palin to a reality different from the one she had known in Alaska, itself no easy political terrain. In every respect, her profile as a woman, which had worked for her so well at the local level, had not translated.

As a gubernatorial candidate, Palin had used gender to her advantage, making the case that as a woman she would enact change. That strategy had worked for women at various levels of politics before, and it worked for Palin in 2006, helping her—a fresh-faced young woman with a seeming spirit of reform— unseat the Republican incumbent, Frank Murkowski, in the primary and then defeat the former governor Tony Knowles. ("Voters are clear that women seem more honest—a potentially significant advantage in a climate of corruption," the Barbara Lee Family Foundation brochure declared, citing Palin's 2006 gubernatorial win as an example of how women can use the argument of change to their advantage precisely because it plays *into* gender stereotypes.)

But in moving to the national ticket, Palin lost control of the change message. Like Clinton before her, Palin failed to straddle critical lines—between being enough of an insider to have credentials and enough of an outsider to bring about change. Between feminine and tough enough to be taken seriously. Whether that failure was her fault or her advisers'—the battle for who was to blame rages to this day—may be impossible ever to gauge.

One thing is certain: other female political figures were watching Palin's missteps from a distance and, when they weren't busy rolling their eyes at her, they were taking notes. Several of them saw themselves as future rivals of Palin's, in a national race or within the Republican party. And all of them, lesser known figures but in many ways more promising as politicians, were waiting in the wings.

Chapter 4

The Prosecutors

"Speak Softly and Carry a Big Statistic"

To understand one formula for getting elected as a woman on rough terrain, it helps to consider the case of Amy Klobuchar in Minnesota.

A quirky state that prides itself on being progressive—the home of Bob Dylan and Garrison Keillor, a land that gave rise to the wrestler-governor Jesse Ventura, Senator Paul Wellstone, and Vice President Hubert Humphrey—Minnesota had, until 2006, nonetheless proven a near-impossible electoral battleground for women.

It was not that women didn't run, or try to win. Two qualified women had mounted viable campaigns for the Senate—Joan Growe in 1984 and Ann Wynia in 1994—and been beaten by Republican men despite their seemingly sufficient political experience and, in Growe's case, explicit appeals to voters that it was time to elect a woman to a job that had been held by dozens of men. But more than a decade after the supposed "year of the woman" elsewhere, Minnesota still had never elected a woman to the Senate. Only two women in its 148-year history had ever been elected to the House—and one of them was Coya Knutson, the congresswoman famously summoned home by her husband in an open letter, entitled "Coya, Come Home" and published in newspapers nationwide, in 1958.

It was understandable, then, that Democrats were nervous about putting Amy Klobuchar, a young mother, on the ticket for Senate in 2006. Though she was a distinguished graduate of Yale and the University of Chicago Law School, and a practicing lawyer with statewide name recognition, Klobuchar faced questions that seemed incredible at the dawn of the twenty-first century. "I was asked repeatedly, 'Do you think a woman can win? Can a woman really win?'" Klobuchar told me in an interview in her Capitol office one afternoon. "I was asked that in Duluth. I was asked that all over the place. This was in *2006*."

By the time we talked, it was 2009, and Klobuchar had not only won her Senate race but also become Minnesota's senior senator; the other seat had not yet been filled by the comedian Al Franken, who was locked in a legal dispute. A petite, dark-haired woman with the unadorned look of someone in her twenties—she wears so little makeup and hair spray she has been mistaken for a Senate aide around the Capitol— Klobuchar had gained national renown for her early support of Barack Obama in the Democratic primaries. She also earned a reputation for being ambitious, so much so that within months of her arrival in Washington she was discussed as a potential presidential candidate, even more so after Hillary Clinton lost and women's groups went back to the drawing board.

Klobuchar had managed something difficult in her Senate victory: she presented herself as the tougher candidate without becoming unlikable. Her eventual triumph, it appears, was largely due to a silver bullet on her résumé: her work as a prosecutor.

Elected Hennepin County attorney in 1998, Klobuchar crafted a law-and-order persona that instantly addressed the underlying questions about whether she was tough enough to be an effective lawmaker. There is a saying among advisers to female candidates: "Speak softly, and carry a big statistic." Klobuchar seemed to get that instinctively. As prosecutor, she began publishing regular reports of law enforcement activity—the amount of time it took to charge nonviolent property cases, for example. She accumulated a run of accomplishments that made for a compelling laundry list on her résumé: nearly three hundred homicide convictions, a drop in serious crime in the county, a redoubling of efforts to solve burglaries. And she started studying other successful female prosecutors, especially Arizona Governor Janet Napolitano, whose specificity and responsiveness she admired. "Our backgrounds were similar, and our states were a lot tougher for Democrats," Klobuchar said. "What I noticed about her is she would answer every question. She had specific proposals for things."

The Klobuchar name was already familiar to many—her father was a longtime columnist for the Minneapolis *Star Tribune*—and the senatorial hopeful made herself even more accessible by campaigning frequently with her husband and young daughter. She also performed another balancing act: repeatedly assuring voters she was not running because she was a woman while quietly cultivating the women's groups—and some female voters—who were eager to elect one finally. "I told people, 'I'm running on the fact that I've been a successful prosecutor for eight years," Klobuchar said. "Because the last time I checked, half the voters were men. And if I was just running as a woman, I wouldn't win."

She had to work to win over the women as well. Klobuchar recalled a town hall meeting in northern Minnesota, full of shouting mine workers and union members, that came screeching to a halt when an elderly woman got up to comment. "This woman stands up, she goes, 'My name is Mrs. Bradovich, and I am eighty-some years old, and I have never voted for a woman before. Because I got to tell you I kind of think they should be home with their kids. That's where I am. But I've listened today and I've decided, in your case, I'm making an exception.' Like that," Klobuchar said. "And everyone cheered."

Klobuchar's emphasis on being a prosecutor was noticed across the board. There were some efforts to attack her on it— she was criticized for being difficult to work for, and for being less effective than she claimed—but she secured a lead early and kept it. Whereas strategic toughness had failed to work for Hillary Clinton, and to a lesser extent Sarah Palin, as she boasted about her athleticism and frontier grit, it was integral to the Klobuchar strategy. Simply the word *prosecutor* conveyed the message. "She ran a very effective campaign. Her campaign very much stressed her prosecutorial experience," said Kathryn Pearson, a political science professor at the University of Minnesota who watched the race closely. "So many things she said connected to the cases she had won, fighting crime, her everyday experiences, coming to Washington and cleaning up the Senate, ending corruption." In one vivid example, Klobuchar reminded voters that she had prosecuted a popular appeals court judge for siphoning more than $300,000 from a trust fund he managed.

The effect was so striking it was quantifiable. Media coverage of Klobuchar portrayed her in terms usually reserved for men, according to an analysis conducted by Danny Hayes, a senior researcher at Syracuse University who has studied gender and politics. Hayes went through the news coverage of Klobuchar to see how gender might have affected her in the general election campaign against Republican Mark Kennedy. He was surprised by the results. "The coverage was strikingly counterstereotypical. Klobuchar was significantly more likely to be covered in 'masculine' terms than Mark Kennedy. Klobuchar was routinely described as a strong leader, as ambitious, tough, hardworking, and so on. These are traits typically associated with men—and Republicans," Hayes said. "This appears to be related, at least in part, to Klobuchar's background as a prosecutor and the role that experience played in the campaign." It is impossible, he said, to know whether it contributed to her triumph. "But if we suspect that some voters are reticent to cast a ballot for a candidate who they feel will be 'weak,' then it's probably the case that women and Democrats benefit from coverage that portrays them in the opposite terms," he said, adding, "My research suggests this is true for Democratic presidential candidates."

But if she is tough, she is not intimidating. Two months into her term, in early 2007, Klobuchar and two of her staff members stepped into the senators-only elevator in the Capitol. An older male senator, now retired, approached the elevator doorway and looked at the three women.

"And he says, 'Do you three get grief for going on the senators-only elevator?'" she recalled.

It was a story she had told many times before, and she

clearly loved it. "And I stop and look at him, and they go, 'Well, she *is* a senator.' And I look at him, and I know exactly who he is, and I say, 'But who are you?' Like that. And then the elevator doors close and he never gets on. That was the best part. He just stood there."

"Janet Has No Family. Perfect."

Amy Klobuchar is one of a number of female prosecutors who have gotten on the glide path to electoral politics through law enforcement. Fred Thompson may have miscalculated in thinking his role as District Attorney Arthur Branch on *Law & Order* would help his presidential campaign, but a growing number of women with real-life prosecutor jobs are reaping real benefits. Current and former female law enforcers are, in fact, in the vanguard of national politics these days; among their ranks are Homeland Security Director Janet Napolitano, Senator Claire McCaskill of Missouri, Governor Christine Gregoire of Washington, Governor Jennifer Granholm of Michigan, Attorney General Lisa Madigan of Illinois, Attorney General Martha Coakley of Massachusetts (who is running for the late Edward Kennedy's Senate seat), Attorney General Kelly Ayotte of New Hampshire (who is running for the Senate as well), and District Attorney Kamala Harris of San Francisco (who in 2010 will run for attorney general of California).

Napolitano is the towering giant of the group in terms of credentials and fame (though not height-wise; she is five foot four, much smaller than she looks on television). Her prosecutorial work includes domestic terrorism investigations and pursuit of a Gambino crime family member, giving her résumé a hint of Hollywood flash. Her expertise on immigration makes her a rare Democrat, let alone woman, who can speak on the subject across party lines. Her first steps as Homeland Security director were applauded within the Obama administration, and the president considers her a friend: like Klobuchar, Napolitano was an early Democratic endorser of his campaign, announcing her decision to support him over Clinton in January 2008, long before the outcome was clear.

On the afternoon I met her, Napolitano strode into her office at the Department of Homeland Security bustling with enthusiasm. She had just given reporters a successful tour of Union Station, showing off her agency's K-9 unit. Her recent work managing severe flooding in North Dakota had gone smoothly and to acclaim. White House officials were buzzing about her as the "valedictorian" of the young Obama cabinet so pleased were they with her efforts to integrate the disjointed department after just a few months. Several weeks later, a swine flu scare would sweep the country, and Napolitano would become an even bigger star as she calmed people's—and other administration officials'—nerves.

But on this Wednesday afternoon, she pulled up a chair and, for my benefit, contemplated a different matter: How hard had it been, as a woman, to rise so quickly in the political ranks?

Napolitano arched one eyebrow skeptically, a trademark look of hers, signaling an impending laugh. And then, with disarming directness, she volunteered that she had to overcome one stereotype when she first ran for public office: false rumors that she was a lesbian. "They said, 'Well, Arizona is never going to go for a single woman,'" Napolitano told me. "The subtext of that is because, of course, you must be gay, which is not true."

It is difficult to imagine too many other cabinet secretaries offering that information up to a reporter within a few minutes of sitting down for an interview. But people close to her say it is classic Napolitano. Her candor and confidence helped boost her to victory in that race for Arizona attorney general in 1998 and earned her the lasting affection of Arizona voters, who elected her to two consecutive terms as governor, in 2002 and 2006. A rare Democrat running a Republican state during the Bush era, she became the first woman ever to win reelection in the job. *Time* magazine named her one of America's five best governors after just two years. She evolved into one of the nation's top experts on immigration and border security, one of the most prominent women in U.S. politics, and, by the time Obama chose her as his Secretary of Homeland Security, a leading contender to be a future presidential candidate.

How Napolitano overcame questions about her personal life and, more important, her party affiliation in a conservative western state is another illustration of the power of prosecutorial street cred. Her willingness to discuss her personal situation suggests she has given her political hurdles serious thought—as she would have to if she were considering an even higher office.

A terrorist attack or major natural disaster, if one were to occur in the next few years, would severely test Napolitano. With the exception of then–Attorney General Janet Reno's handling of the Oklahoma City bombing or the Branch Davidian siege, or perhaps Condoleezza's Rice role in guiding President Bush past the 9/11 attacks—the latter two of which did not help either woman's popularity—few women have served in important national security jobs at a time of crisis. It is impossible to say how Napolitano would fare in such a situation, or how the public would respond.

But at the outset of the administration, at least, Napolitano seemed as well-positioned as any woman in politics for a higher run. She appeared primed for it, in fact. Describing politics as a "kick in the pants," Napolitano said her biggest fear for younger women is that they hear only the downside of running for office—the media bias, the double standards—not the sheer joy that it can provide. And she rolled her eyes at the doubts women have about whether they are qualified to lead.

"As opposed to, you know, *what?* Look at these yahoo guys that have been in public office for two hundred years," she said, as her press aide's jaw dropped. "You think we cannot do as well as they do? I mean, give me a break."

"Badge of Courage"

Like so many women, Napolitano was drawn into public service following the testimony of Professor Anita Hill during the Clarence Thomas confirmation hearings in 1991. But Napolitano was sitting behind the witness stand, serving as one of Hill's lawyers. A partner in a private Phoenix law firm at the time, Napolitano flew to Washington for just a few days to help with the witnesses. It was long enough for her to get a glimpse of the climate back then. "It was outrageous to sit in that hearing room and watch what happened," she recalled. "The professor had no supporter on the committee and nobody who really was sympathetic to the issue of sexual harassment as a bona fide workplace claim. Now, since then, that has changed, and I do not think the committee would handle it the same way again, and members have said as much. But at that time it was very, very frustrating to watch."

Bill Clinton appointed Napolitano U.S. attorney upon her return to Arizona, giving her an entrée into the public sphere. (In our interview, she said she had debated running against

John McCain for his Senate seat in 1992 but decided not to.) After a brief delay during the nomination process by senators still piqued by her role in the Hill hearings, she went on to have a successful prosecutorial run. She had a hand in investigating the Oklahoma City bombing after it was discovered that Timothy McVeigh had contemplated bombing the federal courthouse in Arizona before moving his target eastward and that he still had cohorts in her jurisdiction. She also developed an immigration platform by prosecuting border cases, exposing at least one elaborate underground tunnel that had been built between Mexico and Arizona. Four years later, when she ran for attorney general, those high-profile cases helped neutralize doubts about her toughness and effectiveness.

That would be the case in each of her three statewide elections—and as her star as a prosecutor rose, so did her electoral prospects. As attorney general, she filed racketeering charges against Sammy "the Bull" Gravano, a mob underboss who had started a new drug business while in the witness protection program in Arizona. She brought several financial fraud cases, including one against the now-defunct accounting firm Arthur Andersen. At the same time, she oversaw the state's Consumer Protection Division, becoming a regular presence on television as she warned Arizonans about faulty products and claims.

Along the way, Napolitano developed better-than-usual ties with other law enforcement officials in the state, which helped her in her next elections as they vouched for her credentials—or at least did not support attacks by her opponents. "She ended up fairly early in her public career developing very strong relations with people in law enforcement and being respected by them, and each position got her to the next level," said Dennis Burke, Napolitano's longtime chief of staff, who said it was clear that law enforcement work "insulates you from attack as a woman politician. And in her case, it not only insulated her. It was not only a shield but a sword," he said. "Because she was able to really run on a record of what she had done."

Even as governor, Napolitano kept law enforcement and immigration issues at the forefront of her administration—putting together a task force on fake IDs in her first term to stem the tide of undocumented workers obtaining phony licenses, and in her second term signing a law, billed as the toughest in the country, to punish companies that hired undocumented workers. She made sure more National Guard troops were sent to the border with Mexico, drawing attention across the country just as immigration was heating up in Washington; on the more moderate side, she also backed a comprehensive immigration overhaul proposal, championed by President Bush in his second term, which was defeated.

Though conservative critics complained that she had done too little on immigration—she opposed building a border fence, saying it would not work—that objection was not enough to dent her popularity. After winning her first governor's race by a close margin, 46 to 45 percent, in 2002, she beat her Republican opponent in 2006 by a landslide, 63 to 35 percent. Her nomination at the Department of Homeland Security sailed through the Senate by a voice vote a few hours after Obama was sworn in on January 20, 2008—making her one of the first, and most easily confirmed, members of his cabinet.

For all her law-and-order street cred, Napolitano has avoided the trap of being seen as "too tough" or "unlikable"—in part thanks to her expansive sense of humor. Her wry laugh is irresistible. "She cracks herself up by quoting *Monty Python*. Indeed, she's constantly smiling and laughing, from giggles to deep belly laughs to ironical gasps," one profiler wrote in *The American Prospect*.

And in the delicate balancing act between soft and tough, Napolitano has had one other advantage, if it can be called that. She has survived breast cancer. This puts her in an elite but growing league of female politicians. Once a taboo subject, breast cancer—and survival of it—has become a political factor for more women in public office, as detection and life expectancy rates have dramatically increased.

The disease has led to some heroic stories. The most stunning came from Representative Debbie Wasserman Schultz of Florida, who sent shock waves through the political establishment when she disclosed, in early 2009, that she had spent the previous year as a high-profile campaign surrogate speaking on behalf of Hillary Clinton and then Barack Obama all while secretly undergoing seven breast cancer operations, including a double mastectomy. No one but her husband and a few close friends knew. Only when the treatment was complete and she had been given a clean bill of health did she share it with the world—alongside a related legislative push to educate the public about cancer risks. "I didn't want it to define me," she said, explaining her decision to hide her cancer. But she openly embraced it in hindsight, holding a press conference in the Capitol with other breast cancer survivors. She broke down in tears at one point. "I cannot end my remarks without thanking my wonderful husband," she said, a moment that was splayed across the Style section of the *Washington Post* the next day. But instead of being recorded as a measure of her weakness, the moment was described as one of human vulnerability. The only criticism Wasserman Schultz received was on the substance of the cancer legislation she proposed, which some advocates said might mislead young women about their prevention options.

Five years earlier, in 2004, Jodi Rell of Connecticut, a Republican, was diagnosed with breast cancer not long after she assumed the governorship; like Wasserman Schultz, she did not pause for a period of treatment or (as most of us might) self-pity. Rell had a mastectomy and, days later, delivered her State of the State address. She became one of the most popular governors in the country, her approval rating cruising above 80 percent two years later.

Napolitano, in that sense, was a pioneer. Three weeks after undergoing a mastectomy in 2000, she threw herself back into politics at the most exhausting level: as a speaker at the Democratic convention in Los Angeles, where Vice President Al Gore was accepting the nomination. "I was on the [operating] table like seven hours or eight hours by the time they got all done, so I just physically was still wiped out," Napolitano recalled. "And convention days are exhausting. You are expected to be up early and stay up late and you are not eating regularly. But as the statewide-elected Democrat, I really thought it was important to be there. And also part of it was just beginning that process of people understanding that nothing had really changed. That I was fine." She added: "But that was a stretch. I remember when I told the doctor what I was planning to do, and he was like, 'Umm, really?' And I said, 'Yes.' He goes, 'Well, you can probably do it, but it will not be as fun as it might otherwise be.' And I said, 'Well, frankly, Doctor, this whole breast cancer thing is not so fun.'

Another former prosecutor, Washington Governor Christine Gregoire, had an even more consequential conversation with her doctor about her political future when she was faced with a similar diagnosis in 2003. Just one week after announcing her candidacy, Gregoire, a Democrat, went for a routine checkup assuming she would receive a clean bill of health, which she could then report to the public. Instead her doctors detected breast cancer and recommended that she, too, have a mastectomy. It almost forced her out of the race. "I assumed that the race was over for me, that I couldn't run for governor. I was prepared to drop out," Gregoire said. "The doctor was wonderful and said, 'Why would you assume that, why don't you wait and see?'" Gregoire also consulted with Napolitano and another gubernatorial candidate–survivor, Heidi Heitkamp of North Dakota, stayed in the campaign, and won.

At the time, Gregoire was facing an uphill struggle to persuade voters that she was not *too* tough. She had already built up a strong law enforcement profile during three terms as the state's attorney general, winning consecutive statewide elections and earning national recognition as the lead negotiator for a massive settlement with the tobacco industry. That helped build her credentials for her gubernatorial campaign but also, according to strategists, hurt. "When she was running for attorney general, people didn't think she was tough enough to be attorney general, and then when she was running for governor, people thought she was too tough to be governor," said Barbara Lee, an expert on women governors.

In the end, Gregoire won by the narrowest margin in the history of the state, after a protracted legal fight. Whether or not her status as a survivor affected the outcome, one pattern seems to be emerging: breast cancer survival is perceived as proof of resilience in politics as in life. While the "politics of breast cancer" is not quite a separate academic field, strategists have found that voters respond well to women who face, and overcome, the disease. People seem to be aware that breast cancer is treatable, and that it is not necessarily a sign of old age or fragility.

In some instances, breast cancer has actually redounded to a candidate's benefit. Surviving is almost comparable to withstanding a war wound. Geoff Garin, the Democratic pollster, said it sends several messages at once. "For women it confers courage, that you've faced up to something really difficult in your life," he said. "It confers a real-world knowledge of the health care system. And there's an expectation that going through a personal crisis like that tends to make somebody more empathetic. The most important thing is that it's really seen as a sign of courage. It is described very much in terms of fighting a battle, and women who have gone through this successfully are described as survivors, and what it means to be a survivor goes beyond just a medical term."

Indeed, when Napolitano arrived in Washington in 2009, fellow Arizonan John McCain advertised her role as a survivor as one of her key selling points. "Not only does Janet Napolitano possess a 'no-nonsense' attitude, she also possesses remarkable stamina and unlimited energy. She has hiked the Himalayas, climbed Mount Kilimanjaro, and battled cancer," McCain said in introducing her to Congress. "She will need this same energy to lead a department that was created five years ago through the merger of twenty-two agencies. After some time on the job, she may find climbing Mount Kilimanjaro far easier than navigating the halls of the department." It was quite a compliment, from a senator whose own history of cancer had been a dark cloud over his candidacy, raising questions about his age and whether he would survive a term in office—or leave it in the hands of Sarah Palin, his vice presidential nominee.

In her last television ad during her first run for governor, Napolitano subtly turned her breast cancer experience into a window onto her personality. After the requisite footage of her seated behind a desk, addressing issues of education and the budget, the ad showed Napolitano at the end of a Race for the Cure marathon with her supporters. It showed her giving a high five to her team—"classic Janet," the Democratic pollster Celinda Lake recalled. "She looked very happy, her team won, and they were all high fives—women of all ages and sizes and shapes, and just very warm footage. It was absolutely candid, speaking directly to who she really is. And people thought, 'Oh, okay, cool, she's got a likable and soft side.'"

Still, the image of her as a lone woman has followed Napolitano. "She always had to run against a whisper campaign. Even though she said she was not a lesbian, they said she was," said Kim Fridkin, an expert on women in politics at Arizona State University, who has watched Napolitano's career. Even Texas Governor Ann Richards, who had four children, had been the subject of such a campaign.

When she was picked to head Homeland Security, Napolitano was the subject of a controversial remark by Pennsylvania Governor Ed Rendell, who said she was "perfect for that job. Because for that job, you have to have no life. Janet has no family. Perfect. She can devote, literally, nineteen, twenty hours a day to it," Rendell, a Democrat, said. He later apologized—and insisted that he would have said the same of a man with no family, and that he himself is a workaholic—but the comment was a reminder of how prominent Napolitano's status as a single woman is.

Would that status affect Napolitano's long-term prospects? An informal survey of Democrats suggested they are divided, with some quietly saying being single would hurt her if she decided to run for president and others disagreeing, saying it would eliminate questions, about problematic husbands and children who aren't being adequately raised, that other women would face. And, some of her defenders added, if the country is ready for an African-American president with Muslim relatives, couldn't it handle a single woman born in New York?

Napolitano has thought a lot about women in politics, more than many of her counterparts. In our interview, she declined to talk about where Hillary Clinton had gone wrong or whether she had been mistreated in the press, claiming she had been too busy campaigning for Obama to keep a close watch on Clinton's style. But on virtually every other subject—from lower recruitment rates for women House contenders to the conflicting demands on female candidates—she was full of opinions.

On Sarah Palin, with whom she had made several joint public appearances, including on the *Charlie Rose* show, before Palin was picked for the Republican ticket: "She is very attractive. She is a good speaker. You know, she hits her points. You disagree with her or not, but she has some real political skill and it should not be underestimated."

On why there aren't more women in politics: "There is still a fundamental conflict, particularly at the level of governor or president, Congress, Senate, with the demands of raising a family. In a way, it is similar to 'Why aren't more women partners in big [law] firms?' They join big firms in the same numbers. There are more of them graduating from law school now than ever before. But you look at who actually makes partner, and it is a very small percentage. Because the legal profession has not changed to kind of match with the competing demands on women, particularly women of childbearing age. If anything, our campaign seasons have gotten longer and more rigorous and we have not resolved that conflict."

On why being a prosecutor helps women running for office: "It is kind of counterstereotype. So if the concern is that women are going to be too nice, when they are used to seeing you announcing arrests and sentences . . . you are nice but you are not that nice." She continued: "The second thing is it brings you into contact with groups that normally would vociferously oppose a Democratic woman—law enforcement groups, for example. And that is good, because you have a good shot of either getting their support, or at least they stay pretty quiet."

And as a matter of substance, Napolitano said, being a prosecutor allowed her to run a major office and learn to make decisions on the fly, then to communicate her decisions to the public—all invaluable political skills. "If you are good, you get used to talking about fairly complicated legal concepts in a way that people can understand, which is a skill that is transferable in a lot of ways in public office," she said. "Breaking things up in a way that people get their arms around. Barack Obama is a genius at that. And I think all of those things happen when you are an A.G. or U.S. attorney. Maybe a district attorney, too."

It is interesting, then, to note that Napolitano originally wanted to be U.S. attorney general, but Obama persuaded her to take the Homeland Security job. Perhaps another stepping-stone?

Napolitano insisted that she is not thinking about higher office—yet. "It is not something that I really have thought too much about. I mean, people mention it now, obviously, because of my résumé," she said, with a twinkle in her eye. "But my view is, do a good job on this job, and then see what happens."

"Daughter of Rural Missouri"

Claire McCaskill of Missouri is another former prosecutor who, like Amy Klobuchar and Janet Napolitano, is often mentioned as a potential presidential candidate. Sitting on a sofa in her Senate office one evening in 2009, her shoes kicked off after a long day of meetings and votes, McCaskill sounded wary of the campaign crucible, having just spent many months traveling to promote Obama. "I've now seen the process up close, and it's a brutal, brutal process. And I don't know if my energy or my passion will reach that far," she said. "Right now I'd say no."

Friends of McCaskill's say that she is probably downplaying her ambition, that she has all the necessary skill and drive to campaign for president at some point down the road. And she has a long time to consider it: if Obama runs for reelection as expected in 2012, it will be 2016 before another Democrat has an opening.

Still, it is possible to believe that McCaskill has real qualms. After two rough, close statewide campaigns—one for governor, which she lost; another for Senate, which she won—she still chokes up when she talks about the effect the races had on her husband, whose business dealings became the focus of Republican attacks.

First elected to the Missouri House at age twenty-nine, McCaskill has experienced some of her most important life events in front of the electorate: she gave birth while in office, the first woman actively serving in the state's legislature to do so. After she became the Kansas City prosecutor, her first husband was arrested on drug charges; they later divorced. As a single mother in the years that followed, McCaskill faced public scrutiny as she met, dated, and married her current husband, Joseph Shepard. "I've done everything while in public life, you know. I've gotten married, I've had babies, I've gotten divorced, I've dated, I've remarried. I had personal tragedy," McCaskill said, shaking her head as if in amazement at all that had happened.

Her ability to survive in politics despite so much tumult is thanks in large part to her personality—she is brassy and talkative, in a winning, midwestern way—but it also stems from her profile as a tough operator, which has its roots in her work as a prosecutor. A graduate of the University of Missouri Law School and a former assistant prosecutor in Kansas City, she started her career in the Missouri House of Representatives in the 1980s—the first woman attorney in the chamber in decades—and made criminal justice her emphasis. During her first campaign, she walked door to door in her district. "I'd pull my hair back, and the first thing I'd say when people would open the door was 'I'm assistant prosecutor,'" she said. Once in office, she pushed a measure that required criminals to spend a mandatory percentage of their sentences behind bars before early release could kick in; she would later run with that as an important part of her record.

In 1992, she was elected the first female Jackson County prosecutor and earned a reputation in the local press for "aggressive prosecution" (*Kansas City Star*) and as "tough and fair and innovative" (*Columbia Daily Tribune*), words that would become a part of her biographical narrative. She claimed national recognition for putting more criminals behind bars than other prosecutors; she created a special drug court and was picked by President Bill Clinton to serve on a national drug panel.

By the time she ran for governor in 2004, after five years as the state auditor, people in Missouri knew McCaskill as a no-nonsense, experienced political force. And that was how she ran: as the tough, ready candidate. She took the bold step of challenging an incumbent Democratic governor, Bob Holden, in the primary. Her media team, led by David Dixon—a partner in one of the best Democratic firms in the country at helping women candidates, including Representative Chellie Pingree of Maine, CFO Alex Sink of Florida, and former Governor Kathleen Sebelius of Kansas—and her direct mail organizer, took her brand as a prosecutor and translated it to voters as evidence that she was a "reformer on the side of average people," in contrast to her entrenched Democratic rival.

It worked. McCaskill defeated Holden, setting the stage for a general election showdown against Republican Matt Blunt, the thirty-three-year-old secretary of state whose father, Roy Blunt, was Republican majority whip in the U.S. House of Representatives.

But in the general election, McCaskill suddenly found that the prosecutor profile was not enough, despite the yawning age gap between the candidates. She campaigned hard against Blunt's inexperience, beating him, her advisers felt, in substantive debates. Male voters, in particular, were impressed with her "kick-ass, take charge, take names brand," one adviser said. Yet it was difficult for her negative messages about Blunt to penetrate. Voters in focus groups were reluctant to believe even the most basic negative facts about his thin record. He also did spectacularly well in rural areas, and in a year in which George Bush beat John Kerry in Missouri 53 to 46 percent, Blunt got a down-ticket boost.

Did gender play a role in McCaskill's defeat—her first and only in two decades in politics? In a variety of ways, it appears it did. The job of governor, for one, may have put her at a natural disadvantage; many strategists in the Democratic party believe that there is built-in resistance to electing women to the top executive job. Other women, including Senator Mary Landrieu of Louisiana and Senator Debbie Stabenow of Michigan, had tried to run for governor and lost, encountering the same phenomenon. It is just easier for some women to run for Senate and win. "It's not easy to be a woman senator, but it's a lot easier to be a woman senator than it is to be a woman governor, because you just don't get some of these questions about strength," Celinda Lake, the Democratic pollster, said. "People are just very comfortable with women in collective leadership. They're just a lot less comfortable with them in solo leadership. And they have all these questions. 'Okay, well, fine, she's tough enough, but then can she lead the state legislature? Are they going to listen to her?' You know, 'Can she order people around? Can she protect our state?'" Lake said.

McCaskill had another even more disturbing disadvantage: women voters who expressed skepticism about her.

If she had been elected in 2004, McCaskill would have been the first female governor of Missouri, yet that fact earned her little enthusiasm from female voters, who narrowly preferred Blunt, 50 to 49 percent. She would change the gender dynamic—boosting her margins among women to claim victory in her Senate race two years later—but in her gubernatorial bid it seemed she had failed to reach women on a fundamental, human level. Perhaps the prosecutor image had gone too far. "We never let the voters know who she was as a woman," one of her advisers said afterward. "They didn't know her as a mother, a daughter." It was an early foreshadowing of the dilemma Hillary Clinton would face.

Female candidates, far from enjoying universal support from women in the electorate, had met resistance in a variety of ways over the years. Sometimes, the problem was educated, elite women (as in Hillary Clinton's first Senate race) or younger ones (as in Clinton's presidential bid). More often, though, resistance came from older female voters, suspicious of a younger woman candidate—or even one roughly their age—who did not seem to share their values. And while minority women in the Democratic party have tended to vote for women candidates reliably, white women who are more centrist, independent, or Republican have been a harder sell. In Florida's Senate race in 2004, for example, Democrat Betty Castor split the white women's vote evenly with Republican Mel Martinez; that was enough to doom her. Martinez won men by a wide margin, as expected, and, with sufficient support from women, won the race.

Academic research on the complicated subject of women voters and women candidates is mixed. The difficulty of measuring the way women vote lies in separating gender from party affiliation: female voters have increasingly aligned themselves with Democrats in recent elections, regardless of the candidate's gender. That means that, in some contests, women are voting for a Democratic man at higher rates than for a Republican woman. In Maine in 2008, Republican Senator Susan Collins won reelection with overwhelming support from both men and women but beat her male opponent with a higher margin among men.

Paradoxically, while some data show that women support Democratic women in certain races, strategists report the opposite phenomenon—having to work harder to win support from women. The trend is difficult to quantify, given how few races are available to study.

In races with a gender component, the female candidate is a Democrat. And in those races with Democratic candidates, female voters have often been a decisive force: in 2000, Debbie Stabenow defeated the incumbent senator, Republican Spence Abraham, with strong backing from working-class women voters in Michigan. In 2008, Democrat Jeanne Shaheen beat Republican John E. Sununu for the Senate seat from New Hampshire by winning 60 percent of the female vote, compared with

37 percent of women who backed Sununu, though he had won men, 53 to 45 percent.

A Pew study in 2007 analyzing exit poll data from forty Senate and gubernatorial races since 1998 found that, on average, the Democratic female candidates captured 55 percent of the female vote, compared with 47 percent of the male vote. At the same time, the Democratic female candidates won 51 percent of the overall vote, compared with a control group of Democratic male candidates, who won 47 percent. That meant, in other words, that Democratic women enjoyed a slight gender gap in their campaigns. There was, the study found, no similar advantage for Republican women.

But are women in those cases voting for women candidates because they are *women*, or because they are Democrats? Kira Sanbonmatsu, a researcher at the Center for American Women and Politics at Rutgers, says the effect of a female candidate on women voters is small. "It's nothing like the effects you find with race and especially party. Party is much more important," she says.

So support from women is not a given; at times it is hard to earn. Strategists who work with female candidates describe women voters—across the political spectrum—as a constant challenge even when the voters' ideas and values align with the candidate's. Chris Esposito, a Democratic consultant who has worked with many women over the years, said he always spends a "disproportionate amount of time" in focus groups with women, trying to understand their fears and disapproval of female candidates. "Women voters are the toughest nut to crack for women candidates, which some people find to be counterintuitive because they assume women vote for women," he said. "Women have trouble voting for other women because of the history of this country being run by men; there's a default brain wave that politics is a man's world, not a woman's world, and they've been bombarded with that over the years. There's also a group of women, it doesn't matter where you are in the country, who think a woman running for higher office is too ambitious. Other variants of that are, there are women who view women candidates as trying to become like men. There's a subset of women who view these women campaigning full-time as being irresponsible at home, related to marriage or children or both."

He continued: "And then it sounds crazy to say, but there's always a group of women who don't like the way she looks, how she talks, what she's wearing. I've literally been in ad testing focus groups where we think we've got something to put up on the air and we test it with the women, and they don't like the clothes, the hair, the makeup. Just crazy stuff."

Women seem to be tougher on other women in other industries as well. On Broadway, a recent study found that there is a real gender gap, as many had long suspected: it is harder for female playwrights to get their works produced than for men. But the fault lies almost entirely with female literary managers and artistic directors, according to Emily Glassberg Sands, the Princeton economics student who conducted the research. She sent out identical manuscripts to the people who stage theater productions, some of them under female names and others under similar male names. Women in positions of power were less likely to approve of scripts with women's names on them, in contrast to the men, who approved of male and female scripts at the same rate. "I suspected it wasn't pure discrimination, but I was surprised that women were driving it," Sands said in disclosing her findings.

The pollster Celinda Lake said that while women experienced a burst of support from women voters in certain elections—such as 1992—the enthusiasm has dimmed in recent years. Women often put up resistance to female candidates in focus groups. "They are often like, 'I can't handle it, how could she?' Or, 'Is she really taking care of her kids?'" she said. "With blue-collar women, we've tested the language 'balancing work and family.' They don't even like that language. They say, you know, that's career woman talk. Those are the kinds of women who carry briefcases to church." Instead, Lake said, lower-income women say, "We work *for* our families. We don't *balance* our work and family, we work *for* our families."

McCaskill encountered resistance on that front; women in Missouri were suspicious of her motives and her ambition, and they scrutinized her closely. She was careful, in our interview, to express empathy for the women who had doubted her. "It's hard to paint with a broad brush, because my mom's an older woman, and she loves strong women that are swimming upstream in terms of what's expected of them in society. But I think that for many women—I don't think it's malevolent; I don't think it's that they think about it from a negative place— but it's like, 'Well, her frame of reference is so different than mine. How can I really trust her to understand who I am? She's actually done all this stuff and she thinks she can be a United States senator and I don't see myself as doing those kinds of things,'" McCaskill said. "And so I think women are harder on other women. I think women are *very* hard on women. And I think that you just have to work a little harder at getting their trust that you do understand and that you do get the choices they've made, and why, and that you respect those choices."

The McCaskill example is instructive because she ran two campaigns close together—one, emphasizing her professional traits and her experience, which she lost; another, just two years later, that painted more of a personal portrait, which she won. McCaskill's victory in 2006 can be explained in other ways as well: the mood of the country, and of Missouri, had begun to change after a term and a half of President George W. Bush; she was running against a different male candidate, for a different seat; her Republican rival, Jim Talent, drew negative national attention for opposing a popular stem-cell initiative that was also on the ballot. And by 2006 McCaskill simply had more practice at running for statewide office, and she focused on rural areas in a more disciplined way.

One thing is for sure: McCaskill made gains among women in her Senate race, one of three races that year that Democrats said were decided in their favor by female voters (Virginia and Montana, with male candidates, were the other two). McCaskill won women 51 to 45 percent, enough to offset her opponent's 51 to 46 percent victory among men. Her support among unmarried women surged in the final weeks, her campaign polling found, further demonstrating what they felt was a built-in age gap.

After adjusting the way she ran, advertising herself as a "daughter of rural Missouri" rather than the sharp, experienced officeholder, McCaskill said she learned a critical lesson about running as a woman: that it was not all about compensating. "I had come from the position that I had to prove that I was competent," she said. "Because I worked on this notion that people would assume I probably wasn't either old enough, smart enough, tough enough, or male enough to do the job. And some of that probably comes from the fact that the early years of my career I spent in the courtroom in a prosecutor's office. And for part of that time I was the only woman assistant prosecutor in the office. . . . And so I always felt this need to show that I was up for the job, that I was smart enough and strong enough and knew enough to do the job. And that kind of carried with me; you know, this notion that somebody's going to tap me on the shoulder and say, 'What do you think you're doing here?'

"So I ran for governor that way," she continued. When it was over, McCaskill said, a reporter told her that she had reminded her of an obnoxious *Jeopardy!* contestant—always knowing the answer, always raising her hand, a teacher's pet type. "And this same journalist said to me—a woman journalist, by the way, who covered the race—who said, 'You know, I think that everybody figured out that you knew the answers. They just weren't sure you were a human being,'" McCaskill said. "And then I thought about it and I realized that, in my rush to be smart and competent, I'd probably forgotten that it was important for people to see me as a well-rounded person who had the same fears and hopes that they have, and that I have the same problems in my family and same concerns and worries about my kids. So in the Senate race, I quit worrying so much about giving the smartest answer and tried to make sure people saw that I really did understand Missouri, and the people of Missouri, and what they worried about and what they looked for."

McCaskill started to tell voters a little more about herself—the years she spent as a waitress, earning money to help pay for college; her time as a single mother, raising three kids; her relationship with her own mother, who became a fixture of her Senate race, campaigning on her daughter's behalf. Her strategists also reduced the amount of time McCaskill was featured in her television advertisements, a trick that women had learned in other races, having discovered that voters just did not like hearing their voices as much. (Another industry secret: voters enjoy listening to women more when they drop their voices into a lower range.)

But her biggest adjustment was just opening up—and worrying less about proving her credentials. "I figured out by '06 my problem wasn't that people didn't think I was tough enough. My problem was the opposite. You know, in one focus group I think one woman called me Cruella De Vil. That's plenty tough," McCaskill said, laughing.

On a Monday afternoon in December 2005, in the midst of the Senate race, witnesses inside a day-care center in Kansas City, Kansas, heard gunfire on the street. They ran to the window and saw a man lying facedown on the sidewalk, dead from a single bullet through his neck at close range. The victim was David Exposito, McCaskill's ex-husband. Police said the sixty-four-year-old might have been carjacked in the high-crime neighborhood; his 1979 Thunderbird was recovered the following day, missing its decorative gold rims. McCaskill, who was out campaigning, paused her travel to spend time with their three teenage children as they mourned their father's sudden death. She recalled the episode as "awful."

More than a decade earlier, while still married to McCaskill, Exposito had been caught smoking marijuana on a gambling boat while his wife was out of town. McCaskill was the Kansas City prosecutor at the time; such a scandal could have ended her political career. "You know, the prosecutor's husband, caught smoking pot on a gambling boat—it doesn't get any juicier than that," McCaskill told me. Rather than cover for him, she flew home and publicly chastised him.

She laughed, reliving her response: she went on the radio to conduct a previously scheduled interview, which all her aides wanted her to cancel. "I walked in and I sat behind the microphone and I just said, 'It's going to take me a year to get over the urge to kill him,'" she said. "I just said what I really felt, and it was genuine. All of a sudden I start getting flowers and teddy bears." Her husband was sentenced to community service, and they were divorced the next year. McCaskill did not know it at the time, but her real husband issues were yet to come: a decade later, her second husband, Joseph Shepard, would become a focal point in her gubernatorial and Senate races.

Across the country, candidates and their advisers were finding that husbands were stubborn focal points of media coverage, which did not seem to budge even as other dynamics shifted. Their anecdotal evidence was backed up by academic research. Dianne Bystrom, a professor at Iowa State University who studies media coverage of female candidates, said the news media treatment of women candidates had, by 2006, begun to reach parity in other ways. "There was dramatic improvement in the coverage of women in the late 1990s and early 2000s," Bystrom said. In 2000, in fact, her research found that women received the same quantity and quality of coverage as men in statewide races. Even "hair and hemline" coverage wasn't excessive for women—mainly because news accounts had started to focus on men's appearances, too, a trend exemplified by the treatment of Vice President Al Gore's wardrobe shift to earth tones during the 2000 presidential race.

But an imbalance remained in one area: coverage of candidates' families. The third *h*—husbands—was still an issue. "From 2000 to 2006, what we found was that women were covered much more in terms of their marital status and their husbands and their families," Bystrom said. "That carried forth."

Like Hillary Clinton, Dianne Feinstein, and Geraldine Ferraro before her, Claire McCaskill would spend an inordinate amount of time defending her husband's work. Shepard, a wealthy real estate developer, co-owned and operated a string of Missouri nursing homes, among other properties. He had also built numerous low-income housing projects in the state. Her Democratic rival in 2004 and her Republican opponents in both races made an issue of Shepard's work—including lawsuits over negligence at some of the nursing homes and citations by inspectors—and a $1.6 million loan he made to his wife's campaign. "Claire McCaskill has taken more than $1.6 million in campaign money from her husband, a nursing home owner whose homes were investigated, cited, and sued for substandard care, sexual assault and wrongful death," one ad by Bob Holden charged in 2004.

Two years later, the same script: "It's a new low, even for Claire McCaskill—exploiting the medical tragedy of others just to get votes," a female narrator said in one Republican National Committee ad in the Senate race. "But when rape, poor care, even wrongful death were going on in her current husband's nursing homes—nursing homes she pledged to sanction—where was she? And the profit from the family's nursing homes? She used it to try to buy an election and build her mansion." A vivid flyer showed up in mailboxes with a picture of a tombstone inscribed: "DIED due to NEGLECT in a Nursing Home."

A truth-squadding report by the news organization Fact Check.org found the ad misleading. There *had* been a rape in one of Shepard's nursing homes, and as state auditor, McCaskill *did* oversee the agencies that monitored nursing homes. But she did not regulate the nursing homes themselves, and she had, in fact, investigated and turned up errors by state nursing home overseers. Still, as the Senate race wore on, the attacks accelerated: Jim Talent's allies suggested Shepard had beaten his ex-wife and dodged taxes.

McCaskill said that, after the first campaign, her husband

was "absolutely a mess. We hadn't been married very long," she said. "And he had this like, ridiculously naïve notion that this was going to be fun; it was going to be great for me to be doing this."

Nonetheless, immediately after the narrow gubernatorial defeat, Shepard encouraged McCaskill to run again the following cycle. Her eyes welled with tears as she talked about it. "Talk about a guy that you could stay in love with. You know, the governor's race is over and he's been through all that, and then they start pounding on me to run for the Senate and— I'll never forget it. I will never forget it because we're driving along and he just grabs my hand," she said, pausing as her voice cracked.

"I get choked up talking about it," she said. "He grabbed it really hard and he said, 'You've got to get back out there and fight. You've got to do it. You've got to do it. The country needs you.' And I was like, 'Oh my God.' Because I knew what it meant for him. I knew that he had to suit up and go out there and have it done all over again to him."

She added, laughing: "Suffice it to say, he's not a Republican anymore."

Chapter 5

Mother of Five in Pearls

As Nancy Pelosi prepared to take over as House Speaker in early 2007, her rivals were planning a counterattack. Though they had just lost control of the House, Republicans thought they had been handed a gift in the new Democratic leader: a crusading, batty liberal from San Francisco, her eyes glued wide open, in their caricature version of her.

But in planning a swearing-in ceremony that would introduce her to much of the country for the first time, Pelosi, then sixty-six, added a sentimental flourish. Over the objections of House officials, she insisted that young children be allowed up on the dais at the end of her maiden speech. "I was told, 'Maybe you shouldn't do that,'" she later recalled. "There was a question as to whether it would even happen." Past protocol be damned, Pelosi decided. Rather than wait for permission, she waved the children up to the front of the chamber.

In all, some fifty boys and girls—her own grandchildren and the sons and daughters of House members—swarmed her desk that day. As she raised the gavel, with an adorable passel of little boys and girls gazing up all around her, the moment was frozen in a snapshot and splashed around the world. "For all of America's children, the House will be in order," she said, hammering the session in with a huge smile.

That intuitive bit of stagecraft became a lasting image, telegraphing what would become the trademark Nancy Pelosi image of leadership: a disciplined but nurturing grandmother, proud to be a woman in power. "It did turn out to be quite a picture," Pelosi told me, laughing, two and a half years later. "I laugh because every place I go in the country, people say—the women, especially—'I cried when I saw those children up there. We cried when we saw that,'" she said. "Now I'm realizing the Republicans were crying, too, because they just can't get over it. You know, our success for children, our success on our legislation has driven them to distraction." She laughed again, leaning forward in her chair—but this time it was a devilish laugh, the idea of infuriating Republicans clearly filling her with delight.

On the afternoon I came to see Pelosi in the summer of 2009, her grandmother routine was in full swing again. Her waiting area table was stacked with crayons and coloring books, alongside a bowl filled with purple aluminum-wrapped chocolate Kisses. Two young girls—the daughters of the ABC host George Stephanopoulos and the actress Ali Wentworth, it turned out—were busy drawing while they waited for their mother to finish meeting with Pelosi inside. Another child, belonging to a member of the House staff, showed up to play later on. It was as if the Speaker's office had become a day-care center, albeit a swank one with security guards and stunning views of the Washington Monument.

Yet inside her office, there was another scene. Dressed in a lilac pantsuit, Pelosi stood in front of a bank of televisions, intently watching the day's news coverage of a shooting at the Holocaust museum, a few blocks away. When we sat down to talk, she started with the happy subject of electing more women to office, a mission she described as "wholesome." Within minutes, however, she had adopted a tone that was more *Godfather* than *Sound of Music*. Women can survive in politics, Pelosi said, only if they "don a suit of armor." She had a glint in her eye. "It's very tough for women, because you go in, in such good faith about what you believe in, and in a positive way, and all of a sudden, boom-badaboom-badaboom," she said with a boxing gesture. "As I say to my members, if they punch you in the stomach and they feel flab, you're going to get pounded. If they feel hard, they're going to hurt their hand," Pelosi continued, punching one hand into an open fist. "It's not a nice thing to say, I know. But it is what it is."

Pelosi raised five children, born within six years, and made the experience the backbone of her life in Congress. She describes using her "mother of five voice" to quiet a room, shooting recalcitrant lawmakers what others call her "grandmother look" to get them back in line. She has the maternal habit of serving Ghirardelli chocolates in meetings. "Having five children in six years is the best training in the world for Speaker of the House," Pelosi said not long before the swearing in. "It made me the ultimate multitasker and the master of focus, routine, and scheduling."

In truth, Pelosi rose to become the first female House Speaker in history with the skills of a hardened political operative, trained at the knee of her father, the three-term mayor of Baltimore. A canny negotiator and a partisan, one of the most ideologically committed members of the Democratic caucus, she possesses ruthless strategic instincts. "Reptilian," her friend Representative George Miller said when asked what some of her favorite mantras are. "She thinks every now and then we should be reptilian in our thinking. Cold-blooded." Like her most successful male predecessors, Pelosi can be politically polarizing; Democratic voters love her as much as Republicans love to hate her. A strict vote counter with a long memory, Pelosi has taught colleagues to strive to stay on her good side; even her allies concede she has a vengeful streak. "Nancy is incredibly fucking tough," White House Chief of Staff Rahm Emanuel said with open admiration. "She has a spine of steel," her friend Representative Rosa L. DeLauro of Connecticut said, putting it more gently.

Her steeliness comes wrapped in extreme femininity—delivered with a ladylike smile and a moral certitude that have proven infuriating to her opponents over the years. Impeccably dressed at all times in designer suits and expensive pearls, adamant about decorum (her office has a no-jeans rule), Pelosi has dodged most of the basic public image problems that plagued Hillary Clinton and Sarah Palin. She is neither too masculine nor too feminine, neither too tough nor too soft, neither too aggressive nor too demure. It becomes easy to forget that she was dismissed by opponents many years ago as an "airhead" and a "dilettante." Her long service on two weighty House committees, Appropriations and Intelligence, gave her a complete policy grounding. In her personal life, she has the benefit of a stable family and being "comfortable in her own skin," in the words of one friend—and, on the clothing front, of having a tasteful and affluent husband to help supply it; he even does her suit shopping.

Above all, Pelosi has done something that neither Clinton nor Palin successfully managed during their time in the spotlight: she has unabashedly embraced children, and grandchildren, as a positive political force. It is a hand-that-rocks-the-cradle-rules-the-world kind of approach. Democrats may be ambivalent about being the "Mommy party"—worried about being perceived as soft on national security and defense, limited to the realms of health care and education, which presumably only mothers care about—but not so Pelosi. "The children, the children, the children," she has been known to say when asked about congressional priorities.

Pelosi will almost certainly never run for president herself. "Me? No. I love my job," she told me. "And the reason I'm successful at what I do here is I have no other agenda. You know what? This is where I am. This is where my political life is and will end." Her friends say she is sincere in her denial. "What? I hadn't thought of that. No," George Miller said when asked if she might ever run.

Does having a female Speaker put a woman any closer to winning the presidency? Strategists expressed skepticism, noting that the Speakership is by definition a very different role in the national imagination. Seeing Pelosi wield the gavel does not carry the same vividness, in voters' minds, as watching a woman stare down a foreign dictator or command the military. (One Democratic strategist told me, only half jokingly, that the character of the female President Allison Taylor on the Fox show *24* could have as much of a psychic impact.) Some supporters of Hillary Clinton would also argue that Pelosi actually helped block the first female president by quietly putting her thumb on the scale in President Obama's favor during the Democratic primaries.

She is, however, as of 2009, the most successful woman in American electoral history, with a track record worth examination. And her style could be instructive for future female presidential candidates. It appears effortless, burdened with little of the gender-related anguish that other women in the national spotlight have displayed. "She is a mother and a grandmother, but because she is so comfortable with who she is, she is not defensive about it," said the senior Obama adviser Anita Dunn, who followed Pelosi around during her swearing-in week with a video camera to capture the moment for party archives. "She clearly feels that that element brings an important aspect that she is not scared to talk about in terms of how she views public policy issues. But at the same time she is never arguing—and she never has argued—that it is the reason she should have a seat at the table. Or a reason she should be Speaker or a member of Congress. It has never been the rationale, but it has been value added. And I think that is the code."

Still, more than Clinton or Palin, Pelosi has made a coherent, public case for why having women in politics matters: she argues, explicitly, that women, and especially mothers, represent an underserved constituency. If it is feminism, it is cloaked in the selfless language of public service. "I firmly believe that nothing has been more wholesome for the political and governmental process than the increased participation of women. This is absolute, without any question," she told me.

Pelosi does not limit the argument to domestic issues but applies it across the board. During a budget debate against Republican Minority Leader John Boehner, she held up a photograph of a newly born grandchild (her eighth) and instructed him to reconsider his opposition to the bill. "First of all, I can't take my eyes off of her. And second of all: this is what our commitment is about. It's our commitment to the future—to these children," she said.

She has applied it to national security. "Think lioness when you think of women in politics. You threaten our cubs, you're dead," she said during the 2006 campaign. In our conversation, she told me: "We have to impress upon the public that women are here for the national security of our country, for the economic security of our country, in addition to issues that relate to children and health care and education. It can't be, like the women are over there taking care of the children and the men are taking care of national defense."

Pelosi has also argued, as a matter of both policy and politics, that women inherently represent change. In short, the argument goes: if you don't like the way things are going, why not try something that has not been done in the last few hundred years? It is not a new assertion, and its effectiveness is the subject of great debate in political circles. But no one before Pelosi had made the argument so vehemently at the national level. So enthusiastic was she about the political power of womanhood that she proposed having Democratic women members wield brooms at a campaign event in 2006, to make the case that it "will take a woman to clean out the House." Her aides objected to that prop, but the language became a hallmark.

Claiming gender superiority can, of course, be hazardous. If women are more pure, does that mean men are stronger or better at math? Such an argument risks a backlash. Furthermore, it does not always work. After all, in 2006 a staggering number of Democratic women lost in close races.

Still, Pelosi appears to have a point, at least when it comes to male politicians' lack of discretion. A string of high-profile affairs involving male officeholders—from Bill Clinton to Newt

Gingrich to Eliot Spitzer to John Edwards to Jim McGreevey to John Ensign to Larry Craig to Mark Sanford—has left many political observers wondering why women in power are rarely caught in similar acts. It may just be that there are fewer women in office, reducing the pool of potential female transgressors. Or maybe they know they are held to a higher standard and thus behave. Or maybe they face fewer temptations—or lack the necessary degree of testosterone.

In fact, women more often have the opposite problem: being attached to an unfaithful spouse. Beyond Hillary Clinton, at least one other elected woman, Senator Debbie Stabenow of Michigan, has lived through public humiliation by her husband; in 2008, Stabenow's husband was implicated in a prostitution sting, a mortifying episode. Not too many male politicians have suffered a similar betrayal by their wives back home.

Pelosi may be unique—a "transformational historic figure," in the words of Massachusetts Representative Edward J. Markey—but she shares certain traits with other successful women in politics, starting with political family ties. She was born into the business, and it is impossible to understand her without acknowledging that key fact. Her father, Thomas D'Alesandro, Jr., a five-term congressman and popular mayor of Baltimore, was a bread-and-butter politician who practiced coalition building—among the Italian, Irish, Polish, and Jewish factions in the city—and constituent services, two trademarks of his daughter's House today.

Even when he became a famous mayor with national reach, D'Alesandro ran his political operation out of the family home, employing his six children as helpers. At age thirteen, each child learned to manage the "front desk," receiving visitors and marking down every request or complaint. The mayor kept a "favor file," tracking who needed what and remembering it at election time through pieces of yellow paper tucked in a folder. It was a house in constant motion. Pelosi once told an interviewer that, in her childhood home, "it was always campaign time, and if you went into the living room, it was always constituent time." By the time she was in her early teens, Pelosi knew how to direct visitors in need of medical care to a hospital, or where to call to help someone find public housing. The door was always unlocked, with constituents dropping by first thing in the morning or at night for a home-cooked meal.

Today, it is the daughter of that Baltimore mayor that Pelosi's colleagues see at work. "You look at her, and everybody sees a very attractive woman, well-dressed, who, yes, has children and grandchildren, all that, and she's proud of her children. She's an Italian mother. And proud of her grandchildren," Rahm Emanuel said, rattling off the Pelosi pedigree in an interview. But, he said: "She is her father's daughter. You do not make it to the top of a man's world just on the heels of your children and grandchildren. That's not who they elected. And don't think that the chairmen and the old bulls don't know that—and they still can't believe it. She is her father's daughter and always will be, in the political world."

Male politicians often seem to be on a quest to fulfill their fathers' aspirations, or gain paternal approval; if you look at the last few presidents, you could almost say the psychological profile requires some deep father-related twist (think of Bill Clinton's deceased father and alcoholic stepfather, George W. Bush's effort to outdo his father's one-term presidency, Barack Obama's adult journey toward reconciliation with a missing father he had never known). From the former vice president Al Gore (whose father was a senator) to Senator John McCain (whose father and grandfather were four-star admirals), recent male presidential candidates have been shaped by their fathers' experiences, good and bad. It seems logical that ambitious political women would have similar parental issues. Pelosi seems to have inherited skills from both her mother and her father, channeling Mayor D'Alesandro's political instincts and Annunciata D'Alesandro's capacity for hospitality and mothering. But she also lived out the dreams of her mother, who had no choice but to be a stay-at-home caregiver. In her autobiography, Pelosi said her mother "had dreams of her own, and part of what makes me so receptive to new possibilities, I suspect, is knowing that she could not pursue hers." She has also been quoted as saying that she likes having her own power base. "I'm not into derivative power," she once said, when asked if she might seek a cabinet position—something I heard repeatedly from the next generation of women officeholders.

Pelosi talks about her days as a stay-at-home mother with great nostalgia; her stories of ringing a dinner bell to summon her many offspring in from playing, or of lining them up to inspect their shoes and uniforms before school, conjure postcard images of another era, a kind of upscale *Cheaper by the Dozen* set in San Francisco's Presidio Heights. Tales of how she ran the household are by now legendary: to prepare school lunches, Pelosi laid out ten slices of whole wheat bread on a counter, along with deli meats and condiments, and had the children march through in an assembly line to make their own. She hand-sewed costumes for school plays, baked cookies, and drove the children everywhere in a station wagon.

But though she was technically a housewife—and her children attest to her constant, doting availability to them growing up—Pelosi began building a robust political career while the kids were in diapers. She volunteered for the Democratic party, opening the family house for social events. She attended protests, marching against the Vietnam War and repression in the Soviet Union, sometimes with children in strollers in tow. Her children recall being taken to the mayor's office in 1973 for her swearing in on the library commission. Most significant, in 1976, when all five children were still under eighteen, she threw herself into helping California Governor Jerry Brown in his bid for the Democratic presidential nomination. She convinced Brown, a high school friend of her husband, to mount a serious campaign in Maryland rather than wait for the later primary in California. Then, with the help of the D'Alesandro machine, Pelosi helped Brown orchestrate his first—and biggest—primary victory. Brown hailed Pelosi as his political "architect," launching her to fame within the party.

Pelosi was not, then, as quaintly domesticated as her mother-of-five talk sometimes suggests. She may have gone unpaid for many years, but politics was not quite a second career that she broke into in her forties. "I remember going to state conventions with her since I was eleven years old," Christine Pelosi recalled. Her mother's work during her stay-at-home years was "probably similar now to what some working moms are able to do, which is to telecommute a lot," she said.

Nor was her climb in the party as simple as she makes it sound. Roadblocks for women were firmly intact in the 1970s and '80s, when she began moving up the ranks, and Pelosi encountered them, too. How she handled the sexist slights and efforts to undercut her as a woman—incidents she downplays today—laid the groundwork for success in her congressional life.

A seminal moment in Pelosi's early career came in 1985, when she ran for chairwoman of the Democratic National

Committee—and lost. It was her first, and so far only, major defeat; it was also tinged with gender. Running against Paul G. Kirk, Jr., a former aide to Senator Edward M. Kennedy, Pelosi encountered men who were miffed she was running. It did not help her that Geraldine Ferraro, another Italian-American woman, had just been on the presidential ballot as the vice presidential nominee and lost. Some Democrats felt Ferraro had driven white men away from the ticket, helping Ronald Reagan win a second term. "People tell me that I was the best-qualified candidate. But some of them tell me that it's too bad that I'm not a man," Pelosi told people, according to a biography by Vincent Bzdek of the *Washington Post*. "If I had known I would be judged as a woman, I wouldn't have entered it." She became determined then, according to Democrats who know her, to come back and eradicate the closed-shop mind-set of the party establishment.

It was in that DNC race that Pelosi heard she had been described, by a union official allied with her rival, as an "airhead." She was "furious," according to a biography of her by the long-time *San Francisco Chronicle* reporter Marc Sandalow, and she recounted the insult to reporters in Washington. "I can take the knocks. But [that] made me angry," she was quoted as saying at the time.

Pelosi was described dismissively again the following year, when she ran for Congress for the first time. Signs went up around San Francisco asking voters if they wanted "the legislator . . . or the dilettante?" But by then she had two important forces on her side: a winning stint as the finance chair for the Democratic Senatorial Campaign Committee, which reclaimed control of the Senate in 1987, and the blessing of Representative Sala Burton, whose seat she sought to fill. Burton had recruited Pelosi to replace her shortly before she died; in the special election that ensued, Pelosi cobbled together a coalition of older Democrats,

Republicans, and young women. It was enough to overcome the negative billboards. She won by just a few thousand votes, in what would be her last hotly contested race to represent the Eighth District.

Pelosi laughed as she recalled getting the who-will-raise-her-children questions as a first-time candidate. "My youngest child was going to be a senior in high school. I had four kids in college. And they were saying, 'Who's going to take care of your children?'" she told me. "And I was saying, 'My children? My children are taking care of me.' But nonetheless, it was always, 'You're a mom. Who's taking care of your children?'"

In the two decades since, Pelosi, her allies say, encountered all the traditional pitfalls for women in politics: being stereotyped as too naïve or too soft or focused only on women's issues; being given short shrift for her strategic contributions; being referred to in diminutive terms, as though she were a little girl, or caricatured as a wacky, out-of-control liberal. She was, perhaps more than anything else, dismissed as too pretty to be a serious legislator or powerhouse. Dick Armey, the former House Republican party leader, once said that "one of the reasons Nancy's abilities are not appreciated is that she's a beautiful woman." If she has "a negative in her political career, it's that she's too attractive," Agar Jaicks, a Democratic activist in California, once said. (In more recent days, male members of Congress have sometimes referred to her as "hot" behind her back, but never with the same leering drool reserved for the younger mother of five, Sarah Palin.)

These impediments seemed only to reinvigorate her drive, Pelosi's allies say. Rather than complain about sexism, her approach was to plot a more cunning strategy—to help raise more money, win more Democratic seats, build more experience, accrue more favors. She earned a reputation for graciousness, sending chocolates and gifts to colleagues, visiting them and sending handwritten notes when relatives fell ill. When it was necessary, she killed older members of Congress with kindness, deploying a flirtatious charm. She surrounded herself with loyal male allies—men respected across the caucus, such as Representative John Murtha and Representative Barney Frank and, later, Rahm Emanuel—who lent her greater support and credibility still. Pelosi emerged from the DNC defeat embracing a new motto that might as well apply to her whole life: "Organize, don't agonize."

"She's not a dweller," her youngest daughter, Alexandra, said. "She moves on very quickly. It's a mechanism of survival and self-preservation."

Pelosi told me her political background prepared her for the decades of battle that lay ahead. "I had no illusions about how difficult politics is," she said. "I mean, I grew up in a political family. I know it's very, shall we say, competitive." She said she received, and now doles out, two pieces of advice: to be yourself, and not to get caught up in the insults. "You have to defuse—some people would call them lies, but in polite society we'll call them misrepresentations that they put out about you. You can't ignore it," she said. "You fight it. But you do not let it get to you. It's just like, that's their problem."

She continued: "When I was coming through all of this, I knew one thing. I don't care what they say. I do care that the record be made straight, but I don't care what they say. And that's why I say you have to don a suit of armor, because they're coming after you. Power has never been relinquished without a fight in the history of the world. It's hard for men. It's much harder for women."

. . .

Nothing proved this like the 2006 midterm elections—in which so many Democratic female House candidates lost. Many of them were women handpicked by Pelosi and Emanuel, encouraged to run—and warned about how difficult it would be, to no avail.

Tammy Duckworth was the greatest disappointment. A veteran of the Iraq war who lost both her legs and an arm in combat, Duckworth, then thirty-seven, was seen as an almost perfect female candidate when she launched her campaign to replace the retiring Illinois representative Henry Hyde. She had the trappings of a winner: a compelling personal story, a military background, national support, the political winds at her back. Though she was a political newcomer who needed practice on the trail, her media coverage was overwhelmingly positive. Celebrity endorsements rolled in: former President Bill Clinton, then Senator Barack Obama, and Michael J. Fox all made appearances on her behalf.

And then the attacks began. "Taxes or diapers?" one Republican congressional mailer dismissively asked, accusing "liberal Tammy Duckworth" of wanting to raise taxes and, thus, deprive families of needed diaper funds. Peter Roskam, her Republican rival, criticized her on national security. But Democratic officials believe it was immigration that hurt her most. "Tammy Duckworth supports a plan to give amnesty to 11 million illegal immigrants. Does she have any idea what that will cost us?" a male voice ominously warned in a television spot produced by the National Republican Congressional Committee. A photograph of Duckworth was juxtaposed with video footage of illegal immigrants, handcuffed with their hands over their heads, being led away at night. "Tammy Duckworth: Wrong on immigration. Wrong for Illinois."

Hers was the most visible defeat, but it was not an isolated case. Other women, tagged with being soft on immigration and other issues typically associated with men, also lost. Lois Murphy, a cum laude Harvard Law School graduate and popular Democratic candidate, lost by three thousand votes to Jim Gerlach in Pennsylvania. In Connecticut, Diane Farrell came within a few percentage points of unseating Republican Representative Christopher Shays, who was the only Republican elected to the New England delegation that year. (Shays lost two years later—to a male challenger.) Darcy Burner, in Washington State's Eighth Congressional District, was locked in a tie against Republican Dave Reichert until the end, when he beat her with fewer than eight thousand votes. In New Jersey, Linda Stender lost to the incumbent Mike Ferguson by less than four thousand votes. The list went on.

The year was a severe letdown, especially for Democrats, who had fielded the vast majority of the women candidates. "Women really underperformed in 2006 dramatically," said Richard Fox, a political science professor at Loyola Marymount University who studies House races. "There were about ten races across the country where you could see that Democratic women lost by two to four points, races they thought they had a chance in. It looked like women did worse in close races than they usually do."

No one could quite explain it. Some thought it was simply the Iraq war—that women were seen as too weak on defense—but that did not account for antiwar victories such as that of Carol Shea-Porter, an antiestablishment Democrat in New Hampshire. At EMILY's List, the Democratic group dedicated to electing pro-choice women, strategists were concerned enough about the 2006 results that they quietly conducted an after-action report, looking at the districts where their candidates had been defeated. They concluded—somewhat defensively—that it was because those districts skewed slightly toward

Republicans. "We looked at the difference between where the men were running and where the women ran, and the men's districts were very slightly more Democratic, had more of a union presence in them," Ellen Malcolm, the head of EMILY's List, told me. She vehemently denied that any one issue—or sexism in general—had felled women that year and pointed to the fact that the overall number of women in Congress has continued to rise, if slowly.

But Pelosi and Emanuel, in separate interviews, told me they believed that gender *was* at the crux of their candidates' defeats—and that immigration, in particular, had been used to crush the women who ran. Immigration was an area where women could be portrayed as weak, emotional, sentimental. "Women were seen as more vulnerable to that charge," Emanuel told me. Republicans, he said, argued "that they would take public dollars and take care of illegal immigrant children, and women were more vulnerable to that charge; even a former Iraqi war vet who lost two legs and an arm.

"It was a very successful strategy to use against women," he said. "Now when I said it, EMILY's List went crazy, but you know, the fact is you just don't put your head in the sand."

Pelosi had a similar interpretation. She told me she used to lie awake at night, counting the congressional districts with female candidates the way other people count sheep. She had factored the women into her overall plan for taking control of the House. "I thought many more of those women would be here. We made a major investment in them being here," she said in an interview. She agreed that opponents used the issue of immigration "very effectively"; it was impossible, she said, for women to fight charges that they would spend tax dollars on illegal immigrants, even in cases where such spending was against the law. Voters just believed women were softhearted that way. "If you make the charge that a woman supports feeding poor children, people believe it," Pelosi said. "They might not believe it about a man, but they would believe it about a woman."

The *New York Times,* in an article anticipating a "year of the woman" House sweep in 2006, suggested the midterms would foreshadow the presidential campaign two years later. "This midterm election may offer some hints on the kind of climate that awaits Senator Hillary Rodham Clinton of New York if she runs for president in 2008," the reporter Robin Toner wrote. "At a time when voters have grown accustomed to women as secretary of state, House minority leader, governor (there are currently eight) and the like, this year's campaign could provide insight into the power of gender stereotypes that have been charted by scholars and political experts over many years."

And so it did.

Just weeks after Pelosi debuted as Speaker on Capitol Hill, the other towering Woman in Politics made an announcement. Hillary Clinton declared that she was running for president, instantly sucking the oxygen from the rest of the Democratic universe as the front-runner and the candidate of the establishment.

For the next year and a half, Pelosi claimed a position of virtuous neutrality. She had a legitimate excuse: as leader of the unwieldy House Democratic caucus and chairwoman of the Democratic National Convention, she could not risk alienating any segment of the party by choosing among Clinton, Obama, and all the other candidates. As the race narrowed, however, Pelosi began dropping not-so-subtle clues about her preference for Obama. A top ally, Representative

George Miller, endorsed Obama in early January—a move her circle knew would be interpreted as a reflection of the Speaker's wishes. Pelosi gave Kansas Governor Kathleen Sebelius a prominent national platform—as the lawmaker who responded to George W. Bush's State of the Union address—the night before Sebelius announced she, too, was endorsing Obama. Pelosi even at one point joined the critics who suggested Clinton was playing the gender card, "trying to take advantage" of the perception that she was under siege.

The tacit Obama-Pelosi alliance made sense on many fronts: His grassroots style suited hers, as did his message of enacting institutional change, and Pelosi had never joined the friend-of-the-Clintons club in the 1990s anyway. Pelosi and Clinton had also disagreed on the Iraq war, an extension of a more basic gap in ideology. They had no special personal rapport; people around both women suspect a range of cultural differences would have kept them from ever being close. It is easy to imagine Pelosi, the devout Catholic mother of five, looking askance at some of the Clinton family choices.

Pelosi's thinly disguised favoritism enraged the Clinton camp, already suffering from so many other perceived slights. Bitter Clinton advisers—who kept a running tab of snubs by prominent women, from Oprah to Caroline Kennedy—groused that Pelosi just did not want another woman in the limelight (suspecting she enjoyed being the "most senior skirt in the land," as one Clinton loyalist was quoted as saying in an account by Michelle Cottle in *The New Republic*).

Philosophically, Pelosi might have faced a dilemma about whether to back another woman, given her spoken commitment to the sisterhood. But politically, she paid no price for failing to support Clinton. Quite the opposite: the base loved it. Liberals had been surly over Pelosi's refusal to start impeachment proceedings against President Bush or to yank funding for the Iraq war after taking back the House. Now, they saw her as a heroine, bucking the Clinton machine.

And she did it with a smile. As anxiety in Hillaryland grew after repeated primary losses, Pelosi cheerfully declined to come to the rescue, even as a neutral arbiter. She ruled out counting the votes in Michigan and Florida, where unsanctioned balloting would have helped Clinton—all in the name of fairness, of course. "I don't think that any states that operated outside the rules of the party can be dispositive of who the nominee is," Pelosi said on Bloomberg Television, her convoluted language fooling no one about what she meant. When Clinton turned to a superdelegate strategy, phone-banking the Democratic officials who count for a portion of the nominating decision, Pelosi gave a warning. It would, she said, be "a problem for the party if the verdict would be something different than the public has decided." The moment a joint Obama-Clinton ticket was proposed, Pelosi rejected it. "Take it from me, that won't be the ticket," she told reporters on Capitol Hill in March 2008.

Some top Clinton Democrats, already in an extreme state of agitation, finally sent Pelosi a letter threatening to withdraw their funding of the Democratic Congressional Campaign Committee if she did not rethink her superdelegate position. Pelosi, who does not respond well to threats, did not budge. The incident left a bitter aftertaste. "I think Hillary Clinton has been very gracious," Pelosi said months later, acidly adding: "I think some of her supporters have been less than gracious." (The tactic also backfired: DCCC donations rose in the wake of the threat, thanks to offended Obama backers.)

Experts on women in politics have a saying: to stay in the game, you must slay a dragon. That can mean a dramatic act, like riding in to restore faith in government after a corruption scandal (as Republican Governor Jodi Rell did in Connecticut) or confronting drug cartels on the Mexican border (as Democratic Governor Janet Napolitano did in Arizona). In her first year in office, Pelosi arguably helped slay two dragons at once: President Bush, by blocking his legislative agenda and driving down his approval rating in his dwindling hours, and Hillary Clinton, though that slaying was more on the sly.

"There were a lot of guys around town who questioned her toughness and ability to do the job three years ago," Ed Markey of Massachusetts said of Pelosi. "No one does that now."

Pelosi expressed notably little sympathy for Clinton when she lost. She acknowledged that "there was sexism" but dismissed its impact. "I'm a victim of sexism all the time," she told reporters. When we spoke, Pelosi seemed to have softened some toward Clinton, and even expressed some concern about the way Sarah Palin had been treated. "I mean, she's governor of Alaska. People think they can make jokes about women and they wouldn't even be funny if they were making the same joke about a man, and how he dressed or something. You know, it'd get tiresome after a while," she said. "I think that when you put yourself on the line, you accept that you invite whatever comes. But there should be a little more respect for the fact that someone is breaking ground here."

Still, in our conversation, Pelosi left the distinct impression that the better candidate had won the nomination in her view. She recounted introducing several of the contenders at the Iowa Jefferson-Jackson Day dinner, and the way Obama had surpassed all the other speakers. Clinton, she said, "could have been president. I think everybody had that impression. It happened to be that another candidate came along who was so spectacular and the public wanting, I think, something new— I won't go into that. I don't think she lost. I think she won the campaign. That is to say the respect that she commands, the place that she has in our country was greatly enhanced, I think, by that campaign. The public had a different idea about who would be the nominee and who could win for president; although I think, if nominated, she would have won. But I think that that was a campaign to be very proud of; that her personal strengths intellectually, personally, and in every way made women and people who supported her very proud. So I don't fault anything that was done there. It's just that it was outdone by a phenomenon; you know, a phenomenon that came along."

And then, Pelosi observed that Clinton had started out with an advantage—or should have. In Clinton's race, half the voters were women, whereas women make up less than a third of the congressional caucus that elevated Pelosi to her current position. "I would have thought, going back some years, that it's easier to be a president of the United States for a woman than being Speaker—because the public was much more ready for women to be at the top than an institution which has been a male bastion," she told me. "Here, we broke the marble ceiling. *This* is the toughest arena you could ever imagine."

Moms in the House

Rahm Emanuel liked to warn Democrats not to get too comfortable with the idea of winning back the majority in 2006. Even when the numbers looked good in the months before the election, he was superstitious. "Jews never put the crib up until the baby is born," he would say. "In the Catholic tradition, we never take the crib down," Nancy Pelosi would playfully respond.

Cribs, children, mothers, grandmothers—it was impossible

to turn around without hitting some new twist on the old classic frame of a politician kissing a baby. That time-honored ritual, dating to at least the era of Andrew Jackson, had long been the necessary human touch for male candidates. (Legend had it that, in 1828, Jackson was handed a baby to kiss, the first such incident in U.S. history; befuddled, he declined, handing the infant to his war secretary.) But what happens when the baby belongs to the candidate, and she is a woman? How does the political calculus of motherhood work?

The answer is complicated. It is one thing for mothers of older children, such as Pelosi or Clinton, to have checked the motherhood box on their résumés in the distant past and wave it as a credential, their grown children evidence of their nurturing sensibilities, their compassion, their devotion to issues like health care and education. It is quite another to be an active mother of children under the age of eighteen, showing up at campaign events with the family in tow.

Yet for the first time, in small but countable numbers, younger mothers are trying to break into—and stay in—politics, at least on the Democratic side. In 2009, there were about a dozen female members of Congress with children aged fifteen or younger, including two women who had recently had babies in office. Several of the Democratic mothers attributed their presence directly to Pelosi.

The new mothers were unusually frank about what having a child in office entailed: Representative Stephanie Herseth Sandlin, cochair of the centrist Blue Dog Coalition, was back at work shortly after giving birth—and, in an interview, praised Pelosi for her decision to install breast-pumping rooms in the House for situations such as hers. Representative Linda Sánchez, the first unmarried member of Congress to announce a pregnancy, elaborated still further, telling reporters about her ob-gyn's advice that, at age thirty-nine, she could not wait any longer if she wanted to have a child. There were also several young mothers in the Senate, including Kirsten Gillibrand, who switched from the House to the Senate to replace Hillary Clinton early that year.

Ever the grandmother, Pelosi has encouraged female lawmakers not to forgo having babies for their careers, and she kept track of which ones were pregnant—an approach that her advisers said is as much a pragmatic way to expand her caucus as an expression of her concern. Pelosi has done small, practical things to make the House more hospitable to young mothers, such as adding an ob-gyn to the rotation of doctors who visit lawmakers. "Somebody like me, as Speaker of the House, has a responsibility to the younger generation of women to say: Don't think of this as a minus," Pelosi has said. "This is a *plus*, being a mother, having an experience of raising a family."

Best known of the "young mother caucus" on Capitol Hill, and arguably the most ambitious, is Representative Deborah Wasserman Schultz, an energetic force representing a safe Democratic district in South Florida. Elected in 2004, she shot to national fame just ten weeks after being sworn in with her ardent opposition to government intervention in the case of Terri Schiavo, a brain-dead patient whose husband sought to remove her feeding tube. Wasserman Schultz knew the Florida case cold from her time as a legislator, and she seized it as an opportunity to confront the Republican leadership then in power. She even took on a House Republican leader on the *Today* show, an early sign of her media ubiquity. "It's just absolutely unconscionable," the then-thirty-eight-year-old scolded the much more senior Representative Roy Blunt.

The following year, Wasserman Schultz raised many millions for her colleagues during the 2006 midterm elections; Democrats were victorious, and Pelosi appointed her to a leadership role, as chief deputy whip. She also won a seat on the influential Appropriations Committee, a coup for a House sophomore. In 2009, she was elected vice chair of both the Democratic Congressional Campaign Committee (in charge of winning House seats) and the Democratic National Committee (in charge of the entire Democratic operation). Her meteoric rise in Washington mirrors her career path from the very outset: at age twenty-six, she had been the youngest woman elected to the Florida state legislature.

Yet, despite her evident drive, at the heart of Wasserman Schultz's profile is her family—three young children and a husband, Steve Schultz. Even though they stay behind most of the time in Florida, her children make constant, lively appearances in the congresswoman's anecdotes. "My congressional life, my agenda, everything that I do is done through the lens of being my children's mom," she said over dinner one night near the Capitol. Her youngest, Shelby, was five years old at that point; the older twins, Rebecca and Jack, were nine.

A petite, curly-haired blonde whose bluntness prompted one colleague to describe her as a "female Rahm," Wasserman Schultz does not just happen to be a young mother; like Pelosi, she considers motherhood a political force. She revels in questions about the work-life balance. She sits for profiles about the Capitol Hill house she shares with other mother-lawmakers. She retells stories about going over her daughter's homework on her cell phone at the end of a long day in the Capitol.

And it works. When a divorced, older opponent in her 2004 race tried to campaign against her ability to raise three kids and serve in Congress, Wasserman Schultz turned the argument on its head, saying that as a young mother she would represent an underserved constituency. Her rival, Republican Margaret Hostetter, even went so far as to argue that Wasserman Schultz was clearly "frazzled" because she had, while looking for a writing utensil during a candidates' forum, pulled a crayon from her purse. Wasserman Schultz still relishes the story.

"My opponent was telling this reporter that that was an example of the frazzled life that I now lead and an example of how I couldn't possibly do both jobs well. The reporter asked me, 'Well, what's your reaction to that?' And I said, 'This is my reaction, and I want you to write this down exactly as I'm going to say it. The only thing that that showed was I didn't have a pen, and as a mom I'm often without a pen. But I can assure you that I'm *never* without a crayon,'" she said, beaming. Being on the defensive about her mothering skills gets her juices flowing. "You can say anything you want about me," she said. "I mean, criticize my record, tell me you don't agree with me, call me an idiot, whatever you want to say about me. But do not question my quality as a parent, especially when you don't know what you're talking about."

It helped that she was running in a solidly Democratic district. Campaign professionals have found that Democratic voters are much more willing than Republican ones to put young mothers in office. And her district—both now and when she was in Tallahassee—gives her no reason to temper her liberal instincts on policies involving gender. As a young state legislator, she tried to force dry cleaners to charge the same amount for women's and men's clothing, and sponsored legislation to put the same number of men and women on state boards. When she backed allowing only gender-neutral language in state statutes, it gave her colleagues an easy opening to needle her with the nickname Wasserperson.

But if she does not have to worry about punishment from moderates at home, Wasserman Schultz does, as a frequent Democratic surrogate, have to mind her image for a national audience. (She was a near-constant television presence in 2008, first as a loyal Clinton champion, then as a just as ardent Obama backer.) She almost certainly has higher ambitions as well; she has been discussed as a Senate candidate someday, or someone who might follow in Pelosi's shoes. All of which makes her style—a mix of hard-charging partisanship and softer mothering—an interesting case study.

The mythology of motherhood is both universal and powerful: across cultures and centuries, mothers have been revered in ways that women more generally have not. In times of crisis, mothers have even greater moral authority, one reason that they have formed the backbone of protest groups from Mothers Against Drunk Driving to the Mothers of the Plaza de Mayo in Argentina. It was no accident that the first civilian Iraq war opponent to gain serious traction was Cindy Sheehan, the mother of a soldier killed in action in 2005. Protest for its own sake was seen as a throwback, even frivolous; protest in the service of a lost child, by a grieving mother, carried weight.

Recently, the mother-on-a-mission model has translated into electoral politics. Carolyn McCarthy, whose husband was killed and son severely injured in a shooting on the Long Island Rail Road in 1993, ran for Congress as a Democrat from a long-standing Republican district in 1996 and won.

But unlike men—who have also seen parental tragedy

accrue to their political benefit, as in the cases of John Edwards and Joe Biden—women do not need adversity to strike; just being a mother can lend stature in the right situation. It also telegraphs other things: family values, normalcy, an adherence to familiar gender norms. And while Pelosi may be the best example of the political authority motherhood confers, she has increasingly had company.

Democrat Blanche Lincoln, elected to the House in the "year of the woman" in 1992 and reelected the following cycle, announced that she would not run for reelection in 1996 because she was pregnant with twins, and could not fathom campaigning in that condition in the Arkansas summer. But two years later, she jumped at the chance to run for Senate when Dale Bumpers stepped aside—and motherhood became a key feature of her candidacy. "Daughter, wife, mother, congresswoman: Living our rock-solid Arkansas values," her ads blared. The television spots showed her balancing the babies on her lap, with her head on her husband's shoulder.

In 2003, Kathleen Blanco used a similar approach to become the first female governor of Louisiana; a mother of six and the only woman in a multiple-candidate primary, she stood out because of her gender, along with her emphasis on education and health care. In the runoff that followed, against Bobby Jindal, Blanco "very effectively suggested that where Jindal could discern only numbers, she saw real people," according to a profile of southern female politicians in *The Atlantic*—something that Blanco, as a mother, was especially equipped to do. She gave an emotionally powerful answer in their last debate, saying that a "defining moment" in her life was the death of her teenage son in an accident.

And motherhood-as-training had been in play for decades. Madeleine Kunin, the former three-term governor of Vermont, made the case that her children taught her diplomacy. "I learned my negotiating skills early, with four children at the table," she told *National Journal* in 1986.

Even Hillary Clinton, once she became secretary of state, incorporated motherhood into her diplomatic rhetoric, comparing a belligerent North Korea to an attention-seeking teenager. "Maybe it's the mother in me or the experience that I've had with small children and unruly teenagers and people who are demanding attention—don't give it to them, they don't deserve it, they are acting out," Clinton said in 2009. (North Koreans replied in equally gendered terms, calling her a "schoolgirl.")

Yet for all its symbolic power, motherhood comes with obvious liabilities in the workplace, as any working mother knows. In some arenas motherhood is still seen as outright problematic: not that long ago, women were advised not to put up pictures of their children in the office for fear of sending out signals that they would rather be at home. (Hillary Clinton, in fact, has recalled getting that advice during her time at the Rose Law Firm, though she said she rejected it, putting a framed photo of Chelsea on her desk.) Similarly, women candidates are cautioned not to feature their young children or husbands in their advertisements—to prevent sending mixed messages about their priorities. Even now, research has shown, women are much more likely to show themselves alone in their ads and campaign literature, whereas men tend to surround themselves with multitudes of offspring.

Furthermore, it is a nightmare to commute between Washington and a home district with one or more babies in tow—and virtually impossible for lawmakers whose husbands have full-time jobs. So the political women become the breadwinners, and that role reversal, in turn, has political consequences: voters in many places are still uneasy about stay-at-home dads, according to several strategists who have worked on these campaigns.

Senator Claire McCaskill said she intentionally cut her young children out of her campaign imagery when she was running for county prosecutor in 1992. "I will confess I kept my kids out of the literature and stuff because I was worried that with young children, particularly—I mean my kids were infant, two and a half, and four and a half—that people would say, 'Well, she's going to be out chasing criminals and she's got these babies at home,'" McCaskill told me.

The most famous "mommy penalty" story in politics dates back to the 1950s, when Representative Coya Knutson, the first woman elected from Minnesota, was defeated after a newspaper ran a letter, supposedly from her forlorn husband, begging her to return home. This was the incident that set the stage for Minnesota's mostly male delegations until Amy Klobuchar was elected to the Senate. "Coya, I want you to tell the people of the Ninth District this Sunday that you are through in politics. That you want to go home and make a home for your husband and son," read the open letter, published at the height of her campaign.

Historians have cast doubt on the authenticity of the letter—Knutson's husband was an alcoholic who had often beaten his wife before she left for Congress—but it worked. Knutson lost by a slender margin that fall to a Republican with the robust slogan "A Big Man for a Man-sized Job."

Much more recently, motherhood—and in particular pregnancy—caused political problems for Jane Swift in Massachusetts, a state that, while politically liberal, has nonetheless never elected a woman to its highest office or to the Senate. Swift advertised her pregnancy with her first child when she ran for lieutenant governor in 1998; three years later, she was pregnant again when Governor Paul Cellucci stepped aside to become the U.S. ambassador to Canada, elevating her to the top state slot. She delivered twin daughters in early 2001, one month into her term as acting governor. Famously, Swift kept executive control during her maternity leave and conducted a meeting of the Massachusetts Governor's Council by speaker phone from the hospital.

She attained, in the words of the *Boston Globe* reporter Stephanie Ebbert, "iconic stature as a working mother." But it was a chaotic tenure, and Swift became infamous for the maternal crises that unfolded during her time in office, from her use of a state police helicopter to rush her home to a daughter with pneumonia to her reliance on statehouse aides as babysitters. Each domestic twist became a new source of public fascination—and a curse, driving her approval ratings into single digits. By the time she was running for governor in her own right, in 2002, the Republican establishment had decided she was not worth the risk; one former member of her administration told the *Globe* the party basically "threw her under the bus." Swift ultimately stepped aside to make way for the entrepreneur Mitt Romney, a father of five, who ran on his successful business record and won.

When Sarah Palin was nominated, six years later, the parallels were so obvious that one blogger said the Republican vice presidential nominee was being "Jane Swifted." Swift herself saw similarities from the moment Palin's nomination was announced. The lesson she drew from both experiences is that women simply cannot open up the "Pandora's box" of their children to the public without risk of being judged and ridiculed. "For mothers, it's just different," she said.

Today, Swift is back at home in western Massachusetts, consulting, teaching, raising her children—and, in the view of many, preparing to stage a return to politics, potentially by running for Congress from her home district. In the meantime, she has developed a platform as a Republican feminist, studying her own mistakes and the systemic flaws that block political advancement for young mothers. "The bitterness for me, if I have any bitterness, is that I actually think that I was a better statewide-elected official *because* I had children," Swift said over diet Cokes at a hotel in Williamstown, the college town where she is teaching. "On a lot of the issues we were deciding, my being a mother gave me great perspective. The work I did fairly quietly around children's protective services, certainly all the stuff I did around education, I think I had enormous credibility and a lot of great insights and saw those issues in the nuanced way you want elected officials to. But the reality is I, in many cases, had fewer choices available to me to be a good mother because I was in politics. Because I couldn't have my kids ride along with me to a county fair on a Saturday, so I either had to not do the event or my kids had to stay home."

The difference between Swift's experience and, say, that of Wasserman Schultz may be a matter of office: it is far easier to escape scrutiny as a mother-multitasker as one of hundreds of members of Congress than it is as the solo chief executive. Geography matters, too: House members are running for office in narrow districts, rather than appealing to voters across a broad partisan spectrum. There are, of course, basic questions about the women themselves. Operatives in Boston dismiss Swift as a lightweight and insist the harsh treatment had nothing to do with gender or motherhood but rather her competence as governor, whereas Wasserman Schultz has built up a reputation as a party leader, away from her domestic profile, that keeps her in good stead.

But if there is a trend to be discerned from Swift's and Palin's experiences, it clearly involves the differences for women between the political parties. It is just easier to be a Democratic female official these days—all the more so if you intend to bear children and raise them in office. All of the quantitative research points to a partisan divide. Anecdotally, political operatives say it has become increasingly difficult for Republican mothers to get elected to local and state office, given that their party base is more conservative and much more likely to expect them to stay home with small children. One Republican pollster has reportedly stopped focusing on female candidates; doing so is just not lucrative enough. And Republican women do not win any points from Democratic voters on the basis of gender or motherhood.

"Republican women are just losing ground, period," said Debbie Walsh, head of the Center for American Women and Politics at Rutgers University, which keeps statistics on state legislatures. "Republican women are down to about 15 percent of the Republican caucus—they're at about the same level women were around 1988."

At the same time, she cautions against Democrats feeling too self-satisfied about their enlightened acceptance of mothers in politics. "I wouldn't want to give the impression that young mothers are flooding into electoral politics, because what we've found is women are still older, still less likely to have children under eighteen at home than their male colleagues are, and motherhood is still a bit of a burden for women when they're candidates," Walsh said. "For a man who's running for office, that picture of himself and the spouse and the kids and the golden retriever is priceless because it shows he is grounded in the community, he's a nice family man. For women, the question is: Who's going to take care of your kids?"

Whatever the reason, the partisan divide helps explain why there is only one Republican member of the House young mothers caucus—Cathy McMorris Rodgers of Washington, who became the first woman to give birth in office in a decade when her son was born in 2007—and why Kay Bailey Hutchison, who adopted two children in 2001, is the only Republican mother of young children on the Senate side.

Representative Stephanie Herseth Sandlin, who as of 2009 was the youngest female member of the House, was single and childless when she first won election at age thirty-three, five years earlier. Her maiden name gave her an added boost: Ralph Herseth, her grandfather, had been South Dakota governor, and her grandmother was once secretary of state; her father served two decades in the state legislature. But her single status and her age came with their own baggage. "I was younger. I hadn't held office before. I was still single. I didn't have children. It was kind of like, 'Well, we like what she's saying. We think she'll work hard. But does she relate to me?'" she recalled in an interview in her Capitol Hill office.

Once she married former Representative Max Sandlin and had a baby boy, Herseth Sandlin's political strategists began to wonder how those changes would affect her career, especially if she chose to run for a higher office, such as governor. So far, she said, both appear to be assets. "I think that when I got married, people were happy for me. And then when I was expecting and then having a baby, I think if anything, my constituents feel, okay, well now she worries about the same things we worry about—and that's affordable child care and what are your options? And how do you balance work and family?" Herseth

Sandlin said. "And we know she's got a demanding job . . . but we think she can relate to us better and it's going to make her a more effective policy maker."

Pregnancy was a bolder move, politically, for Linda Sánchez, who was committed—but not married—to her boyfriend when they decided in 2008 to start a family. But conservative chatter in the blogosphere about her single motherhood mattered little in her heavily Democratic California district, and she was surprised to encounter little judgment even in Washington.

"More career women, I think especially women who work, understand that when you delay childbearing and you get to a certain age, there is not a lot of opportunity there. And the longer you wait the harder it gets," she said during an interview when she was seven months pregnant. "So I've been really pleasantly surprised by how accepting and warm everybody has been towards the idea of my becoming a mother. And I have to say I think a lot of that was made easier by the fact that we have a whole crop of sort of younger women in Congress over the last couple of terms, several of whom have given birth recently. So it's not the once in a blue moon occasion that it used to be." Still, Sánchez did wind up marrying her boyfriend, Jim Sullivan, several weeks before the baby was born. She announced the birth by press release a few hours after it happened, on May 13, 2009.

The fact that it warranted a press release signaled just how novel the concept of a childbearing member of Congress still was. "Nobody talks about how many men in Congress had kids last year. But I can tell you off the top of my head how many women did," said Amy Walter, editor in chief of the daily political newsletter *Hotline*, rattling off the names of Linda Sánchez, Stephanie Herseth Sandlin, and Kirsten Gillibrand.

"Historically, if you were a woman and you were going to run for office, you really had to wait until your kids were grown up. It was your second career. It was, 'What should I do next? I'm going to join the PTA; then I'm going to run for office,'" Walter said. "We've had three women in the last year who've had babies in office. You get this sense that it's not that big of a deal—although it is a big deal—or that they're not paying a penalty for it. This is not the 'Coya, come home' story of women not being able to do both."

And why is that? In part, it may be because Nancy Pelosi has set an unmistakably different tone. In one of the most intriguing scenes of the Pelosi Speakership, she was asked at a press conference in the spring of 2009, as Linda Sánchez was about to give birth, to describe her reaction to having so many young mothers in the House. Pelosi lit up when the subject arose. It was the first time a House leader had discussed lactation on camera, as far as anyone could recall.

"New moms being here are important for a couple of different reasons. First of all, we wanted younger women coming into the Congress so that they could gain their experience and their seniority, make their mark at a younger age than most of the women who had come before, which were usually after our children were grown, in our generation," she said. "Secondly, it's a real message to working moms and young moms across America that someone who shares their experience and their aspirations for their children is a voice for them in the Congress. Certainly, they represent their own constituents. But young moms, I think, across the country, identify with seeing someone in their generation, with their experience, having a vote on the floor of Congress through the prism of the next generation. . . . Is this more on the subject than you want to know?" The gaggle of reporters laughed.

But Pelosi was not done. "For me, it's a very good thing," she continued. "It's good for our country. More young moms in Congress, pretty soon, more women and leaders in the Congress. And who knows? Maybe one of these new young moms will be the president of the United States."

Chapter 6

eMeg and the Business Boom

Early on in the 2010 California governor's race, a Republican donor in Orange County summoned Meg Whitman to a meeting. He had already spent time with Whitman and liked her as a candidate but wanted to talk to her again, this time to pose a blunt question: Was she aware that politics is a male-dominated game? And how did she plan to handle the boys' club culture of Sacramento if she were elected to run the state? "Probably the way I have for the last thirty years," Whitman cheerfully replied, according to people familiar with the exchange. She went on to give her now-common refrain, saying that, as she had in the corporate world, she planned to "work a million hours and deliver results."

If Whitman—a self-made billionaire—was taken aback by the question, she did not show it. She had, in fact, spent three decades proving her ability to play, and win, on men's turf. She attended Princeton, in the fourth class to accept women. She went to Harvard Business School when women in attendance were few, earned her MBA, and rocketed from one prestigious company to the next. Male colleagues doubted her, but never for very long. Early on in a marketing job, she was denied a corporate credit card by executives who were afraid to let women travel alone— and politely lobbied until she got one. More recently, as president and CEO of eBay, Whitman had to sit down with a skeptical Saudi investor just to assure him that she was up to the task.

Along the way, she built an impressive record. Famously, in just one decade, Whitman grew eBay, the Internet auction site, from $4 million in annual revenues to more than $7 billion before stepping down in 2008. As eBay stock rose 5,600 percent, she amassed a personal fortune, at one point ranking among the top three hundred richest Americans. In 2004 and 2005, *Fortune* named Whitman the Most Powerful Woman in Business, and in those years her picture seemed to be splashed across the cover of every business magazine. By the time she formally announced her bid for governor of California in 2009, she was an outright celebrity—not quite of the Arnold Schwarzenegger variety, but certainly among technology leaders and the 1.3 million entrepreneurs who sold items on eBay as their full-time jobs.

Fame and fortune have never led directly to victory in California politics; for every star who has made it, such as Schwarzenegger or Ronald Reagan, there has been a millionaire who failed, such as Al Checchi, the Northwest Airlines executive, did in his gubernatorial bid in 1998 and Bill Simon, the wealthy investor, did four years later.

Yet her acclaim in business and technology has given Whitman an automatic fan base—and a realistic taste of the media onslaught that comes with running for statewide office in California. She has dealt with "constituents" before, leading huge national eBay conventions with the small business owners who rely on the site, and prides herself on being held responsible for results—when eBay's computer system broke down, she spent nights sleeping on a cot inside headquarters until it was fixed.

So Whitman's outside-the-box résumé could set her apart from other women who have run. It is a gamble and a test case that political strategists nationwide are watching. There has never been a female Michael Bloomberg or Jon Corzine, the billionaire mayor of New York and millionaire former senator and governor of New Jersey, respectively. If Meg Whitman were to win the Republican primary in 2010 (which is by no means guaranteed) and the general election that fall (an even bigger uphill climb), she would not only be the first female governor of California. She would also be the first female business tycoon in the country ever to transfer those skills to politics.

Whitman has an instinctive grasp of the fact that, both as a newcomer and as a woman, she must brandish her record. She knows she will face questions about her toughness and experience—much more so than her male opponents—and so she answers them preemptively with lessons from the business world and, in particular, eBay. "I think the skills of business—managing large, complex organizations with big budgets and large numbers of people—are highly relevant," she told me one afternoon in the summer of 2009.

Tall and poised, with a broad smile, Whitman immediately came across as likable. She seemed surprisingly normal for a billionaire but conveyed the confidence of a former CEO—talking decisively and fast, with direct eye contact and sharp hand gestures. To my relief, she described her business experience in ordinary English. Asked to elaborate on the similarities between the corporate world and government, she ticked off the key elements of her assessment. "Cost reduction," she said, saying that, like a foundering company, the California state government needs to get its spending under control. "Prioritization— what are you going to focus on, what are you going to have your administration focus on, what are you going to try to have the legislature focus on," she continued. "Figuring out those priorities and how to lead people up a very steep hill, that's hugely relevant. The people that you hire. I did not run eBay by myself. I will not govern the state of California by myself."

One of the early knocks on Meg Whitman was that she was making too much of her business acumen, that "eMeg," as more than one commentator teasingly called her, was long on corporate platitudes and short on specifics about California. One of her Republican rivals, the state insurance commissioner, Steve Poizner, accused her of wanting to use her marketing background merely to "rebrand" California rather than to fix its problems. It was clear from the outset that, while business experience was Whitman's chief asset, it was also the main lightning rod: her opponents and critics would target her record to undercut her case that she was clearly qualified. Certain business moves, such as her acquisition of Skype at eBay, were ridiculed right away— though it was a relatively weak focus of attack given that it was just one of many such decisions she had overseen.

But from another angle, Whitman appeared to be precisely the kind of woman who *should* make the leap to public office. Smart and accomplished, with plenty of money and time to devote to a campaign, she seems both personable and wonkish and wears her competitive streak on her sleeve. Whitman even likes fund-raising. While many political aspirants dread thinking about asking for campaign money, she sees it as a fun—not to mention necessary—part of the game.

Above all, she has a rationale for seeking the governorship:

once hired for her ability to bring adult supervision to eBay, she would now do the same for California, where relations between the legislature and governor recently ground to a halt and the state edged toward fiscal collapse. The old stereotype of women as better at cleaning house, and bringing people together, could thus work in her favor.

In the summer of 2009, she was still getting used to politics. Once she had exhausted the similarities between government and business, she regaled me with the differences. In politics, she said, so much time is spent talking, instead of doing. There are so few measurable results—no quarterly earnings report to wield, to prove things are getting done. At eBay, when financial reporters doubted her, Whitman simply had to wait until the next quarter's numbers proved them wrong. In a campaign, she has little to thrust in the face of a prickly press corps. Her complaints fit neatly into her outsider argument, but they also have the ring of truth.

"At least in business, whether you are a woman or a man, whether you're African-American, Hispanic or Asian or Caucasian or green, black, red, or yellow, it didn't matter, because if you, in fact, delivered the results, that was enough to recommend you," she said. "There isn't that here. There is a whole different feel to it. It feels to me, thus far, as less of a meritocracy and more of a popularity contest. More of a little bit of an old boys' club, maybe sort of like Morgan Stanley was in the thirties and forties."

And, she said with a hearty laugh, politics—with campaigns stretching out years—feels so slow. "This is sometimes a little like watching ice melt," she said.

· · ·

A careful decision maker, Whitman did not just jump into the governor's race after getting a taste of politics at the national level, as an adviser to former Massachusetts Governor Mitt Romney during the presidential campaign. She had been thinking about it since 2007, when she was still in charge of eBay, George W. Bush was still in the White House, and Governor Schwarzenegger was popular.

The political landscape has changed significantly in that time, for California and for women. If the optimists are to be believed, recent events may work to Whitman's—and other female candidates'—benefit. Hillary Clinton got the country primed to consider a woman as a tough political leader. The 2008 race got voters thinking about women in elected office in general. And in comparison to Sarah Palin, whose sudden departure as Alaska governor in the summer of 2009 reinforced her image as unpredictable, Whitman looks indisputably mature and grounded. Patricia Sellers, the *Fortune* editor at large who has followed Whitman as a businesswoman for a decade, describes her as the "anti–Sarah Palin."

During the 2008 campaign, Whitman served first as a national cochair for Romney, who in 1981 had hired her to work at the consulting firm Bain & Company, when she was fresh out of business school. They remain close friends. After Romney withdrew from the race and endorsed McCain, Whitman joined him; McCain, too, remains loyal to her; he even weighed in on the California race with an early endorsement, saying she "represents another generation of Republican leadership."

What if McCain, in his eagerness to lure women voters, had picked Whitman as his vice presidential running mate rather than Palin? Knowing that she had once been on an extended list of prospects, it is hard not to wonder how events would have unfolded differently. On the one hand, Whitman would not have revved up the conservative core of the Republican party the way Palin did. Whitman is pro-choice and has said she supports public funding for abortions. She is also politically untested, something the press corps would have knocked her for at the height of a presidential campaign. And although she has a down-to-earth bent—she is known for taking Southwest Airlines and renting cars to drive herself to events—her overall image is much more business Republican than populist.

Still, in a general election where Hillary Clinton supporters were allegedly in play, Whitman could have made for an interesting counterpoint—especially when Lehman Brothers collapsed and the economy went into free fall, the moment that the race shifted decisively toward Obama. She is young, in her early fifties, but her sons are now in their twenties and out of the house. There is little apparent personal baggage, of either the Palin or the Clinton variety. Though her husband is a renowned neurosurgeon, Whitman does not derive any of her status from his. Though her father founded a financial advisory firm on Long Island, her résumé is her own, and Whitman is her maiden name.

Another thing is for certain: Whitman would have prepared for the vice presidency in ways Palin did not. Whitman even told McCain, in her capacity as an adviser, that he should give whomever he picked at least two weeks' notice to prepare—a point that another McCain confidante, Senator Joseph Lieberman, also made. When it came to the California race, Whitman was methodical, including, before her campaign announcement, spending nights and weekends with advisers going through individual subjects—the state budget, education, immigration, health care, a proposed water conveyance system.

In some ways, being a Republican woman confers an advantage on Whitman: In studies over the last decade, voters concerned about the economy did not downgrade female Republican candidates, as they often did Democratic ones, according to Barbara Lee, who runs a foundation specializing in research on women's gubernatorial campaigns. And gender is just less of a factor for Republican women running for governor overall.

But being a Republican woman in California is also a big hurdle for Whitman to overcome, both in the primary and, if she were to get that far, in the general election. Although the state made national history by electing two female senators at once, and has sent a record thirty-two women to Congress— not to mention giving rise to Nancy Pelosi—the enthusiasm for women officials has been limited to the Democratic side. California's Republican party, by contrast, has been harsh terrain. Republicans have never nominated a woman for senator or governor in California, and there was recently a long stretch in which there were no Republican women in the state senate in Sacramento. The last Republican woman elected to hold a constitutional office in the state was a treasurer, Ivy Baker Priest, in 1966.

That history embarrasses some—and is seen as a potential opening for the state party, if it can change its traditional course, according to Dan Schnur, director of the Jesse M. Unruh Institute of Politics at the University of Southern California. "Part of her appeal—although it goes unspoken—is her gender," Schnur said. "Donors and activists talk around it, but it's very clear that that's part of their calculation. The party has never run a woman for governor here; there's still somewhat of a gender gap. And the thought is that a female candidate, particularly one with strong business credentials, is a way of putting a new face on the party."

If Whitman wins the nomination, she will face an electorate that is overwhelmingly Democratic, and with a large number of female Democratic voters. There has been little evidence, in statewide races elsewhere, that having a Republican woman on the ticket would lure those women away, even from a male opponent. "In the past, our research found that voters think of a Republican woman as a Republican first, woman second," Lee said. "Democratic women candidates are more often seen as a woman first, then as a Democrat."

Give Whitman credit, then, for tackling a challenge: she is basically running against the odds for a job that, were she to attain it, appears next to impossible. Her advisers say it is entirely altruistic. "Meg isn't deterred by the growing conventional wisdom that California can't be governed," Rob Stutzman, an adviser in California, said.

Whatever the outcome, Whitman has gained a national following of sorts just by joining the fray. Fred Barnes of *The Weekly Standard* floated the idea of her running for president someday. Other Republicans have quietly rejoiced in her participation, hoping she can be something of an antidote to Palin—both as a party moderate and as a credentialed, serious female leader.

In the meantime, California has become another lesson on how voters respond to a woman candidate. Somewhat predictably, in the early days of the primary campaign, Whitman's strategists found that she performed better with Republican men than with Republican women. The men "liked the CEO thing," one told me and expressed few serious doubts about her governing ability—the concern from her donor in Orange County notwithstanding. Republican women were more of a problem, and thus in keeping with the electorate nationwide. In focus groups, they complained about Whitman's hair and clothes—she has a decidedly no-frills look (though it is not nearly as grim as her onetime mantra, "she's frumpy, but she delivers," suggests).

And, more than her appearance, women focused on Whitman's children, despite the fact that they are no longer in the house. "Republican women still want to know that she is a wife and a mother and can relate to them," a Republican strategist told me. Whitman's advisers put her on a training regimen, encouraging her to talk about her family and teaching her, in the words of one, to "fill in the personal gaps."

Whitman met her husband, Dr. Griff Harsh IV, during a visit to Harvard when he was an undergraduate and she was a Princeton freshman. They have been married since 1980, when their engagement was announced in the *New York Times,* under the now quaint headline "Meg Whitman to Wed June 7." The item listed the young couple's already impressive credentials, including the bridegroom's election to Phi Beta Kappa at Harvard and distinction as a Rhodes scholar. They have led an upscale life ever since, something that she is sometimes needled for—along with her second home, near Telluride, and the fact that she did not register to vote as a Republican until 2007 (as chief executive of eBay she wanted to remain nonpartisan, she has said, though she has described her spotty voting record as a mistake).

None of it exactly adds up to scandal. And Whitman's description of her personal life, now that she has warmed up to talking about it publicly, is compelling. Her husband is supportive but not sycophantic; while he travels with her some of the time, he still works as a doctor and plans to keep performing surgeries if she is elected. Over the years they have learned to make their dual high-powered careers work. "In some ways, we took turns," Whitman said. She and Harsh moved together repeatedly, from San Francisco (where he studied at the University of California, San Francisco, and she worked at Bain) to Los Angeles (for her job at Disney) to Boston, so her husband could run the prestigious brain tumor program at Massachusetts General Hospital. That lasted until Whitman was hired to run eBay. "It's about give-and-take, it's about sort of taking turns. We used to joke that we just did nothing but sabotage each other's careers, because no sooner would you get traction than the other one would go 'I got a job,'" she said, laughing. "But we worked it out."

In discussing her husband, Whitman adopted an almost mothering tone, one that I had heard from women as varied as Nancy Pelosi and Debbie Wasserman Schultz. Although she had met her husband long before her career took off, she described him as an integral part of her success—the man behind the powerful woman, much as the other women had. "The advice I give young women in their careers is I say"—and here she broke into a whisper, as if passing on something taboo—"pick the right partner, it's really important. Because [Griff] has been a total champ. I mean, he's been incredibly supportive. He's been willing to do things that I don't know that most husbands would be willing to do, and he has stepped up to the plate. What became really obvious at eBay was that eBay was all-consuming, and all I could do was Griff, the kids, and eBay. And so he took on managing the vacations, managing the finances. You know, households do not run themselves, someone needs to run the household. I had done most of it before. And so it's about sort of commitment, it's about flexing when you see the other person is drowning."

She continued with a riff on the work-life balance that sounded as if it could have come straight from First Lady Michelle Obama. "Maybe fifteen years into being married I said, Okay, I cannot be the perfect mother, the perfect wife, the perfect business executive, the perfect entertainer. My house cannot look like Martha Stewart just left," Whitman said. "I mean, something has to give here. You cannot be this hostess, you can't have a social life where you're out every night; you can't." Even if Democratic women would be a difficult catch for Whitman, it was easy to see some of them in California's power centers relating to her on that level, at least.

The bigger question is how her professional experience will transfer into politics. While moguldom has not always been a silver bullet for men—sometimes it has worked, sometimes it hasn't—political strategists believe the business background may perform powerfully for a woman seeking an executive role. In fact, people in the industry of recruiting women to run for office, at EMILY's List and elsewhere, have long wished for a candidate with Whitman's profile. "There was an effort in the women's movement for quite some time to recruit more of these women business leaders," Celinda Lake, the Democratic pollster, said.

To this day, there are always rumors of a millionaire superwoman jumping into politics. Oprah Winfrey is the most popular of these, regularly rumored as a contender for one office or another. Rod Blagojevich, the former Illinois governor indicted on corruption charges, said he had considered naming Oprah to Obama's Senate seat because "she was obviously someone with a much broader bully pulpit than other senators." In New Jersey, Bobbi Brown, the makeup magnate, has been floated as a possible candidate for Senate. Most realistically of all, Carly Fiorina, the former CEO of Hewlett-Packard, is often discussed as a possible candidate for one of California's Senate seats.

The early efforts to recruit such women did not go far. "They were already pioneers in their area," Lake said. "It wasn't like they were the sixteenth woman on Wall Street, they were the *first* woman on Wall Street, the *first* woman billionaire. So they weren't really interested in moving over and being the first again. You know, being a pioneer is tough, and they had already been a pioneer. And now, maybe, we're starting to get a critical enough mass of women CEOs that it will start to turn, but they have not been interested in it."

There are a few businesswomen currently rising through the political ranks, though none of them is as well-known as Whitman—or as new to politics. In Florida, where Democrat Alex Sink is running for governor, she is doing so on her record as the chief financial officer of the state, in which she oversees state spending and billions in taxpayer dollars. Before taking on that role in 2007, Sink was in the private banking sector for most of her career, most recently as the head of Florida operations for Bank of America. "Before the people of Florida elected me their CFO, I spent nearly three decades in business—creating jobs and economic opportunity in communities all across our state," Sink said in launching her gubernatorial campaign.

North Carolina Senator Kay Hagan came to politics with a similar background, after working as an executive at North Carolina National Bank, an earlier incarnation of Bank of America. Hagan, a Democrat, later became a state legislator—it was from the state level that she launched her senatorial campaign against Senator Elizabeth Dole in 2008—but her banking background remained a key credential.

Still, neither Sink nor Hagan came to politics from business in a vacuum. Sink's husband, Bill McBride, ran for governor of Florida in 2002. Hagan's father was a mayor in Lakeland, Florida, where she grew up, and her uncle Lawton Chiles was a senator and governor of Florida as well—a more distant connection to politics but one that exposed her to the profession early. Globally, over the centuries, women with family ties to politics have fared the best in it. And voters see women with family connections as the most legitimate kinds of candidates—or at least they used to.

Even if Whitman succeeds, Debbie Walsh, at the Rutgers Center for American Women and Politics, expressed skepticism that there will be a flood of women from business—or any other field besides politics—following her. "Women have much more traditionally done the work-your-way-up route, running for school board, then the legislature, then Congress, which can take forever," Walsh said. "It's harder for women, if you come from a really nontraditional place. You can't be an Al Franken. It's that credibility issue. Men still just look like what people think of as a U.S. senator or a governor. Women, unfortunately, have to come to it with a set of credentials. Business would be the way to do that, but women are struggling so hard to make it in the business community. We don't have enough of them to be Fortune 500 CEOs and then switch over to politics. That pool is just so small."

In fact, the pool is almost exactly as small as it is in politics: Women make up about 15 percent of board director or corporate officer positions at Fortune 500 firms, slightly less than the 17 percent who hold seats in Congress.

A few years ago, Celinda Lake conducted a study for the consulting firm Arthur Andersen about the way employees viewed female bosses during times of economic distress. People had mixed feelings. If there were going to be layoffs, they wanted a woman in charge, because they assumed she would be more caring and empathetic about their personal situations. But they also worried a woman would not be tough enough to defend their units from cuts. "They thought if you're being downsized, you need a boss who will fight with the other bosses to hold your unit, and a woman boss will not be strong enough in that fight; she will not be powerful enough," Lake recalled. "It was really interesting and, when you think about it, very parallel to the political situation." Applied to the economically turbulent state of California, that is both good and bad news for Whitman.

So is controversial research from 2003 of top firms traded on the London Stock Exchange, which found that companies with higher numbers of women in leadership performed worse than male-dominated ones. "Companies that decline to embrace political correctness by installing women on the board perform better than those that actively promote sexual equality at the very top," a write-up in the London *Times* read.

But in subsequent years, researchers debunked those findings with an alternate explanation: women were brought in at a much higher rate than men to run companies that were already faltering. "Rather than women leaders causing poor company performance, poor company performance may lead to the appointment of women to positions of leadership," two researchers, Michelle Ryan and Alexander Haslam, wrote in the *British Journal of Management.* Women, in their findings, broke through the glass ceiling only to find themselves at the edge of a "glass cliff"—about to be pushed over. Looked at one way, they were set up to fail. Anecdotally, this seemed plausible; one assessment in the *Harvard Business Review* found several high-profile cases in which women executives had been hired into top jobs just as share prices collapsed—including, at Hewlett-Packard, Carly Fiorina, who was subsequently fired.

The other way to interpret Ryan and Haslam's findings is that women are given historic opportunities to lead only in a crisis. If any state has been in a crisis lately, it is California.

Whitman didn't seem to mind the hassle of being a pioneer much, at least not to hear her describe it. When she tells the story of the time she was denied a corporate credit card, she does it in a tone of great amusement, characterizing it as a "little thing" that happened during her early days at Procter & Gamble, in the late 1970s.

She was new to the company, one of 104 young brand assistants—and four women. "At the end of orientation, they said, 'Okay, here's your corporate credit cards because you're going to have to go see the agency, you're going to have to go see all these other people.' And there were four people who didn't get corporate credit cards," she said, laughing. "They were scared to have us travel. They said, 'No, it's like, gosh, you'll be on a plane by yourself. Like, you would be in Chicago by yourself.'"

She said the four women looked at one another in disbelief—obviously they had to obtain credit cards in order to travel, which was half the job. Whitman discouraged a bomb-thrower approach. Instead they started writing memos up the corporate ladder, enlisting women higher up in the company to aid their cause. "We started doing what you do at P & G, which is you write memos," she said. "It's not so much true today, but they were a memo-writing culture.... You wrote a memo to your brand manager, who put a cover note on it, who sent it to their associate brand manager, who put a cover on it, who sent it to—and you just went all the way up the line," Whitman said.

"So it took three months, but we worked it all the way up the line. And finally the president and CEO of the company said, 'Are you guys nuts? Of course we have to give these women credit cards.'"

Even though the anecdote was, by the time she retold it, thirty years old, Whitman seemed to relish the memory of their eventual triumph. "So we just worked the system, right? And it took a while," she said, adding, with a laugh: "Sort of like watching ice melt."

Chapter 7

Why Women Run (and Don't)

As the midterm elections were getting under way in 2005, a political operative started working on a puzzle: What kind of woman could win the open House seat in Ohio's Thirteenth District?

It was more than just an idle question. The operative, Chris Esposito, worked for EMILY's List—a group whose main purpose is electing pro-choice Democratic women to office—and was on a mission to help them find and recruit viable female candidates across the country.

When the Ohio seat opened up, Esposito started by working backward. Rather than seeing which women *wanted* to run, he compiled a prototype of the kind of woman who *should* run, the kind of Democratic woman who would be most likely to win both a primary and a general election in that district. He contacted data analysts at a political action committee, the National Committee for an Effective Congress, who assessed the district's voting patterns, ideology, and population centers, and came up with an answer: the best candidate would be a woman from the Akron area, someone who had run for office before, and who had a good working relationship with organized labor.

Esposito went through a list of potential candidates and one, Betty Sutton, caught his eye. A Cleveland lawyer with a private practice specializing in labor issues, Sutton had once served in the Ohio legislature—she was, in fact, the youngest woman ever elected to the state House when she first won at age twenty-nine in 1992—giving her some name recognition among voters in the district. Her hometown, Barberton, was a commuter suburb outside Akron. From a recruitment perspective, Sutton was ideal, even though she was not at the top of people's would-be candidates lists at the outset.

Sutton herself thought the idea was crazy at first. "Chris Esposito, who I did not know at all, called me at my law office and introduced himself and posed the question of, 'Have you ever thought or would you think about running for Congress?'" Sutton recalled. She remembered telling him at first: "You have to be out of your mind, I cannot possibly run for Congress.

"You know, I just thought it was evidently so out of reach that it was not even in my view," Sutton told me.

After Esposito and other Democrats persuaded her to run, Sutton came from behind to win the primary with 31 percent of the vote—defeating seven other Democrats, including a former eight-term congressman, a millionaire heiress, and the brother of Representative Dennis Kucinich. Her gender enhanced her outsider status and helped set her apart: she was not as well-known as some of the men she ran against, but voters believed her when she said she would be more honest and eschew favor trading. When she won the general election decisively that fall, Sutton became one of the darlings of the 2006 class—one of the fewer than expected women elected the year Nancy Pelosi became Speaker.

Sutton also became a symbol of the effectiveness of recruitment, which strategists and researchers increasingly believe is the key to bringing more women into office. A landmark study conducted between 2001 and 2008 found an interesting explanation for why there were so many fewer women than men in office. It was not that women were less successful in their campaigns, or at raising money; in both those areas, they had just about reached parity, meaning that women had as good a shot as winning as men. But far fewer women actually ran for office, in part because they were not encouraged to run—whereas men were prodded into politics by their peers, elders, and party officials. "Despite the fact that these women and men were well-matched demographically and educationally, there were two main differences," said American University Professor Jennifer Lawless, who codirected the study of nearly four thousand people in jobs that usually precede higher political office, such as prominent positions in the law, politics, or education. "The first was, women were more than one-third less likely to be recruited to run for office. The second was, they were only half as likely to consider themselves qualified to run for office."

Adding to their reluctance: the perception that, as women, it would be harder for them to raise campaign funds and win. That perception has affected reality, Lawless said. "The empirical reality of a level playing field on election day is almost meaningless if no one knows it," she said.

Several female officeholders I interviewed expressed a related concern: that young women had heard all about the harsh realities of running for office without getting the positive spin.

If the number of women running for office has plateaued in recent years—and there is ample evidence that it has—the negative connotations may be part of the reason.

Anyone who has run for office has a story about how insane the process is, including the long bus rides and the turkey sandwich dinners and the handshaking and the town hall meetings. Barack Obama, during his presidential campaign, joked to his aides about writing a third book, entitled *This Is Ridiculous*. Janet Napolitano's favorite anecdote involves riding in sweltering heat in a golf cart parade during her race for Arizona attorney general. It was too hot for any voters to stand along the parade route, so Napolitano found herself waving to the empty streets. "I mean, I am just waving," she said, laughing. "And that is when I thought to myself, Here I am, a Truman scholar, Phi Beta Kappa, a law firm partner, U.S. attorney." And now, in a golf cart, waving to no one. "Some of it is surreal," she said. "It is a kick in the pants."

Napolitano said she has tried to convey that absurd fun to younger women interested in politics, with mixed results. "I see so many women who say, 'I want to grow up to be the policy person, or I want to help with the campaign organization, or this and that.' And I say, 'Well, why don't you just run? Why aren't *you* the candidate?'" she said. "And they say, 'Oh, I could not do that.' So I say, 'Well, why not?' And it is for all these reasons. There is a conflict with the biological cycle in a way. But also, I think that we have really educated women well on how hard it is."

On the Republican side, Jane Swift said she has seen a similar phenomenon. "We spend so much time talking about the challenges of it we forget to talk about the joy of it—and so we've convinced a whole bunch of women, ten years younger than me, that you have to choose one or the other, which is

completely outrageous," she said, referring to the choice between having a family and having a life in politics. "Still, I don't
just want to blindly send my daughters out and say, 'You can do
anything you want. It's never going to be hard.' I want to share
with them, in some appropriate way, the lessons I've learned
and how hard it is without in any way minimizing their ambition and belief in themselves."

If recent events have diluted the positive message—why
would any sane woman want to run for higher office after
watching what Hillary Clinton, Sarah Palin, and even Caroline
Kennedy endured?—they have not killed off the proliferation of
advocacy and fund-raising groups, at least on the Democratic
side. EMILY's List is the undisputed giant of these. Founded in
1985—at a time when no Democratic woman had been elected
to the Senate in her own right and the number of women in
the House was shrinking—the group started out primarily as a
fund-raising operation. Its name stands for "early money is like
yeast," the idea being that women needed a financial network
to become viable candidates.

Today, EMILY's List still focuses on money, but it is a
sprawling political operation as well, mobilizing voters and ad-
vising potential and current candidates. In the summer of 2009,
it claimed a historic milestone, with the election to Congress of
the eightieth woman it had ever helped (compared with twenty-
four years earlier, when there were just twelve Democratic
women in the House). Other groups—Emerge, a political leadership training program for Democratic women in California;
The Farm Team, a network of Democrats devoted to electing
women to office in Virginia; Running Start, a nonprofit dedicated to encouraging young women to run for office—have
cropped up to encourage women to participate in politics and
society at various levels.

And the White House Project, founded in 1998 by Marie Wilson, the former president of the Ms. Foundation, is still geared toward promoting women's leadership "up to the U.S. presidency," though of late it has focused its ambitions on the more immediate goal of electing women as governors. According to Wilson, her group's goal now is to get forty thousand young women engaged in the political process by 2013—rather than to sit and daydream about the presidency. The pipeline, she said, is all that matters. "It just isn't going to happen any other way," she said. Electing a woman president, in other words, is still a long-term project. It is difficult enough getting women, like Betty Sutton, to run for Congress—let alone for statewide office, or for something bigger.

It is even harder on the Republican side. As Republican women have lost elections at a higher pace, so have they had a harder time recruiting new candidates, a task made more challenging because there are so few Republican organizations devoted to doing so. As a result, the 111th Congress includes fifty-five female Democratic House members and just seventeen House Republican women. A similar imbalance exists in the Senate, where of the seventeen female senators, thirteen are Democrats, compared with just four Republicans. In state legislatures across the country, where women hold 24.3 percent of the elected offices, the breakdown is just as stark: 70.6 percent of those female lawmakers are Democrats, and just 28.6 percent are Republicans.

Republicans, with a deeply held aversion to identity politics, have not devoted resources specifically to electing women the way Democratic groups have. Most Republican organizations are committed to advancing conservative ideas, period, instead of being structured to elect members of a specific demographic to office (or, as they might put it, catering to special interest groups). One of the largest Republican women's groups, Phyllis Schlafly's Eagle Forum, says nothing about electing women in its mission statement. One of its chief goals, instead, is to "honor the fulltime homemaker," according to the statement on its website.

But that alone does not explain why the number of Republican women in elected office has dropped, leaving the GOP pipeline to the presidency much emptier than the Democratic one. Republicans once led the way for women in elected office: the first woman elected to the House of Representatives, Jeannette Rankin, was a Republican from Montana (she served twice, briefly—in 1917 and again in 1941). The first woman elected to the Senate on her own, without succeeding her husband, was also a Republican, Nancy Kassebaum of Kansas.

Not surprisingly, leaders on the two sides offered different reasons for the partisan gap. Democrats suggested that Republicans have failed to be inclusive, and have taken the party to such an extreme place that women no longer want to be a part of it. Republicans suggested that Democratic women were less concerned about staying home to raise families. Some Republican women were more critical of their own party, saying they had grown judgmental of women rather than speaking to all of them. Others were simply at a loss for words. Representative Kay Granger of Texas—who has served in the House since 1996 and was Fort Worth mayor before that—sounded outright melancholy over it. The numbers, she said, have "dropped, and it's not just [about] numbers."

"I lost some good friends in the last two elections," Granger said, citing former Representative Nancy Johnson, a moderate from Connecticut, as one of her newly departed friends. Johnson lost to her Democratic male rival, thirty-three-year-old state senator Chris Murphy, in 2006.

A few weeks after the 2008 election had ended, Dana Perino, the outgoing White House press secretary, sat down with me to reflect on the women in her party, including Palin, and to contemplate what would come next. All around her were boxes; she had started to pack for her departure from the West Wing along with President Bush the following month. It was a poignant atmosphere in which to discuss the future occupants of the place. Perino lamented the scrutiny that anyone—but especially a woman—would undergo in trying to get there. "The problem is, who wants to run for office today?" she said. "Who wants to be called a liar and a loser by somebody like [Senator Majority Leader] Harry Reid? To have your whole background turned inside out? And we all have stuff in our closets that we would not want publicly aired, and I think that's one of the reasons that people shy away from it."

Perino, like many Republicans, was skeptical about Palin's ability to return to her mid-2008 popularity. "If a major television network bumps their prime-time programming to run a special *Saturday Night Live* whose sole purpose is to make fun of you, you have a serious problem. And I don't know how you rehabilitate from that," Perino said, referring to the *SNL* special that ran right before the election. "But I think it could be done. Obviously people have rehabilitated before. Look at Bill Clinton. And she [Palin] wasn't even involved in a scandal, so it could happen. But it would take a lot."

Perino's own press coverage had been fairly positive (though she had been dismissed by people on the Internet alternately as "dumber than Miss Teen South Carolina" and as "really hot"). Still, she saw the collective image of Republican women suffering. "I've been thinking a lot about Republican women, conservative women, because I think that they are misunderstood, miscast, ridiculed," Perino said. Extremely conservative women, like Schlafly, have come to "define what a Republican woman is," she said. Of the decline in numbers, she said: "You know, maybe we did it to ourselves."

It shouldn't have to be such a source of angst, for either party. It isn't elsewhere. Other countries—forbidding places, like Rwanda and Afghanistan—have made recruiting women into politics a priority. By one count, there have been at least sixty-two female heads of state elected in at least forty-nine countries over the last century. The ascent of women to executive jobs has accelerated rapidly around the globe in the twenty-first century, with at least twenty-one women becoming heads of state since 2000. There are currently female presidents and prime ministers across the globe—in Africa, Asia, Europe, South America, even the Caribbean. But not North America. At the parliamentary level, women's representation has surged in a number of countries other than the United States, which ranks no higher than seventieth on various international lists. Finland, for example, has had a female president, Tarja Halonen, since 2000 and also has a parliament that is 42 percent female, ranking it fourth globally.

Other parts of the world, of course, have traditions that the United States does not and would not want—of royal families with female monarchs, as in Great Britain, or of extended family political dynasties, as in India. Many countries have implemented quotas, which would never happen in a nation as uneasy about affirmative action as the United States. Parliamentary systems, in which members elect prime ministers within parties rather than putting the office to a popular vote, are considered friendlier terrain. And in some places, women have risen to power only because all the male options failed—after years of population-depleting war, or incompetence, or devastating corruption.

But the disparity between the rest of the world and the United States is striking, all the more so because it goes unnoticed here. As Americans, we believe that we lead everything, when in fact the opposite is true in terms of women in political power. "The U.S. is increasingly falling behind," said Professor Aili Mari Tripp of the University of Wisconsin, Madison, one of the leading researchers on women in global politics. "And it's kind of shocking. People will every now and then say, 'It's nice that Angela Merkel is chancellor of Germany and Michelle Bachelet is president of Chile.' But people don't seem to realize that we're not part of the discussion at all."

The United States actually *was* part of the discussion for a while, during Hillary Clinton's campaign, which sparked notable excitement abroad—at least until her international popularity was eclipsed by Obama's. Even more so than at home, Clinton had been seen around the world as a leader of women after her many foreign trips as First Lady and her rousing speech on women's rights in Beijing in 1995. Her election as president, when it seemed inevitable, looked as if it would be both the capstone of her life's work and the pinnacle of a new wave of female leadership around the world.

And then it wasn't. Her loss was, among other things, a stark illustration of how much the United States lags, in terms of women, internationally. As secretary of state, Clinton has been reminded of the lag more than once in her travels. A young woman in India pointedly reminded her, during one town hall meeting, "that India has had a woman prime minister as early as in the third decade of its postindependence era, while America has been deprived, if I can say so, of the same privilege."

"*You* can say so, to me," Clinton wryly responded.

When I traveled with former President Bill Clinton to Liberia in the summer of 2008—at the start of his image rehabilitation tour, after the Democratic primaries had ended—it was somewhat painful to watch him meet with the country's first female president, Ellen Johnson Sirleaf. There we were in Monrovia, surrounded by squalor and the lasting effects of civil war, in a country still so lacking in infrastructure that Clinton could not stay there overnight. And yet amid all that stood Sirleaf, whose election as the first woman president of any African country, in 2005, had been interpreted as a signal that a woman could win anywhere. At moments, as Bill Clinton addressed Liberian legislators, he looked at Sirleaf almost wistfully and spoke in the language of the women's movement. "You will burst through a ceiling here if all of you stay together and don't get discouraged and know that the world is pulling for you," he told Sirleaf and her colleagues, many of whom were men.

Sirleaf's presidential campaign in Liberia had been a fascinating meditation on gender politics, a kind of parallel universe to the Clinton campaign that followed three years later. Nicknamed the "Iron Lady of Africa," Sirleaf had been raised in an elite stratum of Liberian society and attended school in the United States, completing a master's in public administration at Harvard. But she was also soaked in her country's strife. Divorced from an abusive husband, imprisoned and threatened by the strongmen who ran Liberia into the ground in the 1980s and '90s, she had held prominent international jobs in finance before returning to run for president. She actually ran for president twice: first in 1997, against the violent despot Charles

Taylor, who "won"; and again the following decade, after the Taylor-led years of civil war were ended with his resignation and arrest. Repeatedly over the years, Sirleaf was summoned home to help the country heal—a form of recruitment familiar to women around the world but perhaps never more vividly than in her case.

Despite her prominence and deep experience in public administration, Sirleaf was not expected to win the election in 2005, by her own account. After years of civil war, political observers thought a young male contender named George Weah would sweep the balloting—not some older woman who had been part of the turbulent political process off and on for decades. "Don't you think this country needs a young, fresh face to lead it now?" Sirleaf was asked by the U.S. ambassador to Liberia before the campaign began. "So many of you have been involved in politics for a long time. Don't you think you ought to give way?"

Sirleaf's reply could have been ripped from Hillary Clinton's playbook a few years later. "Given the level of destruction and the challenges ahead, I'm not sure we do need a fresh, young, inexperienced face to take over," she told the ambassador. But Sirleaf did something else as well: she argued that decades of war could be healed only by a woman's presence in the executive mansion. She appealed explicitly to female voters, who formed the backbone of her victory. The scene on election day was of women nationwide strapping babies on their backs and going to the polls. Sirleaf calls women voters her "secret weapon." Everywhere her pollster went, he heard the same refrain: "Men have failed us." "Men are too violent, too prone to make war." "Women are less corrupt, less likely to be focused on getting fancy cars and fancy homes for themselves."

Sirleaf's sister, campaigning for her, invoked motherhood

and experience simultaneously, in a way that would have made Nancy Pelosi proud. She told people: "Suppose you have a baby. And you have to go out to work or whatnot and you need someone to care for the child. Would you give that baby to an older person who has taken care of children, who knows how to nurture the child? Or would you give it to a young person who has not done it before and does now know what to do? Well, this country is a child, a sick child, and it is hurting. You need somebody who can nurture it."

There were questions, of course, about Sirleaf's toughness—especially about whether she, as a woman, was strong enough to rebuild a postwar nation. But these were counterbalanced by her own image as a survivor—one of her campaign posters juxtaposed a black-and-white photograph of her emerging from prison in 1986, her fist raised, with a similar shot from the present day—and by perceptions about women's strengths. Sirleaf's American consultant, Larry Gibson, a professor at the University of Maryland, found that voters were open to a woman candidate—even in a male-dominated African society—because they saw women as pro-peace and anti-corruption, the opposite of the country's male leadership during prior decades of civil war.

Sirleaf's story is compelling but not unique. Recently, in postconflict countries, female politicians have benefited from the perception of a woman as a "nurturer and family unifier," according to one study. In Rwanda, a country rapidly recovering from the 1994 genocide, women have attained new roles and responsibilities—helped in part by quotas but also by the fact that so many men were killed during the months of horror. In the island nation of Timor-Leste, women played a critical role in the fight for independence and now make up one-third of parliament, including its vice president.

It doesn't take a war for a woman to win. Sometimes just

the perception that a fresh start is needed will do. To rise to the presidency of Chile in 2005, becoming the first woman ever to do so, Michelle Bachelet portrayed herself as anti-establishment and a champion of the common good—two notions that played into traditional cultural ideas of how women behave. A doctor and onetime minister of health, Bachelet sent a dual message: that she was both experienced and an agent of change, despite belonging to the party of power. It helped that she had also served as the minister of defense, the first woman in a Latin American country to do so. In one brilliant public relations flourish, Bachelet had ridden an amphibious tank into a flooded section of Santiago to help with the rescue operation. The image—of her as a rescuer—helped make her a star.

Bachelet, like Sirleaf, banked on overwhelming support from women—and got it. Her ascent was seen as part of a broader elevation of women in society at large. "Something else you see in these countries is that there is pressure from women's movements," Tripp said. "No woman head of state wants to say she's been elected by women. But there had been pressure mounting in Chile for greater expansion of women's rights before Bachelet was elected. Certainly in Liberia, Ellen Johnson Sirleaf owes a lot to the women of her country for getting elected. Women recognized that if they were going to have peace, they would have to have power as well."

As much as any war, the global economic meltdown produced obvious opportunities for women to ride in as saviors. Nowhere did gender play a bigger role than in Iceland. The tiny island in the North Atlantic Ocean had built itself into a financial world headquarters during the frenzy of the real estate bubble, becoming "Wall Street on the Tundra," as one magazine dubbed it, virtually overnight. From 2003 to 2007, the Icelandic stock market had ballooned, multiplying by a factor of nine, as had the average Icelandic family's net worth. But it was all built on a mirage—currency and real estate speculation, primarily—that quickly collapsed when the bubble burst. By late 2008, all three of Iceland's major banks had failed, producing the largest economic failure of any country in history. People owned houses worth a fraction of what they owed on their mortgages; the Icelandic currency became more or less worthless; unemployment rates skyrocketed; people panicked and took to the streets for weeks of protests.

And the male leaders took the blame. Former Prime Minister Davíð Oddsson, who later oversaw sweeping banking privatization as governor of the central bank, was forced out, as was the sitting prime minister, Geir Haarde. In their place rose Jóhanna Sigurðardóttir, the first female prime minister of Iceland, and the first openly gay head of state to win election in any country. "Iceland's women are blaming men for the financial crisis that has brought the country to its knees," the German newspaper *Der Spiegel* declared in April 2009. "They are now looking for a female solution to clean up the mess."

A similar situation unfolded in Lithuania, where the economy contracted and unemployment rose in early 2009 and voters, awash in insecurity, chose a female president for the first time (the country had seen women as prime minister, a lesser constitutional role, but never president). The election of Dalia Grybauskaitė—a right-leaning figure with a martial arts black belt, nicknamed "Lithuania's Iron Lady" by the *Wall Street Journal* and a "Steel Magnolia" by *The Economist*—produced more declarations of female superiority. "Lithuania has decided: The country is to be saved by a woman," the Vilnius newspaper declared.

The notion that women are purer leaders has taken hold globally to such a degree that a provocative piece in *Foreign*

Policy magazine in the summer of 2009 declared "the death of macho," citing the recent elections in Iceland and Lithuania as evidence. "It's now fair to say that the most enduring legacy of the Great Recession will not be the death of Wall Street. It will not be the death of finance. And it will not be the death of capitalism. These ideas and institutions will live on. What will not survive is macho," Reihan Salam wrote. "And the choice men will have to make, whether to accept or fight this new fact of history, will have seismic effects for all of humanity—women as well as men."

Maybe. But there are reasons to doubt that a new world order—a death of machismo—is really about to take permanent hold. Especially here, in the United States.

Condoleezza Rice, the former secretary of state, is among the skeptics. After spending all eight years as a member of the George W. Bush administration, she returned to teach at Stanford, where on a bright spring morning in 2009 I sat down with her in her new offices. Apart from a small security detail, she had returned to normal civilian life. She had been frequently talked about as a potential candidate—one of the few Republican women with national stature, however damaged her image may have been by her deep involvement in the unpopular Iraq war—but sounded more interested in academic pursuits, including mentoring students and writing the two autobiographical books she has under way.

And so we had an academic conversation: about women presidents she had met during her tenure leading the State Department and how their political career paths compared with those of women at home. Rice, who used to teach a class called the Politics of Elites, said she was always struck by the sizable pools of contenders who had arisen in other countries—places where the political parties decided to encourage women to run, and where women were in the pipeline long enough to be able to do so. "People don't emerge full-blown as the leader of a country," she said. "One of the explanations in the United States of why we now have women candidates for vice president, in the case of Sarah Palin, or for president, in the case of Hillary Clinton, is that women have entered the pool from which presidents are chosen. Presidents are senators or governors. It's the only way you get elected in the United States—senators, governors, or military officers, after wars. And women had not been in that pool."

Rice said that, in addition to being groomed, many of the women leaders she met abroad had been drawn to office out of a sense of mission. "They were drawn to a cause, or they were accidental politicians. Dora Bakoyannis, in Greece, is quite a formidable politician. But she got interested in politics when her husband was assassinated by a terrorist. You know, Cory Aquino was an early example of that in the Philippines. Tzipi Livni, in Israel, a child of two resistance fighters for Israel's independence," Rice said. "So, they seem to have been drawn in, not out of just political ambition, per se, but rather out of some connection to a spouse, a parent, or by a sense of a cause."

After a while, Rice turned back to the subject of the 2008 U.S. election. I had heard from several people that she had watched the Democratic primary with great interest and had told people, while the primary was still under way, that she expected it would be easier for Barack Obama to win than for Hillary Clinton. She had seen it through the prisms of both race and gender—and with a degree of dispassion, given that, as a Republican, she had no horse in the race.

Now, in her office, Rice confirmed what others had told me: that she still felt women had a long way to go. It was clear that the election had struck a chord with her, and not just as an

African-American. She described—in terms I had heard from so many other powerful women—her cautious optimism about a woman someday being elected president, but with an emphasis on the caution. This was, after all, a woman whose single status had become such an issue that it was a subplot on NBC's *30 Rock*, and whose tears, during a national security meeting in 2004, had made their way into print.

"I, frankly, think we crossed the bar on African-Americans quite some time ago," Rice said. "I'm not quite sure we've crossed it on women." She did not say gender was a reason she would never run, but it was not a difficult leap to make.

Chapter 8

What Will It Take?

In the Age of Obama, there are two schools of thought about electing a woman president. One school holds that it will be relatively easy, and happen fairly soon. Rahm Emanuel, Obama's White House chief of staff, articulates the optimistic viewpoint well. "I mean, I don't think this is that hard," Emanuel told me, with a whiff of exasperation, in his office one afternoon. "She'll be a chief executive with a proven record to have successfully run something. You'll get a woman who's a governor or something, who's proven in some capacity," he said. Then he stopped.

Fiddling with his BlackBerry, pausing, Emanuel seemed uncharacteristically at a loss for words. "I don't . . . I'm not . . ." He finally conceded, "I'm sitting here stalling, because I'm trying to think of a woman who fits what I just said." Then, snapping back to form, he said: "Well, shit, I wouldn't be, like, pessimistic about it, because the fact is, four years ago you wouldn't have picked Barack Obama."

That's not quite true; immediately after Obama's stirring convention speech in 2004, the Illinois senator started to creep into the public imagination as someone who might run four years later. Still, Emanuel's larger point makes sense: there could, one imagines, be a female Barack Obama out there someplace, a hidden talent lurking just beneath the radar of American politics. The logic, according to this school of thought, is that the country has evolved, Hillary Clinton helped pave the way, and when the right woman emerges, she will be elected, or at least stand a decent chance.

But who, exactly? And where would this magical "right" woman come from, and when would she run? In 2012, against Obama? In 2016, or 2020? And if Rahm Emanuel—one of the most politically connected people in the country, in charge not so long ago of recruiting candidates for office—can't conjure up a realistic scenario involving a female candidate in the near future, isn't that a hint that it may be a little ways off?

The most conceivable scenario in which a woman runs in 2012, barring a major surprise, involves Sarah Palin, whose prospects within the Republican party and at the national level, after serving less than a single term as Alaska governor before abruptly quitting, appear mixed at best. One poll in the late summer of 2009 found that 67 percent of Americans, including 43 percent of Republicans, do not ever want to see Palin as president. Other female candidates may be more popular but appear to be several steps removed from a presidential campaign—or are Democrats, meaning they will have to wait their turn, until the Obama era has run its course.

Ask the open-ended question of who the first woman president will be and you get a range of answers, most of them vague. Once upon a time, the answer was simple: Hillary Clinton. Now everyone has a different answer. Maybe it will be Secretary Janet Napolitano—if Joe Biden does not run for president in 2016 and the country can accept a single woman. Maybe it will be Senator Kirsten Gillibrand—except she is so young, so resented by her colleagues for her early success and, for now, such a relative unknown. Maybe it will be Liz Cheney, if she runs for office in Virginia and displays her father's gift for politics. Maybe it will be Meg Whitman—if she wins the California Republican primary, then survives the general election to become governor, and quickly reverses the fortunes of the state before it slides off the continent in economic and political disarray. All big ifs.

The profile of the first woman president is just as unclear. Will she be a mother of young children, or did Palin's experience prove that is too risky and controversial? Will she be an older woman, someone with experience and stature, or did Clinton prove that too many years in politics undercuts the natural argument that a woman would represent change? Could she be someone single, or a black woman, or a divorcée, or someone else entirely, a kind of woman no one has envisioned in the Oval Office?

Which leads to the second school of thought: that it remains a bigger challenge than anyone wants to admit for women to win in American politics, and nowhere more so than at the level of the presidency. "I'm very pessimistic there will be a woman president in my lifetime, frankly," said Kira Sanbonmatsu, a political scientist at Rutgers University's Center for American Women and Politics, the leading research hub on the subject. "I'm pessimistic because the pool is so small." She stopped and sighed. "There's so much debate about gender bias," she said. "A lot of people in my field think it doesn't exist, or think that any bias that exists is offset by people who are predisposed to women candidates and want to see more women in office, so even if there's bias it washes out at the end. I disagree. I tend to think there's more bias against women candidates, and that it's very hard to measure."

The Pessimist Camp has an edge in this argument, in my view, and not just because there are so few women in the so-called pipeline. Politics, in the twenty-four-hour news cycle, remains an attack sport that thrives on personal mockery and ridicule of the kind that has proven especially devastating for women in the national spotlight. Hillary Clinton did not survive it (though she has made a comeback, thanks to Obama). Sarah Palin did not survive it. Caroline Kennedy did not survive it. Further back in time, Geraldine Ferraro and Pat Schroeder did not survive it. Nancy Pelosi has weathered it best, but even she is in constant danger of being turned into the opposition party's favorite target of caricature. For different reasons, in different ways, almost all of the women who have sought a national profile have eventually succumbed to a stereotype that has rendered them unrecognizable—and unelectable.

The most extreme example is Palin, and it is unclear whether she could grow more resistant to the gender barbs in time for a 2012 campaign. Her political and public relations operations since 2008 have certainly left a lot to be desired. Much of it has nothing to do with gender. Memorably, Palin held a Thanksgiving press availability at a turkey pardoning on a farm several weeks after the election; in the background was the unmistakable sight of a farmer snuffing a live turkey. (One disenchanted McCain adviser dubbed it the "turkey murder video," pointing to it as evidence that her missteps were not products of the McCain campaign's handling since they continued after the race ended.) In 2009, with the election long over, former McCain aides were still feuding openly, in the pages of *Vanity Fair* and elsewhere, with Palin's defenders over who was to blame for the Republican ticket's defeat. Around that time, academic research began to emerge showing that Palin had more of a definitive effect—a negative one—than other vice presidential nominees had over the years, another sign that does not bode well for her future.

And then, in a stunning flourish, Palin unexpectedly resigned as governor. "All I can ask is that you trust me with this decision and know that it is no more politics as usual," she said in a July 3 speech near her house in Wasilla. The media, and the Republican establishment, erupted in shock, declaring her erratic and even unstable.

Even in her departure Palin was treated with extraordinary—and gendered—hostility. In *Vanity Fair* a few weeks earlier, the author Todd Purdum had quoted people who had worked with Palin surmising that she might have narcissistic personality disorder. When she quit the governorship, a blogger on the Huffington Post offered up a different diagnosis, saying she really suffered from attention deficit disorder. Most incredibly, a television commentator asked if she might be pregnant. "Is there anything going on with her that perhaps may lead her to want to make this decision, and the one thing that's still left out there is, hey, could she be pregnant again?" said Rick Sanchez on CNN.

"Could be, Rick," countered the columnist Roger Simon of Politico sarcastically. "Or maybe it was just her time of month, because, hey, that's why woman politicians make the decisions they do, right?"

A Fox News poll shortly thereafter asked people what they thought Palin should do next. Thirty-two percent said she should become a "homemaker," as if that were the natural follow-up to serving as governor—while just 6 percent said she should be president.

Of course, Bob Dole had resigned his Senate seat in 1996 in order to run for president ("And I don't recall anybody accusing him of being a quitter. Or of being pregnant," Simon wrote). Former Republican Majority Leader Trent Lott had quit his Senate seat in 2007 just after winning a fourth term in order to become a lobbyist—without producing much in the way of fireworks. Former House Speaker Dennis Hastert also resigned his seat in 2007, without finishing out his term, just as former House Speaker Newt Gingrich had decided to do after losing the majority in 1998. No one diagnosed them with mental illness as a result.

But Palin still faces hurdles besides a societal double standard, not least of which is her own failure to stay engaged in substantive debates and lack of a vibrant political operation. While she has communicated effectively on Facebook as an ex-governor—in one instance putting the Obama White House on the defensive with her accusation that his 2009 health care overhaul would create "death panels"—her pronouncements have been spotty and rarely shifted the national agenda. In order to mount a campaign in 2012 she would, at some point in 2010, need to begin putting together a serious policy agenda and a political team in Iowa—something other Republican hopefuls began doing in the weeks after Obama won.

Which brings the question full circle: What about Hillary Clinton?

She could, of course, run again someday. She will be sixty-nine years old in 2016, hardly too old. She will have the added experience of having served as secretary of state, and, presumably, the goodwill of even more of the Democratic party. Her independence from her husband will be more pronounced, her résumé tied as much to Obama as to Bill Clinton—meaning she could have much less of a baggage problem than she did the last time.

At one point after the election, Clinton still seemed—at least to her admirers—to be the only potential female president on the horizon. "It's not that Hillary Clinton was at the head of the line. She *was* the line," her adviser Ann Lewis said.

But then Clinton took herself out of the running, seemingly determined to end the speculation about her future in favor of living in the present.

"Will you ever run for president again? Yes or no," NBC's Ann Curry asked Clinton in an interview broadcast on October 13, 2009.

"No," Clinton replied.

"No?" Curry again asked.

"No. No," Clinton repeated. "I mean, this is a great job. It's a 24/7 job. And I'm looking forward to retirement at some point." She repeated the denial again in the days that followed.

Some close Clinton friends refused to believe it. One former top adviser told me that she was understandably preoccupied with her diplomatic work, and wanted to rule out a future presidential bid in order to focus public attention on her current efforts. She could always, this adviser argued, change her mind—as Obama did, running for president less than a year after declaring on *Meet the Press* that he would not.

But others said Clinton seems genuinely at peace with the direction her life had taken, and that her personal ambitions have lessened some. Perhaps she has no interest in repeating the torment of 2008. Perhaps she has concluded that it is just too difficult for a woman to run and win—or for her to, anyway.

Or perhaps she has decided, like so many before her, to leave the task to a future generation.

Notes

INTRODUCTION: YEAR OF THE WOMAN?

This chapter draws on data from a variety of sources, including the following articles: "Women Wage Key Campaigns for Democrats" by Robin Toner, *New York Times* March 24, 2006; "Why Did Women Do So Poorly in 2006 House Elections" by Chris Bowers at OpenLeft, July 10, 2007; "RNC's Below-the-Belt Shot at Nancy Pelosi" by Andie Coller at Politico, May 23, 2009; "What Year of the Woman?" by Marie Wilson, Huffington Post, December 9, 2008.

It also relies on Gallup poll data released on July 17, 2009 ("Pelosi's Image Still Negative, Boehner Not Widely Known"), a postelection survey by the Pew Research Center, published November 13, 2008; the General Social Survey of 2008, and the Inter-Parliamentary study of women leaders around the world from March 5, 2009.

Further material was drawn from academic research, chiefly that of Jennifer Lawless, director of the Women and Politics Institute at American University; Richard Fox of Loyola Marymount, and the scholars at the Center for American Women and Politics at Rutgers, whose website is an invaluable resource. The National Women's Political Caucus also provided information.

CHAPTER 1: TOUGH ENOUGH

For these sections, I relied heavily on my own firsthand observations of the Clinton campaign, which I covered for the *Washington Post* from its official inception in January 2007 until its conclusion in June 2008. I had also covered Clinton for the *New York Times* in 2006, before she formally announced her decision to run. I interviewed her on multiple occasions during that time; I also interviewed then-Senator Barack Obama on multiple occasions in 2006, 2007, and 2008. While I drew on my own real-time notes from the campaign—and stories I had written for the newspaper—as well as contemporaneous interviews, I also reinterviewed key players from both campaigns, party officials, and lawmakers once the campaign was over.

In the section "Mothers vs. Daughters" I relied on interviews with the following: former vice presidential nominee Geraldine Ferraro, March 9, 2009; Senator Amy Klobuchar, January 28, 2009; Melody Rose of Portland State University; and Debora Spar of Barnard College. Although they were not directly referenced, I also drew on interviews with Deborah Siegel, December 2009; Marie Wilson, December 2008; Janet Jakobsen, January 2009; Ann Lewis, December 2008; and Karen O'Connor, December 2008. I also referred to these articles: "Young Feminists Split: Does Gender Matter?" by Eli Saslow, *Washington Post*, January 10, 2008; "Goodbye to All That (#2)" by Robin Morgan, posted on the Women's Media Center site, February 2, 2008.

I turned back to midcampaign interviews with senior Clinton officials for the section "The Iron Lady of Chappaqua," and to interviews with then-Senator Hillary Clinton herself, conducted on October 8, 2007, and June 1, 2008. I also held postcampaign interviews with Clinton campaign officials and outside advisers, eight of whom spoke on condition of anonymity, and with the following people: Mark Penn, March 31, 2009; Senator Jeanne Shaheen, February 12, 2009; Patti Solis Doyle, March 31, 2009; James Carville, January 28, 2009; Doug Hattaway, March 30, 2009; Geoff Garin, May 20, 2009. Outside the immediate Clinton orbit, I interviewed Anita Dunn of the Obama campaign, April 24, 2009; Joe Trippi of the Edwards campaign, March 2009; and Dee Dee Myers, a key Clinton supporter, January 8, 2009.

The work and observations of several scholars are included in this chapter, including, most important, that of Melody Rose of Portland State University and Regina Lawrence of Louisiana State University, whose research on the Clinton campaign was an important resource. I also relied on the work of Kim Fridkin of Arizona State University, Jennifer Lawless of American University, Paul Herrnson of the University of Maryland, Kathryn Pearson of the University of Minnesota, and Linda Witt, the author of *Running as a Woman: Gender and Power in American Politics.* Political scientist Georgia Duerst-Lahti's research is also referenced.

Josh Green of *The Atlantic* published scores of internal Clinton campaign memos in August 2008; I borrowed heavily from them here. Numerous other articles shaped the perception of the campaign, and find their way into this section, including: "Women Feeling Freer to Suggest 'Vote for Mom,'" by Robin Toner, *New York Times,* January 29, 2007; "Caucus Win Could Make Clinton No. 1," by columnist David Yepsen, *Des Moines Register,* January 28, 2007; "Hillary Is from Mars, Obama Is from Venus," by Michael Scherer, Salon, July 12, 2007; "Bam: Our First Woman Prez?" by Lucy Berrington and Jeff Onore, *New York Post,* January 7, 2008; "Damsel in the Debate," by Ruth Marcus, *Washington Post,* November 2, 2007; "Gift of Gall," by Maureen Dowd, *New York Times,* November 4, 2007; "For Democrats, Iowa Still Up for Grabs," by Jon Cohen and me, *Washington Post,* November 20, 2007; "The Salon Interview: Elizabeth Edwards," with Joan Walsh, July 17, 2007; "Lazio Says Debate Critics Are Sexist," by Randal C. Archibold, *New York Times,* September 20, 2000.

CHAPTER 2: UNDER SIEGE

In this chapter I relied on contemporaneous notes and interviews, as well as transcripts of interviews with the following Clinton aides and supporters: interview with Ann Lewis, December 17, 2008; interview with Doug Hattaway, March 30, 2009; interview with James Carville, January 28, 2009; interview with Representative Jim McGovern, Democrat of Massachusetts, December 2008; interview with Representative Debbie Wasserman Schultz, Democrat of Florida, January 3, 2009; interview with Patti Solis Doyle, March 31, 2009; interviews with Howard Wolfson, April 2009; interview with Mark Penn; interview with Celinda Lake, May 14, 2009; interview with Geoff Garin, May 20, 2009. I also relied on interviews with Anita

Dunn of the Obama campaign, April 24, 2009, and Joel Benenson, chief pollster for the Obama campaign, December 9, 2008.

I also drew on the following sources: entrance polling data from the Iowa caucuses (which showed women across all age groups breaking down this way: Obama 35, Clinton 30, Edwards 23); from "Katie Couric's Notebook: Sexism & Politics," by anchor Katie Couric on CBS, June 11, 2008; "Hail to the Chief of Staff" by Richard Cohen, *Washington Post*, February 5, 2008; "Letter from the Editor," by Anna Wintour, *Vogue*, February 2008; "Can Hillary Cry Her Way Back to the White House?" by Maureen Dowd, *New York Times*, January 9, 2008; "Hillary Clinton 1, Chris Matthews 0," by Rebecca Traister, Salon, January 9, 2008; "Critics and News Executives Split over Sexism in News Coverage," by Katharine Q. Seelye and Julie Bosman, *New York Times*, June 13, 2008; "Women Are Never Front-Runners," by Gloria Steinem, *New York Times*, January 8, 2008; "Clinton Escapes to Fight Another Day," by Adam Nagourney, *New York Times*, January 9, 2008;

Biographical material on Hattie Wyatt Caraway of Arkansas came from the Biographical Directory of the U.S. Senate.

CHAPTER 3: HUNTING SEASON

I drew on my own reporting from the 2008 campaign for the Palin chapter, including a trip I took with her and her entourage to several states, including Alaska, after the Republican National Convention. In this chapter I relied on contemporaneous notes and postcampaign interviews with senior aides to McCain and Palin, six of whom spoke on condition of anonymity. Other interviews included: Mark Salter, April 2, 2009; Nicolle Wallace, December 2008; John Coale, March 18, 2009; Elaine Lafferty, March 2009; former Massachusetts governor Jane Swift, April 20, 2009; former White House press secretary Dana Perino, January 4, 2009; Representative Kay Granger of Texas, March 17, 2009. I also relied on interviews from the campaign trail with two McCain advisers who spoke anonymously.

I relied on work by my colleague Dan Balz, who coauthored, with Haynes Johnson, a definitive account of Palin's selection in his book *Battle for America: 2008*. I also conducted and drew upon interviews with Anita Dunn of the Obama campaign, October 2008 and April 2009; interviews with aides to Hillary Clinton and Bill Clinton; an interview with Celinda Lake, May 14, 2009; an interview with political science expert Lee Sigelman at George Washington University; interviews with advisers to Michigan Governor Jennifer Granholm; an interview with Debora Spar of Barnard College; an interview with Dianne Bystrom, a political scientist at Iowa State University; an interview with Geoff Garin of the Clinton campaign; interviews with Barbara Lee, expert on women governors at the Barbara Lee Family Foundation in Boston; and an interview with Danny Hayes, assistant political science professor at Syracuse University, who has studied gender in elections.

I drew on these published sources: "Palin's Pregnancy Problem," by Sally Quinn, *Washington Post*, August 29, 2008; "Sarah Palin and Motherhood," by Dr. Laura Schlessinger, www.drlaurablog.com, September 2, 2008; "As Far as I'm Concerned, Elaine Lafferty Can Go F*ck Herself," by Megan Carpentier, posted on Jezebel, October 28, 2008; "Sarah Palin Painted in the Nude at Old Town Ale House in Chicago," by Emma Graves Fitzsimmons, *Chicago Tribune*, September 30, 2008; "The Insiders: How John McCain Came to Pick Sarah Palin," by Jane Mayer, *The New Yorker*, October 27, 2008; "The Sound of His Voice, &c.," by Jay Nordlinger, National Review Online, August 27, 2007; "Democratic Faces That Could Launch a Thousand Votes," by Shailagh Murray, *Washington Post*, October 14, 2006; "It Came from Wasilla," by Todd Purdum, *Vanity Fair*, August 2009; "Palin Problem," by Kathleen Parker, National Review Online, Sept. 26, 2008; "Palin's Failin'," by Peggy Noonan, *Wall Street Journal*, October 17, 2008; "RNC Shells Out $150k for Palin Fashion," by Jeanne Cummings, Politico, October 22, 2008. I also relied on "Fewer Mothers Prefer Full-Time Work," a study by the Pew Research Center, released July 12, 2007, and transcripts of the Katie Couric CBS interviews with Palin and the Charles Gibson ABC interviews with Palin.

CHAPTER 4: THE PROSECUTORS

In this chapter I relied on extensive interviews with Senator Amy Klobuchar, January 28, 2009; Department of Homeland Security Director Janet Napolitano, April 8, 2009; Senator Claire McCaskill, May 12, 2009; Dennis Burke, spring 2009; Geoff Garin, May 20, 2009; Celinda Lake,

May 14, 2009; advisers to McCaskill and Napolitano who spoke on condition of anonymity; Democratic strategist Chris Esposito.

In the academic community Danny Hayes of Syracuse University did me the invaluable favor of analyzing media coverage of the Klobuchar and McCaskill campaigns; his work, along with his research associate, Rebekah Liscio, is relied on heavily here. I also drew on interviews with Kathryn Pearson of the University of Minnesota; Kim Fridkin of Arizona State University; Kira Sanbonmatsu of the Center for American Women and Politics at Rutgers University; Dianne Bystro at Iowa State University; and the work of Kathleen Hall Jamieson, and Barbara Lee of the Barbara Lee Family Foundation in Boston.

This chapter relies on the following published sources: "Janet Napolitano and the New Third Way," by Dana Goldstein, *American Prospect*, July 7, 2008; "Napolitano 'Great Choice' as Homeland Security Boss," by Christina Bellantoni, *Washington Times*, April 5, 2009; "After Cancer, Lawmaker Urges Tests," by Richard Leiby, *Washington Post*, March 24, 2009; the Almanac of American Politics 2008 edition (pages on Rell, Gregoire); "Gov. Gregoire's Personal Battle," by Jean Enerson, King5 News, October 28, 2007; "Six Women in Primaries for Two Minnesota Seats," by Chris Lombardi, WeNews, September 7, 2000; "Central Casting: The Democrats Think About Who Can Win the Midterms—and in 2008," by Jeffrey Goldberg, *The New Yorker*, May 29, 2006; "Chasing Amy," by Jon Tevlin, *Minneapolis Star-Tribune*, August 31, 2003; "Pearls, Politics & Power," by Madeleine Kunin (Chelsea Green Publishing, pp. 143–44); the Statement of Sen. John McCain before the Homeland Security and Governmental Affairs Committee on the Nomination of Governor Janet A. Napolitano, January 15, 2009; "Sexism Sneaks in Over Open Mic," by Campbell Brown, CNN, November 19, 2008; "A Conversation with Governors Janet Napolitano and Sarah Palin," *Charlie Rose*, October 12, 2007; "Are Americans Ready to Elect a Female President?" by Andrew Kohut, president, Pew Research Center, May 9, 2007; "Rethinking Gender Bias in Theater," by Patricia Cohen, *New York Times*, June 24, 2009; "McCaskill's Husband Is Found Murdered," by Matt Franck, Jo Mannies, and Heather Ratcliffe, *St. Louis Post-Dispatch*, December 13, 2005; "Accusations Fly in Senate Squeakers," by the Annenberg Political Fact Check, Factcheck.org, November 6, 2006;

"Campaign Takes Low Road Through Crucial Missouri," by Jonathan E. Kaplan, *The Hill*, November 1, 2006.

CHAPTER 5: MOTHER OF FIVE IN PEARLS

This chapter is based on interviews with the following people: House Speaker Nancy Pelosi, June 10, 2009; White House Chief of Staff Rahm Emanuel, May 14, 2009; Alexandra Pelosi, April 2009; Christine Pelosi, April 2009; Representative George Miller, April 2009; Representative Edward J. Markey, April 2009; Representative Rosa DeLauro, April 2009; former representative Max Sandlin, April 8, 2009; Anita Dunn, April 24, 2009; EMILY's List president Ellen Malcom, June 4, 2009;

This chapter also draws on data from Richard Fox, political science professor at Loyola Marymount University. I also drew from the following articles: "House Broker: Nancy Pelosi Doesn't Like to Be Threatened," by Michelle Cottle, *The New Republic*, June 11, 2008; "Triumph of the 'Airhead,'" by Mark Z. Barabak, *Los Angeles Times Magazine*, January 26, 2003; "Pelosi: Clinton Camp Played Gender Card," by Rick Klein, ABC News, November 5, 2007; "Grandma with a Gavel," by Ruth Marcus, *Washington Post*, January 10, 2007; "Women Wage Key Campaigns for Democrats," by Robin Toner, *New York Times*, March 24, 2006; "Florida, Michigan Delegates Shouldn't Decide Race, Pelosi Says," by Laura Litvan, Bloomberg, February 15, 2008; Pelosi radio interview with talk-show host Ronn Owens, August 13, 2008.

I relied on the following books: *Woman of the House: The Rise of Nancy Pelosi*, by Vincent Bzdek (Palgrave MacMillan); *Madam Speaker: Nancy Pelosi's Life, Times and Rise to Power*, by Marc Sandalow (Modern Times); *Know Your Power: A Message to America's Daughters*, by Nancy Pelosi (Doubleday); *Pearls, Politics & Power*, by Madeleine Kunin (Chelsea Green Publishing); press release: "Pelosi: Budget Is a Blueprint for the Future," April 29, 2009.

The section "Moms in the House" is based on interviews with the following people: Representative Debbie Wasserman Schultz, January 3, 2009; Representative Stephanie Herseth Sandlin, March 17, 2009; Representative Linda Sánchez, March 5, 2009; Senator Claire McCaskill, May 12, 2009; former government Jane Swift, April 20, 2009; Debbie Walsh, head of the Center for the American Woman and Politics at Rutgers

University's Eagleton Institute of Politics; and Amy Walter, the editor in chief of the daily political newsletter *Hotline.*

The following news stories informed this chapter: "Nancy Pelosi Speaks About Being a Mom," by Kathy Kiely, *USA Today,* May 5, 2007; "New Political Woman," by Scott S. Greenberger, *The Moment,* May/June 2009; "Dixie Chicks," by Alexandra Starr, *The Atlantic,* September, 2004; "North Korea Escalates War of Words, Calls Clinton Vulgar, Unintelligent," by Glenn Kessler, *Washington Post,* July 23, 2009; "Coya Comes Back," by Dan Gunderson, Minnesota Public Radio, November 22, 2001; "Jane Swift Remakes Herself, Juggles Her Passions," by Stephanie Ebbert, *Boston Globe,* October 7, 2007; a posting on www.noquarterusa.net, November 2008; "What's New on Capitol Hill? Motherhood," by Dana Bash, CNN, June 8, 2009. I also relied on the book *The Thumpin,* by Naftali Bendavid (Doubleday, 2007, p. 84).

CHAPTER 6: eMEG AND THE BUSINESS BOOM

This chapter is based on interviews I conducted with the following people: former eBay CEO Meg Whitman, June 22, 2009; Senator Kay Hagan of North Carolina, January 11, 2009; four Republican strategists who spoke on condition of anonymity; Dan Schnur, director of the Jesse M. Unruh Institute of Politics at the University of Southern California, July 2009; Barbara Lee; Rob Stutzman; Celinda Lake.

I drew on the following published sources: "Going, Going, Gone: Meg Whitman Leaves eBay," by Adam Cohen, *New York Times,* January 25, 2008; "eMeg," by Fred Barnes, *The Weekly Standard,* May 25, 2009; "The Gavinator and Meg Whitman's Big Money," by Patricia Sellers on her blog on *Fortune*'s website, July 6, 2009; "Meg Whitman's First Hurdle: State's Male GOP," by Carla Marinucci, *San Francisco Chronicle,* February 16, 2009; "Meg Whitman to Wed June 7," announcement in the *New York Times,* April 20, 1980; Rod Blagojevich interview on ABC's *Good Morning America,* January 26, 2009; statement of Florida CFO Alex Sink, May 13, 2009; "Women on Board: Help or Hindrance?" by Elizabeth Judge, *UK Times,* November 11, 2003; "The Glass Cliff," by Michelle Ryan and Alex Haslam, *British Journal of Management,* May 28, 2004; "The Glass Cliff: Are Women Leaders Often Set Up to Fail?" by Silvia Ann Hewlett, *Harvard Business Review,* August 5, 2008.

CHAPTER 7: WHY WOMEN RUN (AND DON'T)

This chapter is based on interviews I conducted with: former Secretary of State Condoleezza Rice, May 21, 2009; Representative Betty Sutton of Ohio, June 24, 2009; Department of Homeland Security Director Janet Napolitano, April 8, 2009; American University professor Jennifer Lawless; former Governor Jane Swift, April 20, 2009; Representative Kay Granger of Texas, March 17, 2009; former White House Press Secretary Dana Perino, January 4, 2009; political science professor Aili Mari Tripp, University of Wisconsin-Madison; Marie Wilson, director of the White House Project.

The chapter also draws on my contemporaneous notes from my trip accompanying former President Bill Clinton to Rwanda and Liberia in the summer of 2008, as well as from the following published and broadcast sources: "Seizing a Window of Opportunity: The Election of President Bachelet in Chile," by Marcela Rios Tobar, *Politics and Gender* 4(3): 509–19 (2008); "Clinton Reaches Out to a New Generation in India," by Michele Keleman, NPR, July 20, 2009; "Timor-Leste: Women Make a Difference in Politics," United Nations Television, June 2009; "Women Hold Record 18.3% of Seats in Parliament, Group Reports," by Bill Varner, Bloomberg News, March 5, 2009; "Wall Street on the Tundra," by Michael Lews, *Vanity Fair*, April 2009; "Cleaning Up the Men's Mess: Iceland's Women Reach for Power," by Manfred Ertel, *Der Spiegel*, April 22, 2009; "The Death of Macho," by Reihan Salam, *Foreign Policy*, June 22, 2009. It also draws on data from CAWP at Rutgers. Liberian president Ellen Johnson Sirleaf's autobiography *This Child Will Be Great*, was another immense resource (HarperCollins, 2009, pp. 246–50).

CHAPTER 8: WHAT WILL IT TAKE?

This chapter draws on interviews with Rahm Emanuel, May 14, 2009; Kira Sanbonmatsu at Rutgers' Center for American Women and Politics; a senior McCain aide who spoke on condition of anonymity.

I relied on the following published sources: "Would You Like to See Palin as President Someday?" by Susan Davis, *Wall Street Journal*, July 29, 2009; a transcript of Palin's speech, July 3, 2009; "It Came from Wasilla," by Todd Purdum, *Vanity Fair*, August 2009; "Sarah Palin: Is

It All Just ADHD (Attention Deficit Hyperactivity Disorder)?" by Paul Abrams, Huffington Post, July 9, 2009; "The Sins of Sarah Palin," by Roger Simon, Politico, July 7, 2009; a transcript of Secretary of State Hillary Clinton's interview with NBC's David Gregory, *Meet the Press*, July 26, 2009.

Acknowledgments

Thanks first and last to Jon Cohen, my future husband. This was a torturous process, but he patiently encouraged me at every step—even when I wanted to stop. His data analysis, editing, and organizational skills were also indispensable. This book, like so much else, would not have been possible without him.

I am indebted to my sister, Emily Kornblut, who logged long hours researching foreign female leaders and made sharp observations throughout. Her intellectual support and sense of humor were invaluable, as was her practical advice on entering the social networking era.

Thank you to the rest of our families—especially Mom and Edward, Harriet, Betty and Murray, Dan, Susanna, Liz and Jeff, and Oscar—for enduring heated conversations about gender, reading rough drafts, and giving me food for thought. Thanks, too, to my father, the late Arthur Kornblut, for telling me I could be anything when I grew up.

Sally Alexander, my English teacher in the eleventh and twelfth grades, deserves special recognition for volunteering, two decades later, to lend her editing talents to this book. Her encouragement over the span of twenty years is the gift of a lifetime. Although I never imagined I'd see her red pen in the margins of my papers again, I am so grateful I did.

This book in many ways also belongs to my editor, Sean Desmond, who treated it as a collaborative effort in every sense. Special gratitude goes to Richard Abate, my agent, for insisting that I write it in the first place. Both Sean and Richard saw how this book could take shape before I did. I also owe Stephanie Chan great thanks.

Equally important in the creation of this book were my colleagues at the *Washington Post*, including my editors, Marcus Brauchli, Liz Spayd, Kevin Merida, and Marilyn Thompson, who generously gave me time to write. My reporting cohorts were just as selfless. Dana Milbank gave me countless creative suggestions; Dan Balz offered his wisdom on politics and the writing process; Mike Shear read key sections and helped keep my spirits high throughout the year, as he always does. Thank you to Chris Cillizza for both political insights and valuable sources; Alec MacGillis for his expertise on New Hampshire; Paul Kane for his observations on Nancy Pelosi; and E. J. Dionne and Sally Jenkins for offering guidance on how books get done. Tim Curran and Shailagh Murray made 2008 not only bearable but fun. Shani George and Jill Bartscht were endless resources. Thanks especially to Katharine Weymouth and Don Graham for their unwavering support of our journalism, and for continually funding campaign coverage, which is always the first draft.

Bill Hamilton, my former editor at the *Washington Post*, gave me clarity at a critical moment, his special talent. Thanks as well to Peter Baker for his insights on the Clintons and his companionship during the campaign, and to Susan Glasser for hiring me to cover Hillary Clinton for the *Washington Post* in the first place.

Bruce Cain, director of the University of California's D.C. office—and a phenomenal mentor—generously offered me office space and his time, and his insights on politics are woven throughout the book, as are those of my wonderful temporary officemate, Matt Dallek.

Thank you to the many, many campaign operatives who pointed me in the right direction—sometimes literally—over the last three years. Some of the Clinton and Palin advisers who were most helpful spoke to me on condition of anonymity during that time, so I will only thank them by saying: I am grateful for your trust.

Not one word of this book would have been written without the work of Katie Feola, whose research helped get it off the ground. Thank you to Julie Tate for swift, smart fact-checking; Alice Crites, for always finding the very best clips, fast; and Elisabeth Null for her fine research work. Patrick Chisholm and the team at Accentance listened to endless hours of interviews, turning around transcripts within days just as I needed them and patiently taking down all the cursing political operatives seem unable to communicate without.

I am also grateful to friends who devoted time to this project: Barbara Laing, for reading chapters and offering her keen feedback; Campbell Brown and Dan Senor, for talking me through the hardest parts and adding tremendous insight; Frank Bruni, for cheering me up and leading by example; Russ Schriefer and Nina Easton, for reminding me it was just a book; and Peter Reid, for being an eager reader.

I must recognize the work of others in journalism and politics, many of whom helped with the book without even knowing it. Jake Tapper of ABC kept a skeptical eye on gender in the campaign, and provided me with careful observations for those and other chapters. The work of Rebecca Traister at Salon and Michelle Cottle at *The New Republic* provided constant food for thought. Andrea Mitchell and Norah O'Donnell at NBC kept up a running dialogue on women in politics, and Deborah Siegel singlehandedly brought me up to speed on the current state of feminism. Vincent Bzdek, Marc Sandalow, and Mark Z. Barabak are the reigning experts on Nancy Pelosi in the world of journalism, and their writings helped immeasurably. Arianna Huffington, Amy Walter, Amy Siskind, Wendy Button, and Elaine Lafferty all gave me provocative ideas.

Several chapters would not have been possible without the data and expertise of Celinda Lake, Ellen Malcolm, Andy Kohut, and Geoff Garin. Debbie Walsh, head of the best academic center on the subject, patiently walked me through current research. Marie Wilson, Barbara Lee, and Melody Rose provided the backbone of several sections. Thank you as well to Debora Spar at Barnard for her insights into college campus zeitgeist.

Thank you to both Dana Perino and Dee Dee Myers for sharing their views on women and Washington over the course of many hours.

A special thank-you goes to Anita Dunn for her thoughtfulness on this subject and many others, and for her enthusiasm in helping me with the project.

I am indebted to Chris Esposito for several key brainstorming sessions, and for his patience in explaining how gender in politics works at ground level. David Dixon and Steve Murphy, two of the best in the field, also lent their expertise on gender in politics. Colleen Flanagan gave me an important jump-start with our conversations about her work in North Carolina. She was also indispensable in making things happen, as were Sean

Smith, Brendan Daly, Michael Mershon, Stacey Kerr, Jonathan Beeton, Colby Cooper, Alex Reese, Sean McCormack, Rob Stutzman, Henry Gomez, Tucker Bounds, Nichole Francis Reynolds, and Eric Schultz.

Endless thanks goes to these people, and they know why: Jessica Yellin, Sarah Feinberg and Dan Pfeiffer, the Campbells, Darren Kornblut, Ruth and Mark Guyer, Jim Rutenberg and Ondine Karady, Dafna Linzer and Bart Gellman, Jane Black, Richard Wolffe and Paula Cuello, Joe Yonan, Jennifer Loven, David Greene and Rose Previte, Kit Seelye, Mark Leibovich, Dana Bash and John King, Todd Harris, Brian McGrory, Gordon Johndroe, Molly Pisula, Laura Williams, Rebecca Femia, Tracy and Scott Reilly, R. B. Brenner, Tom Sietsema, Nina and Matt Rees, Laura Capps and Bill Burton, Michael Schmuhl, John and Anne Dickerson, Savannah Guthrie, Julie Mason, France Latremoliere, Erin Hartigan, and Marc Lavallee.

I also owe great thanks to the following individuals, each of whom has helped me in a variety of critical ways over the years: Matt Storin, Larry Hackett, David Shribman, Mary Leonard, Joel Benenson, Phil Bennett, Alexandra Pelosi, Laura Nichols, Mark Salter, Mo Elleithee, Stephanie Cutter, Doug Hattaway, Matt McKenna, and Philippe Reines.

James Carville and his students at Tulane tested my theories, as did Jane Swift and her class at Williams College. Thanks to all for sharpening my thinking.

So many women either in or close to elected office shared their time freely, and I owe them for it: House Speaker Nancy Pelosi, Senator Kay Hagan, Homeland Security Director Janet Napolitano, Representative Debbie Wasserman Schultz, California gubernatorial candidate Meg Whitman, former Secretary of State Condoleezza Rice, Senator Claire McCaskill, Senator Amy Klobuchar, former Governor Jane Swift, Representative

Eleanor Holmes Norton, Senator Barbara Mikulski, Senator Jeanne Shaheen, Representative Linda Sánchez, former vice presidential nominee Geraldine Ferraro, former Representative Pat Schroeder, Representative Stephanie Herseth Sandlin, Representative Kay Granger and Representative Betty Sutton all gave generously of their time. And the men, too: Chief of Staff Rahm Emanuel, Representative Jim McGovern, Representative Ed Markey, Representative George Miller, and former Representative Max Sandlin offered valuable insights.

Regina Lawrence of Louisiana State University and Jennifer Lawless at American University offered immensely helpful critiques, as did John Sides of George Washington University. I thank all of them for giving up precious free time to read the manuscript.

It is impossible to give enough thanks to Paula O'Rourke and Matt Calderone, and to Eliza and Adam McGraw, and their children.

To the gang on the plane—Jamie Smith, Eloise Harper, Fernando Suarez, Athena Jones, Beth Fouhy, Peter Hamby, and the rest: We will always have the Middle-Class Express, the Hill-o-copter, and Waterloo.

Index